HOLY
ANOREXIA

HOLY ANOREXIA

RUDOLPH M. BELL

EPILOGUE BY WILLIAM N. DAVIS

THE UNIVERSITY OF CHICAGO PRESS

CHICAGO AND LONDON

Rudolph M. Bell is professor of history at Rutgers University. He is the author of *Fate and Honor, Family and Village: Demographic and Cultural Change in Rural Italy since 1800* and, with Donald Weinstein, of *Saints and Society: The Two Worlds of Western Christendom, 1000–1700,* both published by the University of Chicago Press.

The University of Chicago Press, Chicago 60637
The University of Chicago Press, Ltd., London
© 1985 by The University of Chicago
All rights reserved. Published 1985
Printed in the United States of America

94 93 92 91 90 89 88 87 86 85   5 4 3 2 1

Library of Congress Cataloging in Publication Data

Bell, Rudolph M.
  Holy anorexia.

  Bibliography: p.
  Includes index.
    1. Christian saints—Italy—History.   2. Women—
Italy—History.   3. Women—Italy—Psychology—History.
4. Anorexia nervosa—Patients—Italy—History.   I. Title.
BX4656.B45   1985   305'.90824   85-8460
ISBN 0-226-04204-9

Photos by courtesy of the following individuals or organizations. Figures 1, 2, 3, 4: Alinari/Art Resources; Figure 5: Foto Grassi, Siena; Figures 6, 7, 10, 11, 12: Foto Soprintendenza B.A.S.—Siena; Figure 8: The Metropolitan Museum of Art, Lehman Collection, 1975; Figure 9: Umberto Brandigi, Florence; Figure 13: Foto Soprintendenza B.A.S.—Firenze e Pistoia; Figures 14, 15, 16, 17: Carmelo di S. Maria Maddalena de' Pazzi; Figure 18: Centro Studi *S. Veronica Giuliani*, Città di Castello.

FOR ALESSIA TAMARA

CONTENTS

PREFACE

SEVERAL years ago, while I was at work with the Renaissance historian Donald Weinstein on a study of popular piety, it dawned on me that some holy women in late medieval times were described in terms that were similar in important ways to clinical descriptions of modern-day sufferers of anorexia nervosa. Because of other commitments, I could not pursue the idea systematically at that time. Furthermore, the response of some of my colleagues to my early ruminations was discouraging—had I entered a phase of mild to acute insanity? they wondered. What could Twiggy and Karen Carpenter possibly have in common with Clare of Assisi and Catherine of Siena, or scientifically based behavior modification programs and tube feeding with cloistered Capuchin convents and Jesuit confessors? Recently several scholars—Caroline Bynum, Marina Warner, and Marcello Craveri perhaps are the most significant—have published findings of self-starvation behavior patterns among female saints in places from the Low Countries to Italy and from the twelfth through the seventeenth centuries. And John Demos, in his penetrating study, *Entertaining Satan*, has seen the likelihood of anorexia in seventeenth-century New England even while recognizing how a paucity of relevant documentation may force the historian to limit his exploration. At least, if I am mad, I am not alone in my madness.

Two years in Florence as director of the Rutgers Junior Year in Italy Program provided me with the opportunity to complete the necessary research. Laura Bell, Olivia Cardona, Sandra Fedeli, Katherine Gill, Natalie Marchetta, Beth Price, and Carmela Verga assisted in the gathering of documents. I am especially grateful to Padre Innocenzo Colosio, Padre Eugenio Marino, Padre Giacinto

D'Urso, and Sister Mary O'Driscoll, who graciously corrected my errors and called additional materials to my attention even when they did not share my conclusions. For their comments on various drafts of the manuscript I thank Traian Stoianovich, Philip Greven, Paul Clemens, Bernard Landis, Richard Kieckhefer, Caroline Bynum, Ernest McDonnell, Herbert Rowen, John Lenaghan, and the Rutgers Social History Group. Staff members at the following libraries in Florence were especially helpful: Biblioteca dell'Accademia Toscana di Scienze e Lettere "La Colombaria," Biblioteca dei Cappuccini, Biblioteca del Collegio Teologico dei Carmelitani Scalzi, Biblioteca del Convento di S. Marco, Biblioteca Domenicana, Biblioteca dell' Istituto di Psicologia, Biblioteca Marucelliana, Biblioteca Medicea-Laurenziana, Biblioteca Nazionale Centrale, Biblioteca Provinciale dei Frati Minori, Biblioteca Riccardiana-Moreniana, and the Biblioteca di Spiritualità "A. Levasti." At more than two dozen convents and monasteries around Italy my visits and requests for precious materials were received warmly; I thank them all but mention only two, the Centro Studi "S. Veronica" and the Centro Nazionale di Studi Cateriniani. Marc Singer, then one of those remarkably bright undergraduates willing to take chances, first explored with me the ways of Catherine of Siena.

This essay treats a very special group of people—the 261 holy women officially recognized by the Roman Catholic church as saints, blesseds, venerables, or servants of God (included in the *Bibliotheca Sanctorum*) who lived between 1200 and the present on the Italian peninsula. For about one-third of this number the historical record is so meager that nothing of consequence can be concluded about them for my purposes. Of the remaining 170 or so, more than half displayed clear signs of anorexia; for several dozen the documentation is extensive and highly reliable. These were women who stirred up controversy and commanded attention. For years and even centuries following their deaths they were heroic models and protectors for the believers who flocked to their tombs, fought for possession of their relics, and listened in awe as preachers spread word of their holy behavior.

Accounts of saints' lives are a valuable but complex source for the study of medieval and early modern European culture. Whereas for men's lives, whether saintly or not, there is a great deal of evidence and one might choose to eschew so problematic a historical area as hagiography, for women the situation is different. Apart from a few queens and some noble courtesans, societal restrictions on women's roles made it unlikely that they could generate historical documents appropriate for an in-depth psychological study, unless they entered religious orders or found themselves accused of witchcraft or heresy. Therefore, if we are to explore the feelings of nonelite medieval and early modern women at all, we must use the sources we have, including the tough ones. In *Saints and Society* Donald Weinstein and I considered at some length the difficulties and limitations of working with hagiographical materials, so I will not repeat that discussion here. Boccaccio's opening story in the *Decameron* ridicules a target worthy in many ways of just such treatment, and yet it remains possible to explore these *vitae* (a term I use to refer to the biographical texts, as distinct from the person's life itself) in serious fashion. Just as a tape recording of a psychotherapy session, a political campaign speech, or the pillow talk of lovers cannot be taken literally or at face value, even though it may be rich with meaning, so also the biographies and especially the autobiographies preserved by clerics for purposes of spiritual edification may yield their truths. Exciting work has been done over the last two decades on witches, and recently scholars such as Michael Goodich, Richard Kieckhefer, and André Vauchez have rediscovered the saint. More material exists on Catherine of Siena, for example, both her own utterances and writings as well as biographical accounts by contemporaries who knew her well, than for any other woman who lived in the fourteenth century.

My decision to limit this essay to "Italian" saints is based on my deep sense that the anorexic behavior pattern is not only an intrapsychic phenomenon but also a social perception. In order to analyze in at least a reasonably systematic way the interaction between holy women and the world they responded to and that responded to them, it seemed best to concentrate on an area with substantial internal coherence and consistency. Most of the women whose lives I explore came from the urban centers of central Italy, especially Umbria and Tuscany, at least until after the Catholic Reformation. Certainly there was variety even within this limited region, one that changed substantially over the centuries, but its history is far more manageable for the present sort of study than all of Europe would be. Therefore I leave Mary of Oignies, Joan of Arc, and Teresa of Avila, along with many others who I suspect were anorexic, to the greater expertise of others.

In this essay I hope to address two rather different audiences. The first is composed of students of medieval and early modern

Europe as well as those more generally concerned with the history of women and its psychological dimensions. I seek to persuade them that a historically significant group of women exhibited an anorexic behavior pattern in response to the patriarchal social structures in which they were trapped. My second intended audience is composed of physicians and psychologists concerned with the causes, treatment, and cure of anorexia nervosa. Here I am not out to persuade, only to suggest that the existence of a historical reality, what I call "holy anorexia," may indicate a need to reevaluate certain modern approaches to the disease and in particular to be no less concerned with etiology than with therapy. To this audience I apologize for all the footnotes and some of the detail, encumbrances of disciplinary norms that over the long haul do seem necessary.

The first chapter surveys how anorexia nervosa has been defined and treated over several centuries, attempting to show that it certainly is not a new disease or one that began with ballerinas and dieting fads. The next three chapters explore in depth three distinct types of holy anorexia. In the first, represented by Catherine of Siena, it leads to death as a direct consequence of starvation and related harsh austerities. In the second, represented by Veronica Giuliani, an anorexic teenager recovers or is "cured," usually in a convent with the support of other nuns; she achieves a sense of self and learns to express her need for autonomy in more positive ways. In the third, represented by three married penitents in the thirteenth century, the anorexic behavior pattern is not what today would be called anorexia nervosa; it is relevant nevertheless, because in earlier times so many women were married off by their fathers at such a young age that the usual adolescent contests over identity and autonomy were short-circuited, only to appear years later upon the occasion of widowhood or some other worldly crisis. Among holy anorexics of this type the scars of repressed infantile rage are especially prominent, nurtured by years of household subservience.

The last two chapters shift from a typological approach to the more conventional historical one and trace why holy anorexia emerged and how lay people and clerics responded to such behavior. In the epilogue William N. Davis, Executive Director of the Cornell Center for the Study of Anorexia and Bulimia, explores from the perspective of a clinical psychotherapist what the history of holy anorexia may suggest about contemporary understanding and treatment of anorexia nervosa and bulimia.

CHAPTER
I

RECOGNITION AND
TREATMENT

A N O R E X I A, from the Greek *an* (privation, lack of) and *orexis* (appetite), is a general term used to refer to any diminution of appetite or aversion to food. Everyone has experienced at least temporary anorexia, perhaps when a severe head cold interfered with the sense of smell or as a result of some emotional trauma. Often students cannot eat on the eve of a major examination and athletes may not be hungry as they anticipate the challenge of the big game. A host of somatic conditions, from blockages in the alimentary system to hormonal imbalances, may cause an aversion to food in general. Pregnant women regularly experience changes in food preferences that cannot be dismissed as caprice. A person who arises at 2:00 A.M. with an intense craving for spaghetti topped with strawberries and whipped cream is responding to a stimulus originating in or transmitted through the hypothalamus, that part of the brain which is the center of the autonomic nervous system. We cannot command ourselves to be hungry if we are not, nor to feel satiated if we are famished. The life-sustaining mechanisms of appetite, like the response to pain and the sexual drive, appear to be beyond the individual's control, at least for most people most of the time. Definition of the full range of activities controlled or affected by the hypothalamus is a matter for some disagreement, nor do we know precisely how this collection of nerve cells works, but unquestionably there are close links among the urges of fatigue, appetite, pain, and sexual desire. It is generally believed, although with less certainty, that the hypothalamus also plays a role in the nervous mechanisms underlying moods and motivational states.[1]

"Anorexia nervosa" (aversion to food due to some personality

---

disorder) is something of a misnomer. Many of those who suffer from the disease do not report a "loss of appetite," although obviously they do not eat enough to be healthy. Hungry or not, victims of anorexia nervosa voluntarily starve themselves to the point at which their lives are at risk, and reported mortality rates range from 10 to as high as 20 percent. Long-term follow-up studies show that a majority of those who undergo prolonged treatment for the disease never recover fully. Anorexia nervosa is far more common among females than males, by a ratio of ten or even twenty to one. The most frequent time of onset is adolescence and, although the poor are not immune to this disease, it appears to be the special preserve of well-to-do, white, Western girls. Among "high-risk" private school girls in England the reported incidence of anorexia nervosa is 1 in 200, and a recent survey of aspiring ballerinas suggests a rate of nearly 1 in 6, but estimates in the general population run from 0.6 to 1.6 per year per 100,000. Apparent differentials of gender, class, and age may be attributable in part to patterns for recognizing and treating the disease, and this question will be taken up presently. Earlier literature described the illness as hysterical, a term so vague and ultimately pejorative that it now is in total disfavor, and in many cases it was confused with other serious psychoses, including schizophrenia.[2]

The currently accepted criteria for diagnosing the condition anorexia nervosa, published by J. P. Feighner and his associates in 1972, are as follows:

1. Onset prior to age twenty-five.

2. Lack of appetite accompanied by loss of at least 25 percent of original body weight.

3. A distorted, implacable attitude toward eating, food, or weight that overrides hunger, admonitions, reassurance, and threats; for example, (a) denial of illness with a failure to recognize nutritional needs, (b) apparent enjoyment in losing weight with overt manifestation that refusing food is a pleasurable indulgence, (c) a desired body image of extreme thinness with overt evidence that it is rewarding to the patient to achieve and maintain this state, and (d) unusual handling or hoarding of food.

4. No known medical illness that could account for the anorexia and weight loss.

5. No other known psychiatric disorder, particularly primary affective disorders, schizophrenia, obsessive-compulsive disorder, and phobic neurosis. (The assumption is made that even though it

may appear phobic or obsessional, food refusal alone is not sufficient to qualify for obsessive-compulsive or phobic disease.)

6. At least two of the following manifestations: (a) amenorrhea, (b) lanugo (soft, fine hair), (c) bradycardia (persistent resting pulse of 60 or less), (d) periods of overactivity, (e) episodes of bulimia (binge eating), and (f) vomiting (may be self-induced).[3]

Feighner's list of a set of symptoms is useful as a benchmark for a historical evaluation of the recognition and treatment of anorexia nervosa and at the same time as a reminder of how poorly the condition is understood. The symptoms he listed are derived from empirical observation and statistical frequency rather than from a rational ordering of causal mechanisms. The criteria for age and for weight loss merely reflect what has been observed most of the time; they are not arbitrary, but neither are they part of a logical chain of reasoning. The third symptom obviously is difficult to define in practice since it so heavily involves the observer's subjectivity, while the fourth and fifth conditions merely state what the disease is not. As with most psychiatric disorders, then, the syndrome of anorexia nervosa is known mostly by indirection. But the illness is there, and people die from it. Another immediate observation about Feighner's criteria is that they include both somatic or physical variables and psychic or attitudinal conditions. For many years the recognition and treatment of anorexia nervosa alternated between the extreme poles of somatic and psychic approaches, a bifurcation no more helpful for those who suffered from the disease than for the historian who would attempt to propose an explanation of holy anorexia.

The earliest known case of anorexia nervosa, or at least the one generally cited in the medical literature, is found in Richard Morton's *Phthisiologia: or a Treatise of Consumptions.* He described the plight of a twenty-year-old girl whom he treated in 1686. Her illness had begun two years earlier when

in the Month of *July* [she] fell into a total Suppression of her Monthly Courses from a multitude of Cares and Passions of her Mind, but without any Symptom of the Green-Sickness following upon it. From which time her Appetite began to abate, and her Digestion to be bad; her Flesh also began to be flaccid and loose, and her looks pale . . . she was wont by her studying at Night, and continual pouring upon Books, to expose herself both Day and Night to the Injuries of the Air . . . I do not remember that I did ever in all my Practice see one, that was conversant with the Living so much wasted with the

---

greatest degree of a Consumption, (like a Skeleton only clad with Skin) yet there was no Fever, but on the contrary a Coldness of the whole Body . . . Only her Appetite was diminished, and Digestion uneasy, with Fainting Fitts, which did frequently return upon her.[4]

Morton grimly went on to describe how his patient refused every medication he had to offer (combinations of salts, waters, and tinctures) and how three months later she fainted and died. This seventeenth-century physician was the first to suggest concretely several of the symptoms typical of anorexia nervosa and to distinguish the disease clearly both from the vague diagnosis of consumption and from the specific ravages of tuberculosis. Scattered reports of self-inflicted emaciation appeared in eighteenth-century medical treatises, and Morton's perplexity in dealing with a patient who seemed to choose to starve gave way to consideration of the emotional or psychic basis of nervous disorders.

Among these very early precursors of Freud one of the most important is Giorgio Baglivi, who held the chair of medical theory in the Collegio della Sapienza in Rome by appointment of Pope Clement XI. Baglivi was thoroughly versed in physical medicine and, indeed, adhered to a school of thought that treated the body as a machine composed of many smaller mechanical parts. As Ilza Veith points out in her history of hysteria, however, Baglivi was far from narrowly mechanistic in his treatment of patients, and he believed that passions of the mind might even be the cause of various physical ailments. In his day the prevailing view was that overindulgence in food and drink were the sources of hysterical illness. On the contrary, the good doctor believed that persons of consequence, those of genteel breeding and more delicate emotional substance, mostly had "other things to think of than overcharging their Stomach with Gluttony or Drunkenness." Peasants and other "meaner sorts of persons" were less sensitive and better able to cope with grief and worry, but among Baglivi's clientele "a great Part of Diseases either take their Rise from, or are fed by that Weight of Care that hangs upon every one's Shoulders."

Already a class bias in diagnosis and treatment of nervous disease is evident. With his contemporaries, Baglivi held that mental illness almost invariably manifested itself in gastrointestinal symptoms. The physician believed that these followed on the decreased appetite and lack of interest in food he found so commonly among his patients, especially among young women unrequited in love. Baglivi frankly acknowledged that he could not explain the process by which emotional imbalances led to physical symptoms; he turned instead to therapeutic remedies. His medical regimen involved little more than encouraging the patient's self-recovery with the help of "a Physician that has his Tongue well hung, and is Master of the Art of persuading."[5]

Although some of the symptoms referred to by Baglivi may have been indicative of anorexia nervosa, he did not identify this specific disorder. Rather, he, his predecessor Thomas Sydenham, and such eighteenth-century writers as Bernard de Mandeville, George Cheyne, Robert Whytt (who described *fames canina*, or voracious appetite), and William Cullen groped for general explanations of a baffling variety of physical disabilities that seemed to have a psychic origin. The terms *melancholy, hysteria, hypochondriasis, lowness of spirit, nervous disease, English Malady*, and *affliction of vapors* (perhaps emanating from an unhappy uterus as it floated upward and pressed upon the gastrointestinal organs) were used imprecisely in a literature that never fully escaped from the ancient Egyptian association of emotional disturbance in women with genital disease and the "wandering womb." In virtually all of the eighteenth-century medical literature it is impossible to distinguish anorexia nervosa from other "nervous" diseases. Only the recognition of a class differential remains constant, although in some quarters with an inversion of Baglivi's bias. From the American colonies Benjamin Rush, addressing a well-fed and probably sotted group of dignitaries at a conference on Indian diseases, lamented that the "HYSTERIC and HYPOCHONDRIAC DISEASES, once peculiar to the chambers of the great, are now to be found in our kitchens and workshops. All these diseases have been produced by our having deserted the simple diet and manners of our ancestors."[6]

Even in the early nineteenth century writers describing symptoms typical of anorexia nervosa did so in the context of more general treatments of hysteria and the "genital neuroses of women." Philippe Pinel, head of the famous Salpétrière public mental hospital for women in Paris, identified a pattern of alternation between periods of anorexia (with concomitant amenorrhea) and what he called *nymphomania*. He described one such patient as being "in a state of sadness and restlessness; she becomes taciturn, seeks solitude, loses sleep and appetite, conducts a private battle between sentiments of modesty and the impulse towards frantic desires." Pinel goes on to tell how "voluptuous leanings" win the contest and the girl deteriorates from indecency and provocative solicitation to disgusting obscenity and finally to a violently maniacal condition. Shortly thereafter he relates a specific case history involving symptoms found in typical anorexia nervosa: female age seventeen, loss of appetite and even complete abstinence from food, amenorrhea, bulimia, bradycardia. Pinel also notes several symptoms often associated with anorexia nervosa even though they are not part of Feighner's diagnostic criteria (outlined earlier): disgust with daily life, frequent crying, taciturn behavior, inability to speak, facial discoloration, paralytic muscle spasms and body rigidity, constipation and limpid urine, hyperacuity, and depression. All these Pinel notes in reporting a classic and for him defining case of hysteria, one that may well have involved a patient who suffered from typical anorexia nervosa.[7]

Specific recognition and nomenclature for the disease had to await the reports of William W. Gull and Charles E. Lasègue. As early as 1868 Gull had described a strange malady that seemed to afflict young women; they refused to eat even as they became extremely emaciated. He called the sickness *apepsia hysterica*, an appellation of dubious value since there is no necessary absence of pepsin and because the term "hysterica" at that time applied only to women, whereas self-starvation can occur also in men. Six years later Gull published a revised and updated set of findings and called the condition *anorexia nervosa*, the designation still used in England and the United States. Again he concentrated on the refusal to eat, extreme weight loss, and amenorrhea characteristic of the disease in young women. Moreover, he noted concomitant symptoms including constipation, low pulse rate, slow respiration, and the absence of somatic disease. Gull expressed some amazement at the highly active pace, even hyperactivity, of some of his anorexic patients. (This observation is especially important in terms of the analysis of "holy anorexia" that follows.) In a later report, enhanced with an engraving of the self-starved sickly body of one patient, he wrote about K. R., age fourteen, who walked long distances through the streets despite the fact that she was so obviously emaciated as to attract the stares of passersby. Even with "nutritive functions at the extreme ebb" she and her fellow sufferers persistently wished to be "on the move." Gull suggested that the illness resulted from a "morbid mental state" among young girls at an age when emotional distress was especially likely to affect the appetite. He asserted that the girl's relatives were "the worst attendants" but did not explore deeply the nature of the parents/daughter relationship and its causal or contributory role in the onset of anorexia.[8]

At virtually the same time as Gull's second report in 1874, and apparently independently of it, Lasègue published a lengthy account, based on eight cases, of what he called *anorexie hystérique*. He carefully distinguished this disease both from "hysterical emaciation" and from the sudden weight loss associated with acute depression. None of his patients fasted absolutely, and whereas some developed an aversion to all types of food others objected only to certain items. Lasègue believed that the disease began with some emotional trauma, one the patient was inclined to conceal, usually in females in their later teenage years. He emphasized the relative happiness of his patients; they showed little concern about their extreme thinness and appeared positively to enjoy their condition. They alternated between being ill patients and capricious children, slowly and surely drawing their entire families into a trap in which eating and the refusal to eat became the sole topic of concern and conversation. Lasègue pessimistically observed that the families' responses, limited to entreaties and menaces, often with a confusing and unpredictable mixture of the two, were quickly exhausted and served as a touchstone to exacerbate the illness. Thus the physician tried to place "in parallel the morbid condition of the hysterical subject and the preoccupation of those who surround her." Negative as he was about the family's ability to bring its daughter to good health, he was certain of his own curative powers. Unlike Gull, who reported that at least one of his patients had died, Lasègue happily claimed a recovery rate of 100 percent.[9]

Within a decade of these early reports, of which Lasègue's was the more influential, anorexia nervosa, or *anorexie mentale* as it came to be called in France, was widely known and diagnosed as a specific malady of psychic origin. The preliminary suggestion by Gull and Lasègue that the patient's family was somehow responsible for the disease, or at least for its continuation, became a basis for standard treatment once it received the world-renowned Jean-Martin Charcot's stamp of approval. From his newly won Clinical Chair of Diseases of the Nervous System at the University of Paris, Professor Charcot told the now familiar story: a thirteen- or fourteen-year-old girl from Angoulême, after blossoming nicely for six months, suddenly refused all nourishment, even though she suffered no physical ailment. The girl's distraught parents finally turned to Charcot and begged that he come have a look at their daughter, now hovering near death. Charcot declined; from the written description alone he "knew" that the child suffered from *anorexie mentale*. The only hope was to send the girl to his hydrotherapy clinic in Paris and for the parents to go back home, not even to see their daughter for brief visits. The physician concluded his lecture with the girl's confession, made after her recovery.

> As long as papa and mamma had not gone—in other words, as long as you had not triumphed (for I saw that you wished to shut me up), I was afraid that my illness was not serious, and as I had a horror of eating, I did not eat. *But when I saw that you were determined to be master, I was afraid*, and in spite of my repugnance I tried to eat, and I was able to, little by little.[10]

Charcot's emphasis on who was the *master* (the italics are his) may have been little more than normal professional arrogance, but it does point to an area worthy of much further exploration. Holy anorexia involves a need to establish a sense of oneself, a contest of wills, a quest for autonomy. But before we explore this theme it is appropriate to digress, geographically and theoretically, to consider the work of Charcot's even more influential contemporary.

Although Sigmund Freud did not deal explicitly with anorexia nervosa, his theories have had such a profound impact on all areas of psychiatric medicine that some note must be made of his contributions to the understanding and treatment of this illness. That he and his early associate, Josef Breuer, encountered anorexic patients is beyond doubt. One need look no further than the widely known case of Fräulein Anna O. At the age of twenty-one she became ill and turned to Breuer for help. He described her as intelligent, imaginative, poetic, extremely kind, and formerly of excellent health. Even in her illness, which Breuer diagnosed as hysteria, she looked "after a number of poor, sick people, for she was thus able to satisfy a powerful instinct . . . The element of sexuality was astonishingly undeveloped in her." In her "private theater" she indulged in systematic day-dreaming and during her illness she experienced an "enormous number of hallucinations." Variously she presented severe vision disturbances, paralyses of the limbs, paresis of the neck muscles, paraphasia, and somnambulism. As she nursed her beloved father in his final illness she developed an extreme distaste for food, perhaps, thought Breuer, due to a nervous cough occasioned by her desire to go dancing instead of tending to the patient, her sleeping habits changed, and she went into lengthy periods of autohypnosis. Her condition worsened as she lost all sense of pain in her extremities, showed signs of a split personality, and became unable to speak. Breuer then describes Anna's eating habits more fully.

> She had eaten extremely little previously, but now she refused nourishment altogether. However, she allowed me to feed her, so that she very soon began to take more food. But she never consented to eat bread. After her meal she invariably rinsed out her mouth and even did so if, for any reason, she had not eaten anything—which shows how absent-minded she was about such things.[11]

During this time she lived mostly on oranges, and a year later Breuer had only to hold an orange before her eyes in order to carry Anna O.'s recall back to this time, indeed, to a day by day reliving of the year 1881. Even in the preceding summer, before she became manifestly ill, she had "lived only on fruit, such as melons" and later she experienced intense feelings of nausea. Breuer reported that he sequentially located and "cured" the psychic sources of each of her "hysterical" manifestations and that she made a complete recovery, but recently discovered evidence shows conclusively that Anna O. remained ill for the rest of her life. In considering the holy anorexia of Catherine of Siena the reader may note several important parallels between the saint who martyred herself and Breuer's patient.

Consider next the illness of Frau Emmy von N., a forty-year-old woman in whose condition Freud took a great interest. Her list of symptoms is lengthy and bizarre, ranging from ticlike facial movements to clacking sounds, to amnesia, somnambulism, and animal hallucinations accompanied by severe gastric pains. Freud judged her illness to be "hysterical," and anorexia was certainly only one of many aspects of her malady. In concentrating on this single aspect we nevertheless may gain some insight into Freud's influence on the treatment of self-inflicted starvation. The child of an overenergetic and severe mother, Frau Emmy had been "constantly ill" for the preceding fourteen years, ever since the untimely death of her husband (she would therefore have been twenty-six at the time), and during this period she had had only marginal success in raising two sickly and nervous daughters. Her anorexia began at the time of her husband's death when "she had for a long time lost her appetite completely and had eaten only from a sense of duty; and her gastric pains had in fact begun at that time." After employing a combination of rather traditional treatments, bathing and massages, with regular hypnosis, Freud notes that Frau Emmy became "perfectly well," or at least so she appeared. But one day he happened by at lunchtime and caught Emmy throwing her dry pudding into the garden, where the eager children of the houseporter captured their dessert. It turned out that she had been doing so regularly and also that she ate less than half of her other courses and could not tolerate water. According to Freud the lady did not look noticeably thin but he nevertheless aimed at "feeding her up a little." Suddenly the previously cooperative patient became extremely resistant, eating the whole of her helpings one day but then becoming "profoundly depressed" and "very ungracious" the next and vowing to eat nothing at all for at least five days. For the first time she refused to enter a hypnotic state and was "in open rebellion." Freud had little patience with uppity women, and we may suspect that he did not fully realize that Emmy was involved in a contest of wills, a struggle for self-mastery. All was resolved on another day, when Freud put Frau von N. under hypnosis and quickly located, at least to his satisfaction, the sources of her anxieties about eating: a mother who forced her to eat cold and fatty meat she had refused at dinner, a brother with a horrible contagious disease whose knife and fork she feared she might accidentally use, another brother with consumption who sickened her by using an open spittoon at the table, and a bout of gastric catarrh from bad drinking water in Munich. These fears he removed and two months later Emmy reported that "I am eating excellently and have put on a great deal of weight."[12]

Freud's discussion of Frau Emmy von N.'s eating disorder is a classic statement of one approach to anorexia nervosa. Its refinement over several generations softens the edges but does not change the essence of his analysis.

> Our patient's anorexia offers a most brilliant instance of this kind of abulia [inhibition of will or inability to act due to the presence of an affectively toned and unresolved association which is opposed to linking up with other associations]. She ate so little because she did not like the taste, and she could not enjoy the taste because the act of eating had from the earliest times been connected with memories of disgust whose sum of affect had never been to any degree diminished . . . her old-established disgust at mealtimes had persisted un-

diminished because she was obliged constantly to suppress it, instead of getting rid of it by reaction. In her childhood she had been forced under threat of punishment, to eat cold meat that disgusted her, and in her later years she had been prevented out of consideration for her brothers from expressing the affects to which she was exposed during their meals together.[13]

Elsewhere in his analysis of Emmy's condition (and a matter he obviously expanded upon at length) Freud noted, quite briefly, that it is the sexual element which is "more liable than any other to provide occasion for traumas" and that Emmy's state of sexual abstinence over many years was a "neurotic" factor since such abstinence is "among the most frequent causes of a tendency to anxiety." Later work by Freud and his followers asserted even more clearly a link between self-starvation and the sexual drive. The anorexic patient, according to one influential formulation, in rejecting food is refusing an oral impregnation fantasy involving the father's incorporated phallus. Eating binges, constipation, and amenorrhea, all typical of anorexia nervosa, respectively symbolize oral impregnation, the child in the abdomen, and the amenorrhea of pregnancy. This symbolic sexual approach, as well as the more direct attempt to discover "abulias" arising from early eating experiences, are widespread in the modern discussion of anorexia nervosa. For reasons to be explored more fully in due course, however, they seem to me not to constitute the most useful way to understand holy anorexia. Appetite and sexual drive are related, and the virtually universal presence of amenorrhea in female anorexics is not incidental, but one is not merely a displacement, symbolization, or substitution for the other. Rather, appetite and sexual drive are related but distinct parts of a constellation of bodily urges that the holy anorexic seeks to tame and ultimately to obliterate.

To inaugurate the 1906–7 academic year of Harvard Medical School, its trustees decided to invite the eminent Pierre Janet to deliver a series of fifteen lectures based on his work in France. One of these lectures Janet devoted to anorexia nervosa, or, as he termed the disease, *hysterical anorexy*. Building on the work of Lasègue and Charcot, he described hysterical anorexy as an illness with three distinct stages occurring over a period never shorter than eighteen months and often lasting ten years or more. In the first, or gastric stage, the patient is extremely docile and willing to alter her diet and take her medicines in an effort to rid herself of vague stomach pains. The second, or moral state, finds the girl in conflict with family members who by now suspect her of being a stubborn hypochondriac. In turn the girl becomes resistant, feeling that any concession on her part would betray her as the capricious child her exasperated parents have come to think she is instead of the determined person she wishes herself to be. At the same time she becomes hyperactive; more ominously, she habitually vomits whatever she has been induced to swallow. In the last stage, or period of inanition, life itself is at risk and the patient's symptoms cannot be hidden: foul breath, retracted abdomen, constipation, little urine, dry and cracked skin, quick pulse, shortness of breath. The girl is bedridden and in a delirious, semicomatose state. At this point some patients, including several treated by Charcot and Janet, refuse to eat and consequently die. Others, such as those reported by Lasègue, become frightened, yield to the authority of their doctors, and recover.

Janet's description of the course of anorexia nervosa has a fatalistic quality. He sensed deeply that there was no alternative to watching the patient deteriorate from stages one to two to three before making the hopefully authoritative intervention. The regularity and gravity of the disease's evolution led him to conclude that "it is due to a deep psychological disturbance, of which the refusal of food is but the outer expression." Probably Janet is correct, although he was unable to specify the nature of the deep disturbance. He was especially intrigued by the hyperactivity of anorexics in the second stage of their disease, usually the most protracted by far of the three phases, and lasting ten years or even more. Gull and Lasègue, among others, had noted an extreme fondness for physical exercise among their patients but had seen this as a secondary symptom reflecting the girls' efforts to prove that they were not sick or as part of a conscious effort to become yet thinner. Janet disagreed, for he suspected that hyperactivity was central to the disease itself and involved a suppression of the feeling of fatigue, something much more important than any possible anesthesia of the stomach. The result of such suppression, he told his Harvard audience, was a heightened level of "physical and moral activity, a strange feeling of happiness, an euphoria." "The feeling of euphoria," suggested Janet, "as it is known in the ecstatic saints, for instance, does away with the need of eating. Our hysterical anorexy is to be traced to much deeper sources than was supposed." It is precisely these deeper sources, which

Janet modestly chose not to pretend to explain, that must be explored to reach an understanding of holy anorexia.[14]

The suppression of physical urges and basic feelings—fatigue, sexual drive, hunger, pain—frees the body to achieve heroic feats and the soul to commune with God. Or so I shall propose. Once this new and special reward system is experienced it does indeed become self-induced and self-perpetuating, a classic instance of affect/response, affect/response. But extraordinary physical activity and starvation cannot continue indefinitely. At the critical juncture, stage three in Janet's groping but astute analysis, the holy anorexic heeds, not the advice of a worldly physician, but the call of higher authority. Death becomes a logical, sweet, and total liberation from the flesh. The path of saintly austerity is well marked, and its rewards are ultimate. The end is easier to explain than the beginning. Why did Saints Catherine of Siena, Veronica Giuliani, Mary Magdalen de' Pazzi, Francesca de' Ponziani, and others choose or fall into the way of holy anorexia in the first place?

Before attempting to answer this question by examining the lives of these women, however, let us return to the subject of the present chapter. Shortly after Janet's lecture, which turned out to be something of a stopping point in the psychiatric approach to anorexia nervosa, medical opinion on the causes of self-induced starvation changed dramatically. The occasion for the shift was the publication in 1914 by M. Simmonds of autopsy findings showing destructive lesions of the pituitary gland in a severely emaciated pregnant woman. For the next twenty years the psychological factors isolated by Gull, Lasègue, and others were largely ignored, and most physicians treated virtually all presentments of extreme malnutrition, even if apparently self-induced, as primary endocrine disturbances. Even after Simmonds disease was clearly distinguished from anorexia nervosa in the late 1930s, somatic approaches continued to be prominent in attempts to treat cases of self-starvation.[15]

Physical factors are important, if for no other reason than that starvation, regardless of its cause, produces many of the symptoms typical of anorexia nervosa. Even experts most closely associated with psychiatric approaches to treatment, such as Minuchin, Selvini-Palazzoli, and Bruch, agree that no psychoanalytic work is useful until the severe consequences of undernutrition are overcome. Tube feeding, behavior modification, hyperalimentation, and drug therapy all have been used frequently to bring about rapid weight gain. The result is the disappearance or amelioration of symptoms related to a general slowdown of bodily functions among starved individuals: hypotension, bradycardia, changes in skin and hair texture and color, water retention, constipation, and hypothermia. Endocrine system functions also return to normal levels or at least improve. Moreover, several psychic conditions sometimes associated with anorexia nervosa—extreme self-absorption, psychotic-like thinking, regression to childish ways of reasoning, and splitting of the ego—have been observed widely in victims of externally imposed starvation. These conditions, too, are reported to respond to better nourishment.

The major problem with purely somatic approaches, however, is that a majority of patients who "recover" after such therapy subsequently suffer relapses. Moreover, hyperactivity and amenorrhea often precede weight loss in the onset of anorexia nervosa. Whatever the merits of distinguishing the general effects of starvation from consequences unique to anorexia nervosa, a matter about which there is some disagreement among present-day medical practitioners, it is neither possible nor fruitful to do so in considering holy anorexia. Starvation alone certainly did not cause holy anorexia. Even the most severe authorized regimens of ritual fasting, customary abstemiousness, and regulated diet never turned convents into hunger camps. Nearly all of the specific cases of holy anorexia to be considered in this study involve girls whose families were of sufficient means that involuntary undernutrition is very unlikely. Our problem is both more complicated and more intriguing. Certain holy women set upon a path of rigorous austerity, encouraged to this course by the very same patriarchy that then unsuccessfully ordered them to turn back. Once they did, starvation steadily amplified symptoms which these anorexics and their confessors, friends, families, and followers came to understand as signs of heavenly favor.[16]

Another aspect of the organic approach to anorexia nervosa is the theory that the condition is caused by hypothalamic disease. Experiments with animals show that lesions of the hypothalamus result in aversion to food, behavioral disturbances, abnormal fluid retention, low gonadotropin secretion, and even hyperactivity—in sum, a wide range of psychic and organic symptoms found in anorexia nervosa. One recent study goes so far as to suggest that the disease be renamed "puberal starvation-amenorrhea" in order to be less committed about its etiology.[17] No one doubts that hypothalamic malfunctioning is involved in anorexia nervosa, but there is sharp disagreement, and no resolution in sight, over the nature of this involvement. One possibility is that starvation damages the hypothalamus, an explanation that obviously fails to explain why self-imposed emaciation begins at all but that may be incorporated usefully along with other consequences of starvation into an overall evaluation of the course of holy anorexia. Another possibility is that a primary hypothalamic defect of unknown organic etiology is at work. Even if this turns out to be true, we would be left to explain why and how cultural responses to the disease have varied so greatly over the centuries. The final possibility, the one most widely accepted among present-day theorists and the starting point for the argument of this essay, is that hypothalamic malfunction follows from psychic stress or command. In this view, the hypothalamus is understood as a "crossroads" area of nerve cells that accepts directions from the higher brain centers of the cerebral cortex and transmits them downward and outward. In short, I assume, although it cannot be proved or disproved, that the onset of Saint Catherine of Siena's anorexia was a consequence not primarily of lesions in her hypothalamus but of psychic factors, in her case her will to conquer bodily urges that she considered base obstructions in her path of holiness. Once the pattern of conquest and reward was established, no doubt acting through her hypothalamus, starvation intensified the consequences of her holy anorexia and ultimately she died in a state of inanition, or, as her confessor tells us, exhausted by her holy austerities.[18]

The psychic/somatic approach to anorexia nervosa, as opposed to the purely organic explanation which holds the disease to be of unknown origin, offers several theories relevant to an exploration of holy anorexia. Earlier writers, steeped in the Freudian tradition, emphasized intrapersonal factors. In the beliefs of primitives as in the fantasies of children, Waller and his associates wrote in 1940, pregnancy occurs through eating. The child may repress these fantasies, but they remain powerful at the subconscious level throughout life. Especially in adolescence, girls who feel the unmistakeable biological and social signs of entering the genital-sexual stage of physical and psychic development may regress to the apparent comforts of the oral stage. This in turn leads to a re-awakening of oral impregnation wishes, consequent feelings of guilt, refusal to eat, and life-threatening emaciation representing an inverted aspect of infantile killing impulses, in particular against the mother. In a recent formulation of this drive-oriented psychoanalytic view, Helmut Thomä suggests that the anorexic suffers from an unbearable conflict over the dependency of an inside need, hunger, upon an outside object, food. He then quotes from a revealing treatment session:

> Bottle—child—disgust, if I think of it—injections—the idea that there is something flowing into me, into my mouth or into the vagina, is maddening—integer, integra, integrum occurs to me—untouchable—he does not have to bear a child—a man is what he is—he need not receive and he need not give.[19]

In a recent work, *Saints and Society*, Donald Weinstein and I set forth a major distinction between male and female saints, especially with regard to their ascetic practices, based on their differing perceptions of the locus of sin. For women evil was internal and the Devil a domestic parasitic force, whereas for men sin was an impure response to an external stimulus, one that left the body inviolate.[20] If that formulation makes sense, it follows that the Freud/Waller/Thoma model of anorexia nervosa as a food/sex oral fixation expresses in modern psychoanalytic terms a set of circumstances relevant to the Catholic Middle Ages as well. But specific application of intrapersonal psychological theory in a historical context is fraught with difficulties. The most obvious problem, the one that seems to trigger obsessive-compulsive attacks by some historians on all psychodynamic models, concerns evidence. Even among saints, many of whom were objects of awe and comment from earliest infancy, adequate information on the oral stage of development is lacking. Often the description of adolescent crisis and conversion is much richer, alas, so rich as to invite psychoanalytic speculations that unfortunately cannot be proved. As Freud himself recognized, and as the psychiatric profession is painfully aware, the most practical test of theory is whether it produces results, whether therapy helps sick patients to recover. Historians do not have this luxury; our cast of characters is dead and beyond our help or harm. The result is that psychoanalytic theory, applied to a historical problem, easily becomes purely descriptive or reductionist; and even when it purports to be explanatory, proof is not possible. Snakes, toads, and ferocious beasts abound in the hallucinations of holy anorexics, but why assume that these have sexual as well as religious significance? When Francesca de' Ponziani saw a serpent she believed the Devil was attacking her, and it seems not to be of historical consequence that this serpent may have symbolized repressed penis envy. Given the hopeless inadequacy of the evidence and the descriptive, untestable nature of psychodynamic theory in a historical context, the signs and symbols so abundant in the lives of saints neither support nor refute the Freud/Waller/Thomä approach for understanding holy anorexia. Nevertheless, that approach must suggest a more general awareness of the importance of gender differences and of the particular biosocial experiences that led some medieval adolescent women to extreme asceticism.[21]

Recent medical literature on anorexia nervosa has moved beyond sole consideration of the oral component and toward an approach that offers better possibilities for the consideration of holy anorexia. The recently deceased Hilde Bruch, whose pioneering studies made her the foremost authority in the world on the disease, confessed that she had begun as an unabashed Freudian, but later she deemphasized intrapsychic conflict in favor of a more interactive view. Naturally enough, much of what she wrote applied primarily to the contemporary context, as, for example, her inclusion of Twiggy and dieting fads as possible causes of the rapid spread of the disease in the 1960s. But throughout her technical works, especially *Eating Disorders*, and in her highly readable popular account, *The Golden Cage*, Bruch stressed the larger themes of identity, autonomy, and perfection.

> Anorexics struggle against feeling enslaved, exploited, and not permitted to lead a life of their own. They would rather starve than continue a life of accommodation. In this blind search for a sense of identity and selfhood they will not accept anything that their parents, or the world around them, has to offer . . . [In] *genuine* or *primary anorexia nervosa*, the main theme is a struggle for control, for a sense of identity, competence, and effectiveness.[22]

The typical anorexic girl comes from a two-parent family of middle- or upper-middle-class status. Her mother has read all the correct books on how to be nurturing and loving without smothering the child's initiative. Her father, an ambitious, upwardly mobile, and driving individual, often participates actively in establishing the household's norms. On every matter of consequence to them, they have an opinion: obesity is ugly, unhealthy, and lower-class, so the family eats balanced meals and avoids junk foods and snacks. Dad may not have read Thomas Jefferson's injunction to his eleven-year-old daughter Patsy—"Take care that you never spell a word wrong. . . . If you love me then, strive to be good under every situation"[23]—and surely he knows better than to be quite so openly oppressive, but subconsciously he loves success and detests failure. He demands no less of others than of himself, for he is a man whose compassion is tempered by logic. His wife joins him in measuring her love out carefully.

The girl always has been a favorite of teachers: never docile, just innately eager to learn; never forbidden to engage in foolish child's play, just naturally more interested in music lessons, ballet, and reading Jane Austen; never so brilliant as to be troublesome, just a very good and slightly overachieving student. Adults find her delightfully mature, and she is popular with her agemates as well. In its early stages her anorexia goes virtually unnoticed, for in their different ways both the loving mother and the striving father always wanted their daughter to be independent, to try new things, and to choose the best freely for herself. At worst they see a harmless fad, and quite often a wise and self-reliant decision to give up sweets and fats in favor of modest portions of wholesome celery sticks and protein-rich chicken livers. The girl knows this to be the test of her willpower. Her special goodness as a child was all a fake; she was never truly good enough anyway, and sometimes she wanted not to be good at all. Now she will excel, in an intensely personal contest of her choice, over her feelings and drives. She will be an individual, not a daughter or a pupil. She does not seek to goad her parents into opposing her and resorts to silence, deception, secretiveness, and outright lying to avoid having them enter her contest, her world. Good girl that she is, she goes willingly to the doctor, very calmly explains that nothing is wrong, and dutifully agrees to do just as he says. She refuses rewards for eating heartily and willingly accepts punishments for leaving too much on her plate. In the bathroom she practices sticking her fingers down her throat and regurgitating, quietly, so that no one will be disturbed. Saint Teresa of Avila, the Spanish mystic and spiritual force of the Catholic Reformation who invigorated whole Orders, regularly used an olive twig to induce vomiting so that she might receive the host without fear of rejecting it. Weight loss is very rapid.

How is it that a good girl raised by well-meaning and concerned parents becomes so dangerously ill? In Bruch's view (one shared by Levenkron, Sours, Minuchin, Orbach, and other leading theorists despite their differences on questions of therapy—a matter explored by Dr. William Davis in the Epilogue) the girl always lived for others, judged herself by their standards, and let them define her identity. Raised to strive for perfection and to seek approval from narcissistic parents, she now is able to set for herself a daily, relentless, physically torturing challenge, one over which she alone has control. The immediate cause of her desperate choice may be a lower than expected grade at school or it may be the onset of bodily maturation, the uncontrollable fattiness of developing breasts and rounding hips, or it may be a disgusting sexual encounter, but it is the underlying psychological need to gain a sense of self that is the essence.

The anorexic girl feels hopelessly inadequate and ineffective in dealing with others—parents, friends, teachers, psychiatrists. And yet she has become the master of herself. Regardless of what others see and prefer, she sees her emaciated appearance as normal and likes it very much. Others may tell her that she must be hungry and fatigued, but she feels no need to eat more and is constantly on the go. Others warn her that if she keeps this up she will never be able to have children; she admits to loving children, but the idea of being someone's wife stands in the way. To admit to being sick—not temporarily to be released from the hospital, with its tube feeding or demeaning behavior modification program, but truly to understand that she is ill—means that the girl must give up mastery for slavery. No wonder the recovery rate is so low.[24]

The holy anorexic never gives in, and ultimately she may die of her austerities. She rejects the passive, dependent Catholic religion of mediation through priests and intercession by saints, and so herself becomes a saint. Usually she is a happy and obedient child of well-to-do, perhaps even noble, parents. In various ways she is a special child, sometimes the last and most precious, other times the only survivor, always beloved. Precocious signs of extraordinary holiness may be part of her early *vita*, but even the most fanciful of these do not suggest the bitter struggle that will follow. At first her devout parents encourage her spiritual impulses; she prays for their souls as well. Quickly, however, the conventional nature of their religiosity becomes apparent and they turn against a daughter who rejects not only their worldliness but also the accepted path of an established convent.

The girl, that she may become more beautiful in God's eyes, may cut off her hair, scourge her face, and wear coarse rags. To be more mindful of the Passion she may walk about with thirty-three sharp stones in her shoes or drive silver nails into her breasts. She stands through the night with arms outstretched in penitential prayer and stops eating, taking her nourishment from the host. If so much as a bean remained in Catherine of Siena's stomach, she vomited. Toward others the holy girl is docile and uncomplaining, even servile, and yet in her spiritual world her accomplishments are magnificent. She becomes Christ's bride, not His handmaiden but His bride, and regularly communicates with Him, with Mary, and with the heavenly host. These extraordinary favors she relates to the world through her confessor, assuring him all the while that she is an utterly worthless and debased servant of God. Nonetheless, possessed of supernatural grace, she is perfectly willing to tell popes and kings what to do and how to do it. To be the servant of God is to be the servant of no man. To obliterate every human feeling of pain, fatigue, sexual desire, and hunger is to be master of oneself.

In describing this behavior as "holy anorexia" I mean to draw attention to both the similarities and the differences between it and "anorexia nervosa." The modifier is the key; whether anorexia is holy or nervous depends on the culture in which a young woman strives to gain control of her life. In both instances anorexia begins as the girl fastens onto a highly valued societal goal (bodily health, thinness, self-control in the twentieth century/spiritual health, fasting, and self-denial in medieval Christendom). Her peers, and especially her parents, pursue this goal with only marginal success, more often than not honoring it only in the breach. She, by contrast, emerges from a frightened, insecure, psychic world superficially veiled by her outwardly pleasant disposition to become a champion in the race for (bodily/spiritual) perfection. Her newly won self-esteem and confidence initially receive the approbation of those she depends upon—parents, teachers, counselors—causing her to deepen her self-denial pattern until it takes over as the only source of her sense of self. Anorexia becomes her identity, and ultimately the self-starvation pattern continues beyond her conscious control.

Insecurity (I am no one/I am a worthless, debased sinner) gives way to absolute certainty. The modern anorexic exhibits visual distortion and literally *sees* herself in the mirror as being heavier and wider than she is; she *feels* just fine and in fact accomplishes feats of considerable physical endurance. The holy anorexic *sees* Jesus' bridal ring on her finger and a place for herself in heaven; she *feels* God's love and energetically lives on the host alone. Each pursues her externally different but psychologically analogous, culturally approved objective with fanatical, compulsive devotion. Eventually, however, her self-destructive, life-threatening behavior commands the attention of family, friends, and professionals.

Our own world, imbued with a progressive spirit of scientific rationalism, defines anorexia as a nervous condition and sets out to "cure" its victims. While there is much dispute among medical experts about the most appropriate therapy, all agree that the anorexic must be helped to change her ways. Medieval people, on the other hand, were less sure of their power to control events and to shape the lives of others. Confronted with a young woman who fasted until her very life was at risk, they cautiously tried to determine whether this was the work of God or of the devil. Some of the holy anorexics to be considered in the chapters that follow actually underwent formal trials on charges of heresy and witchcraft, charges made at least in part because of suspicions about their eating habits. All of them, however, even those not formally tried, confronted a deeply skeptical male clerical hierarchy.

Among an unknowable total number of medieval anorexics probably only a small percentage managed to convince parents and then church officials that their strange behavior was inspired by God. Clearly it required enormous charisma and outward self-confidence (despite inner doubts that they never eradicated completely) to initiate and then to sustain such a lofty claim. The few who did so successfully quickly became objects of awe and reverence, people who seemed to exercise the power and might of carrying forth God's work and of knowing His will. Their anorexia came to be seen as part of a wider pattern of heroic, ascetic masochism amply justified in the literature of radical Christian religiosity. This public response, even when the "public" was limited to a small number of nuns and visiting confessors in a cloistered convent, reinforced the anorexic's sense of self, sometimes contributing to her "recovery," other times deepening her self-starvation pattern until it led to death. Either way, it was Christendom's patriarchy, not the girl herself, who had to define her anorexia as saintly rather than demonic or sick. We who seek to understand these women and to explore what that understanding may tell us about our own world can do so best if we keep in the foreground not only the psychological dimensions of self-starvation but also the cultural imperatives of medieval holiness, for it is the intersection of the two that results in holy anorexia.

I, CATHERINE

IN THE NAME of Jesus Christ crucified and sweet Mary.
Dearest beloved Father in Christ sweet Jesus, I Catherine, useless servant of Jesus Christ, entrust myself to you; with a desire to
see us united and transformed in that sweet, eternal and pure
Truth, Truth that cleanses us of every falsehood and lie. I dearest
Father, cordially thank you for the saintly zeal and jealous care
that you have for my soul; because it seems to me that you are
very worried, hearing about my life. I am sure you have no other
motive than the desire to honor God and care for my health, fear-
ing a demonic siege and self-deception. About this fear, Father,
particularly about the matter of eating, I am not surprised; I assure you not only you are fearful, I myself also tremble with fear of
a demonic trick. But I place myself in the goodness of God; and do
not trust myself, knowing that in myself I cannot trust. In response to your question whether I believed it possible to be deceived, saying that if I did not so believe this [in itself] would be a
demonic deception, I answer you that not only in this, which is
merely a bodily function, but in this and in all my other actions,
because of my frailness and the devil's cunning I am always afraid,
thinking that I may be deceived; because I know and see that the
devil lost beatitude but not knowledge with which knowledge, as
I said, I know he could deceive me. But I turn to and lean upon the
tree of the most holy cross of Christ crucified and there I wish
to be nailed; and do not doubt that I will be pierced through
and nailed with him for love and with deep humility, that devils
will not harm me, not for my virtue but for the virtue of Christ
crucified.

You wrote to me saying in particular that I should pray God that

I might eat. And I say to you, my Father, and I say it to you in the sight of God, that in every possible way I could I always forced myself once or twice a day to take food; and I prayed continually and I pray to God and will pray, that he will grace me in this matter of eating so that I may live like other creatures, if this is his will, because mine is there. I say to you that many times, when I did what I could, then I look[ed] into myself to understand my infirmity, and [the goodness of] God who by a most singular mercy allowed me to correct the vice of gluttony. It saddens me greatly that I did not correct this weakness [myself] for love. As to myself I do not know what other remedy to try, other than that I beg you that you beseech that highest eternal Truth to grant me the grace of allowing me to take food, if this be more for his honor and for the health of my soul, and if it pleases him. And I am certain that God's goodness will not disdain your prayers. I beg you that whatever remedy you see in this, you write to me, and as long as it is the will of God I shall take it gladly. And further I beg you that you not be too quick to judge, unless you have cleared yourself in the presence of God. I say nothing further. Remain in the holy and sweet love of God. Sweet Jesus, loving Jesus.

[CATHERINE BENINCASA, to a Religious in Florence][1]

C A T H E R I N E Benincasa was a woman of about twenty-six when she dictated these words, sometime in 1373 or 1374. Already a person of considerable reputation for outstanding holiness, she was also a center of controversy. Typically she confronted her enemies and detractors with the subtle mixtures of defiance, irony, sarcasm, and exasperating claims of total humility that mark this letter. Always she acted in every matter as she said her spiritual bridegroom Jesus Christ told her she should, and not as earthly men might order or advise. That she ate almost nothing was widely known; such behavior not only was scandalous in itself but led some of her contemporaries to believe she was possessed by the devil. Her abstemiousness went far beyond the austere or ritual fasting of even the most holy men and women of her day and often was in direct violation of the explicit directions of her confessors. Various of these men assigned to watch, control, and guide her in the path of holiness (and to protect the Church from a possible heretic in its midst) ordered her to eat. For a time she obeyed, but the presence of even a mouthful of food in her stomach caused her to vomit, and after a while she simply refused.

Warned that by such eating habits she was bringing about her own death, Catherine shot back that eating would kill her anyway so she might as well die of starvation, and do as she wished in the meantime.[2]

The most important source of our information about Catherine Benincasa, apart from her own writings, is a biography composed during the decade or so after her death by Raymond of Capua. He became her confessor and spiritual guide in 1374, shortly after Catherine had been summoned from Siena to Florence to appear before a formal Church commission and give an account of herself. Although she managed to persuade her inquisitors of the correctness of her thought and behavior, nonetheless both the Master General of the Dominican Order, of which she was a tertiary, and the Pope decided jointly to appoint the somewhat worldly, occasionally skeptical, and already powerful Raymond to be her new confessor and to watch closely over her. During the next four years their spiritual and personal relationship was intense. For Catherine confession was no perfunctory accounting of sins followed by absolution and penance but a long and detailed theological and psychological examination of all the extraordinary experiences of her religious life. Raymond served as Catherine's counselor no less than Freud did for his favored patients centuries later, nor did the Dominican friar fail to record carefully all that he observed or heard from Catherine during their extended sessions. After her death Raymond collected his own notes and those of her earlier confessor, as well as the testimonies of many other people who had known her.

From these sources he constructed a *legenda*. The term to him had its original meaning of a thing to be read rather than the modern connotation of a fable; he meant it to be the fundamental, documented account of her life, for the edification of the faithful and with an eye to Catherine's possible canonization. He left out stories he could not verify from multiple firsthand witnesses (whose names he listed in his text) or that to him seemed exaggerated or fanciful. Still, like nearly everyone in his day, his belief in the supernatural was unquestioned and he certainly never intended to be a rational, scientific historian. As he must have anticipated in taking time out from his many duties to write the *vita*, for by this time he himself had become Master General of the Dominican Order in Italy, it was the basis not only for Catherine's ultimate canonization in 1461 but also was read widely and became a source of inspiration for preachers and artists alike.

A vernacular translation by Neri di Landoccio soon followed and appeared in print in 1477, one of the earliest published books; that three other editions rolled off the presses before the end of the century clearly indicates Catherine's popularity among both clergy and laity. Her life became a model consciously imitated by holy anorexics over the next two centuries. Raymond of Capua's *Legenda* consists of thirty chapters of which the seventeenth, running to fifteen good-sized printed pages in the modern edition, is devoted to Catherine's eating habits.[3]

As a youth Catherine had fasted rigorously but not to excess by the standards of this age of heroic asceticism. Then at the time of her conversion to radical holiness, beginning when she was not yet sixteen, she restricted her diet to bread, uncooked vegetables, and water. About five years later, following her father's death and visions in which Christ told her to give up her solitary ways and go forth in the company of worldly men and women, she lost her appetite and could not eat bread. By the age of twenty-five, maybe a bit earlier we are told, she ate "nothing." Elsewhere it becomes clear that Catherine did not in fact eat nothing and that total suppression of hunger did not come to her easily or involuntarily (as her letter quoted earlier ingenuously claims) in the absence of her religious impulses. While dressing the cancerous breast sores of a woman she was tending, Catherine felt repulsed at the horrid odor of the suppuration. Determined to overcome all bodily sensations, she carefully gathered the pus into a ladle and drank it all. That night she envisioned Jesus inviting her to drink the blood flowing from his pierced side, and it was with this consolation that her stomach "no longer had need of food and no longer could digest."[4]

Raymond bases his account of Catherine's anorexia both on her confessions to him and on the writings (subsequently lost, although "Caffarini" may have incorporated them in his work) of her previous confessor, a relative named Tommaso. Divine grace so infused her body and deadened her life fluids that the nature of her stomach was transformed, is how Raymond begins. "Not only did she not need food, but she could not even eat without pain. If she forced herself to eat, her body suffered greatly, she could not digest and she had to vomit." Her family and friends immediately suspected a diabolic trick. Even her earlier confessor, who (Raymond tells us) meant well but was not very discerning, ordered her to ignore what he suspected was a demonically inspired impulse and to eat at least once a day. Catherine obeyed reluctantly, because she felt stronger and healthier when she did not eat; she grew ill and tired but still he commanded her to eat until she was reduced nearly to the point of death. Only then did Tommaso accept her reasoning that it would be better to die from fasting than from eating and tell her to "do as the Holy Spirit suggests to you."[5]

Freed from the command of her early confessor, Catherine had to face the world. Concerning her inability to eat, writes Raymond, "everyone had something to say against this holy virgin." Certainly her habits were difficult to understand. She drank only a little cold water and chewed on bitter herbs while spitting out the substance. To Raymond and others she seemed about to die at any moment, yet, until the very end, at the opportunity to honor God or do an act of charity, and without medicine, she became robust, vigorously outwalked her companions, and never grew tired—in short, she became hyperactive. She took nourishment from the host alone, a connection not lost on her ever-probing confessor and biographer. One day Raymond asked Catherine whether when she did not receive communion her appetite was stimulated. Her answer suggests a concentration on the host that is found among virtually all holy anorexics, one that reveals continued mental effort to suppress bodily urges that in fact are not entirely dormant: "When I cannot receive the Sacrament, it satisfies me to be nearby and to see it; indeed, even to see a priest who has touched the Sacrament consoles me greatly, so that I lose all memory of food."[6]

Detractors stated flatly that the whole self-starvation routine was a fiction she perpetrated to aggrandize her reputation and that secretly she ate very well indeed. Other skeptical observers recalled the biblical warning against Catherine's behavior, reminding her of Jesus' command to his disciples: eat and drink that which is placed before you (Luke 10:7). Who was she to refuse to do what Christ on earth, his glorious Mother, and the Apostles did? They ate and drank; a truly holy person ought to seek never to be singled out for attention and therefore in all matters follow common customs. Il Bianco da Siena, a follower of the harshly ascetic *gesuati*, who joined her compatriot Giovanni Colombini, wrote a *laude* to rebuke Catherine on this very point. Even a brief excerpt conveys the sarcastic and serene disrespect with which many men of religion greeted the Benincasa girl:[7]

| Now watch out, sister of mine | *Or ti guarda, suora mia* |
| | *Che no caggi in gran ruina:* |

That you not fall in great
    ruin.
If you have grace divine
Make sure that you keep it

Se tu hai grazia divina,
Fa che l'abbia conservata

Sister of mine, with cross
    ahead
Beware of the oiled praises
That already have led many
    astray
From goodness uncreated

Suora mia, con croce in fronte
Guardati dalle lod' unte:
Molte n' hanno già disgiunte
Dalla bontà increata

If the Spirit guides you
For earthly praise do not
    look,
By it the soul gets loose
If by her it is desired

Se lo Spirito ti mena
Non cercar loda terrena,
Per la qual l'anima sfrena,
Se da lei e disiata

He receives a big blow
Who follows one not
    keeping himself low,
If by praise your mind is
    fattened
With pain it will be
    flattened

Grande riceve spatassa
Chi segue chi non s'abassa
Se d'onor tua mente ingrassa
Con dolor fie dimagrata

More disconcerting to Catherine, and certainly more dangerous, was the suspicion of demonic possession or witchcraft. According to the beliefs of her day, Catherine's ability to live on
without food might well mean that she was being fed by the devil
in a symbiotic rapport with a familiar or an incubus. If this were
so, again according to a logic that made as good sense to Catherine
as to her detractors, she would not accept earthly food. The obvious way to silence her enemies, and all others who in one way or
another were scandalized by her fasting, was to prove that at least
she would try to eat like anyone else. Thus, to demonstrate that
she was not possessed, or possibly the even more serious charge
that she might be a witch, Catherine began to eat once daily and
in the company of her companions. Raymond of Capua at this
time apparently was already her confessor, which indicates that
she was at least twenty-seven years old. He describes her new life-
style as follows:

As we have said above, her stomach could digest nothing and
her body heat consumed no energy; therefore anything she
ingested needed to exit by the same way it entered, other-

wise it caused her acute pain and swelling of her entire body. The holy virgin swallowed nothing of the herbs and things she chewed; nevertheless, because it was impossible to avoid some crumb of food or juice descending into her stomach and because she willingly drank fresh water to quench her thirst, she was constrained every day to vomit what she had eaten. To do this she regularly and with great pain inserted stalks of fennel and other plants into her stomach, otherwise being unable to vomit. Because of her disparagers and particularly those who were scandalized by her fasting, she maintained this life-style until her death [about six years later].

Raymond, who one suspects may have advised Catherine in the first place to accept this eating/vomiting pattern both because he himself was unsure about her and to quash rumors of diabolic influence that inevitably cast a shadow on him, finally urged Catherine to ignore her detractors and abandon such agonizing ways. She refused, telling her confessor that the painful vomiting was penance for her sins and she much preferred to receive her just punishment in this world than the next. Raymond is left speechless by such inspired wisdom and closes his chapter by urging readers to reflect upon how this strange gift of God— Catherine's loss of appetite and inability to eat—became by her will and understanding a response pattern to be imitated.[8]

Catherine recognized fully that penitential routines and self-punishment did not in themselves bring her closer to spiritual perfection. In *The Dialogue* she urged "holy hatred" of oneself and "love fixed more on virtue than on penance." Penance, she wrote, must be measured according to one's need and capability. The essential effort had to be the destruction of self-will, not the accumulation of superficially meritorious acts. Further on in *The Dialogue* God warned her: "Reprove yourself if ever the devil or your own short-sightedness should do you the disservice of making you want to force all my servants to walk the same path you yourself follow." Notwithstanding the vast differences between Catherine's drive to be united with God and the modern-day anorexic's quest for a sense of self, the psychological dilemma is similar. The fourteenth-century saint, like the twentieth-century patient, says she *cannot* eat and denies that she is asserting her will or being stubborn. But it is her will that is at stake, and unless something works to deflect the contest, its logical outcome is death.[9]

From all this testimony—Catherine's own words, the disparaging comments of her detractors, and especially the lengthy, often perplexed, and inadvertently revealing *Legenda* by Raymond of Capua, not to mention the briefer or less reliable accounts discussed in the endnotes—a composite summary of Catherine Benincasa's anorexia emerges. What may have begun as religiously inspired fasting at some point escaped Catherine's full conscious control. As with present-day anorexics, she could be very active physically, slept very little, and claimed that she gladly would eat but had no appetite. When her fame grew, enemies fastened hard on her well-known refusal or inability to take food and variously charged her with being a liar, an unholy egotist, and a witch. Supporters and confessors urged or ordered her to eat; when she did so it was only to enter into an eating/vomiting cycle such as is common among acute, long-term anorexics. Whatever the primacy of physical circumstances involved, it was Catherine's *will* that shaped the course of her infirmity and gave it meaning. Throughout, she consciously countered the urges of appetite by concentrating on the host. No one, including Catherine, saw her diet in itself as something heroically ascetic. On the contrary, by the sheer power of her conviction she convinced people that behavior commonly thought to be insane or demonic was holy. None of the efforts of Catherine's friends, confessors, or enemies succeeded in changing her ways and curing her anorexia, and in the end she starved herself to death.[10]

To understand the personality that exuded such iron will and self-assurance is yet more difficult and problematic than the effort thus far to establish that Catherine's anorexia was not merely a case of excessive asceticism. At most I hope to offer a way, not necessarily the only way, of explaining why this young woman behaved as she did, how she understood herself, and how people reacted to her. I have no useful quarrel with those who would begin with a supernatural explanation, but mine will be a human analysis and the causes asserted will all be earthly. Therefore let us begin with breastfeeding, a subject as fascinating to hagiographers as to psychoanalysts.

Catherine was a twin, and both babies were weak. Her mother, Lapa Piacenti, was in her early forties and previously had borne twenty-two children, of whom less than half are known to have survived their infancy. Lapa did the right thing and quickly had both girls baptized lest they die without grace. Then she made the difficult choice of sending the sickly Giovanna out to a wet nurse while taking Catherine to her own breast. Giovanna died within a short time, but Catherine gradually gained strength and soon was robust. Lapa recalled that never before had she been able to complete nursing her children because always she had found herself pregnant, but with Catherine this did not happen and she nursed the infant for at least a full year before weaning her. Only then did Lapa become pregnant and give birth once more, probably when Catherine was about two, to a girl she named Giovanna in the memory of Catherine's dead twin. The new baby, affectionately called Nanna, died on April 18, 1363, the very year of Catherine's dramatic conversion to radical holiness. The source of these intimate details is Lapa herself, who lived to the ripe age of eighty-five or so and told them to Raymond of Capua as he was working on his biography of Catherine. His portrait of Lapa is generally unflattering, as are those of all other testimonies, but he does note that he believes her fully because "as everyone who knows her agrees, and notwithstanding her eighty years, she is so unaffected that even if she wanted to tell a lie she would not be able to."[11]

Whatever the accuracy of Lapa's recollections, it is unlikely that Catherine retained into the crucial years of her adolescence any direct memory of how she was nursed. If her presumably favored infancy left a permanent psychological impact on the girl, the surviving records cannot establish this fact beyond doubt. I believe Erik Erikson's theory on oral contentment may be applicable here to explain Catherine's enormous capacity for faith, but I do not know how to prove it from historical documents. Readers willing to consider the matter might begin with the following quotation from one of Catherine's confessions, as she described a vision in which she received Christ's succor: "Do you know, father, what God did for my soul that day? He did as a mother does to the child she loves the most. She shows her breast, but keeps it out of reach until he begins to cry; then she smiles benignly and takes him to her breast and, kissing him, presents the food happily and abundantly. This is what God did to me. That day he showed me from far away his holy side, and I cried with great desire to place my lips on the most sacred wound." It was "in exchange" for this consolation that Catherine believed God made her suffer a sharp and continuous pain in her breast.[12]

Moreover, some evidence we shall look at presently suggests surprisingly hostile feelings on Catherine's part about weaning. What is very likely, however, given all we are told about Lapa's ways, is that when the teenage Catherine began experimenting with radical and highly individualistic religious expressions, her anxious mother quickly and often flung at her daughter the *obligation* of having been a special infant, a child chosen to survive when her twin did not. Later, in a letter to her brothers in which Catherine reprimanded them for their lack of filial devotion, she explicitly reminded them of the "obligation" they owed to their mother because she had tried to nurse them.[13]

The year in which Catherine's mother weaned her favored girl, 1348, was a year of death. The plague struck with a virulence that terrorized the entire population, killing its victims within three days and striking one household or another without apparent reason. Murder, sorcery, lawlessness, and prayer all coexisted in a society where the dead seemed to outnumber the living. The general pandemonium of people escaping the city, corpses piling up on the streets, and survivors driven mad with fear that they would be the next to fall surely affected the Benincasa household. We need only to recall the vivid description by Catherine's contemporary, Giovanni Boccaccio, in his introduction to *The Decameron*. "This disaster had struck such fear into the hearts of men and women that brother abandoned brother, uncle abandoned nephew, sister left brother, and very often wife abandoned husband, and—even worse, almost unbelievable—fathers and mothers neglected to tend and care for their children as if they were not their own." Even if little Catherine was not a victim of neglect or abuse, the times were bad.[14]

Whether the family left Siena for their country home a few miles away we do not know, but it is not unlikely that their pressing business concerns led them to decide to stay in their town quarters and hope for God's protection. Giacomo, Catherine's father, was a dyer of some means, known for his patience and good sense. To join the fleeing throng offered no hope if God's will was that they should die, and to attempt escape meant abandoning his business. It was a particularly bad time to do that since only a year and a half earlier his eldest son had entered into a partnership with two other Sienese dyers and they had started their own firm, with Giacomo's help and blessing. The venture must have been going badly; sometime before August 1349 both partners died. Their heirs and Giacomo's eldest son on July 30, 1349, lost a major legal suit brought against them by Tomuccio di Iacobo di Colombino before Siena's Market Council. Exactly how much direct financial loss the infant Catherine's father suffered cannot be determined for sure since the accounts indicate that he established his son in business but do not prove that they were also legal partners;

still, Giacomo was not one of the many plague survivors who prospered as massive population decline left a relatively constant amount of wealth to be shared among fewer people. All descriptions of Lapa suggest that this worldly woman was very concerned with financial success, and the legal record testifies that her son soon was to become responsible for a debt more than twice as large as his original investment. The evidence of such business misfortune suggests little likelihood that the understandably distraught Lapa and Giacomo handled the weaning process in a way that would assist, or at least not profoundly affect, Catherine's emotional development. And then there are Catherine's mother's physiological circumstances to consider.[15]

Lapa was in her forties and yet "never before" had weaned her children, apparently because always she had found herself pregnant. When this happens a mother's milk becomes watery, losing its rich sweetness, and it is the child who soon rejects the breast in favor of more satisfying nourishment, not the mother who denies it. There is no triumph of the mother's will over her child's desire, but a physical change that neither controls nor even understands instantly but that both soon must accept. With Catherine it was different—Lapa first weaned Catherine and only then became pregnant. This mother's no-nonsense ways may have been hardened when she found herself so inexperienced in a matter that most women of her age knew how to handle. In so ordinary and seemingly trivial a contest of wills as weaning, it had to be mother Lapa who triumphed over daughter Catherine, but as an adult this particular child made sure never to lose such battles, often redefining a situation in her mind so that what might appear to others as obedience in this world was to her a triumph in the next for the bridegroom with whom she was united.[16]

Catherine never wrote about her own weaning, nor is there reason to suggest that any person has a direct and conscious recollection of such early experiences, but her mature understanding of the process is plain enough. She was in Avignon, France, in the late summer of 1376 on the most important mission of her public life, both as a special envoy for the warring city of Florence and to persuade Pope Gregory XI to return the Papacy to Rome. After an elaborate face-to-face meeting with the Supreme Pontiff, Catherine's most cherished desire was about to be realized, and we may understand that she saw this triumph as the result of her personal efforts rather than as the conjuncture of geopolitical considerations that historians know it was. Then at the last moment

Gregory wavered, asking Catherine for her opinion about a letter he had received from an unnamed holy man warning him that he would be poisoned if he returned to Rome. Her response is filled with livid anger and rebuke, certainly for the supposed holy man (whom she calls "less than a child," a "simpleton," and an "evil devil") and at least by implication for anyone who would follow such advice. She continues:

> I think he wants to do with you as the mother does to her child when she wants to take away the milk from his mouth. She puts something bitter on her breast so that he tastes the bitterness before the milk, so that for fear of the bitter he abandons the sweet; because a child is deceived more by bitterness than by anything else . . . And I pray you on behalf of Christ crucified not to be a timid child but manly. Open your mouth and swallow the bitter for the sweet. It does not become your Holiness to abandon milk because of the bitterness.[17]

In all her writings Catherine uses metaphors with abandon, mixing them freely and spontaneously; yet patterns emerge and it is hardly coincidental that at this crucial moment in her life, when her will that Gregory should return to Rome is being challenged by a powerful enemy, she uses maternal imagery. Nor is the choice of particular words without meaning. The simple word for weaning does not come to her mind, nor the commonly understood phrase for "breaking the habit" that Italians know means weaning; instead, she attempts to describe literally what happens by saying *tollere il latte di bocca*. Taking away or "removing milk from the mouth" is not precisely what happens, but that is how Catherine understands the matter. Shortly thereafter she uses the word *ingannare* to explain that a child is most easily "deceived" by bitterness. The word is a powerful one, generally reserved for the work of the devil or for adultery and other such familial deception and treachery. From the context of Catherine's letter to Pope Gregory it is impossible to be certain about how and why she uses this particular word; her letter is filled with references to the devil and also with very personal familial imagery. Maternal weaning and diabolic ruin of the Papacy have become one in Catherine's thought. Then, in a complete reversal of reality, she equates manliness with refusing to give up the breast and timidity with the usual growth process. Finally, the last phrase, in which Catherine uses the words "vostra Sanctita" (your Holiness), might also be read as "your Sanctity." If it were anyone else writing to the Pope this phrase might be passed over as a common form of address, but we know that this young woman regularly called Gregory her "Daddy," even her "sweetest Daddy," and neither knew about nor cared for proper form. Saint that she would be, Catherine had to be too humble to consider herself a saint and not so presumptuous as to grant this designation to Pope Gregory; and yet the words, and the weaning context, refer to both of them.[18]

We are on speculative ground here: a devastating plague, but one during which babies other than Catherine were weaned; business misfortunes not all that uncommon in the fourteenth century; a mother no worse or better than many; and an adult metaphor that may be read in several ways. And yet the combination of circumstances and words does tell something, especially if the question of *why* Catherine behaved as she did looms large. I suggest that Catherine's adult reference to weaning (one of many) is neither immaterial nor a simple carryover of common wisdom, but rather a possibly subconscious recounting of her own infant experience, and much more probable and significant, a conscious retelling of what her mother has made her feel deeply many times over, especially during their battles over Catherine's self-destructive asceticism: the comfort of the breast cannot be a safe haven or a place of return, for the exit is too painful. Catherine's self-starvation was not regression to oral delights (as some of the modern theories discussed in the preceding chapter would suggest) because for her the promise of being a special, chosen child always meant the death of another. Survival was a contest requiring manliness and the path of sanctity was bitter. For the young Benincasa girl it came to include sustained anorexia.[19]

Catherine spent her early years in the crowded Sienese district of Fontebranda, where she appears to have grown up much like other girls her age in the 1350s. She was a happy child, out of the house a lot and with a ready smile. The precocious religious expressions told by her biographers all seem quite natural. It is said that at the age of five she was found genuflecting and saying a Hail Mary at each step as she climbed to her bedroom. Such delight in ritual repetitiveness is quite common among children and this particular practice, which originated in Ireland, was widespread among the Sienese. Neighbors and playmates called Catherine "Euphrosyne," perhaps because the child reminded them of this legendary virgin or else because Catherine herself spoke with such incessant eagerness of her heroine. She learned about Euphrosyne from the widely popular *Golden Legend* of Jacopo da

Varazze, which recounts how centuries earlier a beautiful young girl, to escape an unwanted marriage and an angry father, changed into man's attire and retired to a monastery. Only on her deathbed, wasted by severe austerities, did Euphrosyne reveal to her grieving father her true identity, and he afterward spent his remaining ten years in her cell. That Catherine should have been so taken with the tale that she answered to the name Euphrosyne shows only a healthy and childish imagination. As an adolescent she faced the same difficulty as Euphrosyne, yet she forged a very different solution. That often she was seen frequenting local churches, gazing at images of saints, transfixed by candles, and inhaling incense does not surprise us. Her alternative was to sit at home with her busy, scolding mother and the noise and smell of her father's dyeing works on the floor below.[20]

At the age of six or seven, as she returned with her brother Stefano from an all-day errand to her married sister that took them beyond the city gates, Catherine experienced her first vision. In the sunset sky ahead of her she saw a *loggia* full of radiant light; Jesus, robed all in white like a bishop with the pastoral staff, smiled at her. Behind him were several saints, also dressed in white, and a shaft of light, a sunbeam, came from him and fell on her. Catherine stopped in her tracks, only to be rudely shaken by her brother when she did not answer his call. When she looked back up at the sky the vision had disappeared. The sunset, the tiring and exciting long day, the white imagery—it is all very natural and shows none of the extraordinary and embellished qualities so common in accounts of saints' lives. Even more revealing for our purposes is Catherine's reaction afterward. She said nothing to Stefano nor for several years to her parents or anyone else. Instead, she meditated in solitude, tried to understand whether the vision was good or evil, and what to make of it. The expected reaction of a religious seven-year-old who experiences a clearly happy and reinforcing vision would be to run home to tell her parents, perhaps also the local priest. Adults might be skeptical or patiently amused, but even a child who fears such a reaction usually would not be able to avoid bursting with excitement and telling someone. Why did this outgoing, exuberant girl who lived in a culture that believed readily in the supernatural and thirsted after favorable signs keep this vision to herself? What we have here, I suspect, is an indication that even as a young girl Catherine began to develop the capacity to rely for inner strength solely on her personal relationship with God, ignoring or opposing as necessary the dictates of the world around her. She cares very little for the confirmation and support of parents, friends, and confessors (and therefore becomes immune to their criticism as well). While in earthly matters she is an obedient and good child, her soul, spirit, psyche, or what you will, is becoming hers alone, nourished by a fusing of God's design and her ego that she alone interprets and arbitrates.[21]

From biographies written after her death and intended to show that a supernatural light shone upon her from her earliest years we cannot expect to extract a full psychological portrait of Catherine's development. And yet the fragments we have are quite rich. Others have noticed, and at this point their work deserves mention, how early she expressed a strong sense of self. When Catherine was about ten her mother scolded her for coming home late from an errand. She had stopped off to pray at a local church and may have lost track of the time as she went through her prayers and attended Mass. Upon her return Lapa greeted Catherine with: "Cursed be the evil tongues that said you would never come back!" And the child responded:

> My lady mother, when I do less or more than what you re-
> quire of me I beg you to beat me as much as you will, so that I
> may be more careful another time; this is your right and your
> duty. But I beg you not to let your tongue curse other folk,
> whether good or bad, for my shortcomings, because that
> would not befit your age, and would grieve me too much.

The modern scholar Arrigo Levasti rightly emphasizes the considerable moral sophistication and sense of self carried in this reply. By taking all guilt onto herself and willingly accepting physical punishment she effectively isolates herself from the psychological effects of obedience to her mother. It is Catherine the child, not Lapa the mother, who will determine the appropriate punishment, thereby changing its meaning completely and turning a beating into a personal moral triumph, one from which she might derive great psychic satisfaction.[22]

Catherine's religiosity, however, still was tentative. We are told that she formed a group of playmates who secretly flagellated themselves using ropes tied into knots. Such imitation of an adult practice not unknown in a Siena driven to extremes in the aftermath of the plague suggests misplaced enthusiasm on Catherine's part. Taming of the flesh for her never would be a group activity; she was engaging in a painful game, but still a game. On one occa-

sion she decided to become a hermit and with a bit of bread took
off beyond her sister's house to what she thought should be an appropriate desert. For an entire day she sat in a grotto and concentrated her most fervent prayers that her vision of the radiant Jesus
should return. Instead, she felt herself levitate and feared that this
was the work of the devil. Hungry, tired, and very confused she
returned home to her parents that same evening. Perhaps she simply told a little fib and said that she had gone to see her sister, for
no one even bothered to question where she had been all day. At
some point, most likely on the day of her first communion, she
secretly vowed her virginity to Mary. How many hundreds of
Sienese girls had the same thoughts we cannot know, but Catherine's promise certainly was not exceptional, nor was she prepared
emotionally at that stage to act on it in a meaningful way.[23]

Considering that all the firsthand accounts we have of Catherine's childhood were written by people who believed she was a
saint and worked for her canonization, the most remarkable thing
about them is how ordinary they are. Ritual prayer, fascination
with tales of heroic saints, an easily explained and certainly be-
nign vision, an episode of running away for a few hours to a cave,
an impulsive consecration of her virginity, a period of group-
inflicted physical punishments—certainly these are not so unusual for mid-fourteenth century Siena, nor, with minor modification of the cultural details, for children in our own time. There
are traces of a desire for solitude and a personalized sense of guilt
for the sins of others, but most observers correctly saw Catherine
as an obedient, happy, outgoing child.

So also the stories of her brief interlude with outright worldliness ring true. When Catherine was about twelve her ever-
practical mother began to prepare her for marriage. This meant
keeping after her to scrub her face and put on makeup, and teaching her to dye her hair blond and curl it. Such prettiness did not sit
well with the child and so the exasperated Lapa called upon her
married daughter Bonaventura, the very sister whom Catherine
had been visiting when she experienced her first vision several
years earlier, to try to bring the girl into line. Where Lapa's nagging had been rather ineffective and even counterproductive, the
more patient Bonaventura seemed to have success. The older sister made Catherine understand that every young woman had a
right to adorn herself and that such beautification was in no way
displeasing to God. The girl much admired and loved Bonaventura, and under no circumstances could she consider her sister's

advice sinful. Gradually Catherine became more worldly, yet never evil or unmindful of the Church's teachings, a shy and hesitant participant in the doings of Siena but increasingly a participant. This slow turning from childish religious exuberance to adolescent reality continued for two or three years, during which time Catherine's vow to preserve her virginity for God may less have been abandoned than relegated to a clear but not pressing memory. Both Giacomo and Lapa were happy at the prospect of a devout and proper daughter who soon would make a good wife. Whether Catherine was in accord with this design we do not know; in her later years she denied any wavering of her true intentions, yet in reality she appeared to be following in the footsteps of her pious yet worldly sister.[24]

Then everything changed. Bonaventura died in childbirth; the date listed in the burial register of San Domenico is August 10, 1362, so that Catherine was about fifteen. Death was not an uncommon or hidden experience in fourteenth-century Siena, yet for Catherine the blow must have been severe. The elder sister she so admired, whose ways and good counsel she slowly learned to accept, was dead, a victim of an earthly woman's main purpose, certainly according to Lapa's example. Catherine's biographers convey an essential fragment of her reaction; the future saint blamed herself for Bonaventura's death, convinced herself that it was her own brief flirtation with worldliness that had brought God's just wrath not upon her but upon her sister. Once again, as in her infancy, Catherine lived in the place of another. This time she was old enough to respond in ways that would make everyone notice.[25]

Immediately she turned inward, meditated deeply upon how her sin had brought about the death of someone she loved, and determined to have no more to do with the world. But her parents and brothers were of a different persuasion. "They put it in their heads to acquire a new in-law by finding a husband for Catherine at all cost. Spurred by the loss of their other daughter, they wanted to repair the damage immediately with the live one" is how Raymond of Capua sums up their wishes. The description sounds as if it comes from one of Catherine's general confessions; she understood that she was to be the next asset placed in her family's business. To whom was she to be wed? We cannot be certain. However, from *I miracoli di Caterina*, an anonymous panegyric written during Catherine's stay in Florence in 1374 when she appeared before the annual general meeting of the Dominican Order, we learn that Lapa openly discussed the possibility that Catherine might have wed none other than Niccolò Tegliacci, the dead Bonaventura's husband. He too was a dyer, and an important personage in the political faction to which the Benincasas belonged; all that we know of their ways suggests that finances counted heavily. The technical problem of marrying one's brother-in-law was real but surmountable, especially considering the precarious state of the family enterprise, and the psychological implications certainly never occurred to anyone but Catherine. In her old age Lapa may have realized what a saint her daughter was, but her own testimony reveals that as a concerned mother she considered her teenager little more than a potential investment, apparently worth a dowry price in order to maintain an ally in the dyeing trade. Theirs was a family business, and the family's needs at this point were obvious.[26]

Certainly Niccolò's character was not one Catherine could have admired, and to the extent that to her he seemed typical of any prospective husband it becomes understandable that she wished to marry no man. Early in his marriage to Bonaventura he often had his friends at the house and all quickly fell into ribald jokes and foul language. Much to his bride's dismay, for she never had heard such words at home, he started cursing habitually. At this Bonaventura became physically ill and "visibly thin," and warned Niccolò that unless he changed his ways he soon would see her dead. He reformed and prohibited his companions from using bad words in his wife's presence, yet she died anyway.[27]

The evidence here is necessarily fragmentary and inferential— parents clearly devoted to making money, a dead sister and an unattached, rather old and uncouth, but influential brother-in-law of the same trade, an utter revulsion for marriage by a girl who before had been groping toward acceptance of the world, a child now twice burdened directly and personally with the guilt of being a survivor, the recurring alternative of radical holiness. And yet one or another detail may be stricken from this scenario and still the outcome makes sense. Following the death of her older sister, for which she blamed herself, Catherine was repelled by all worldliness, absolutely refused to take any bridegroom but Christ, and entered upon the conquest of her body.

During the months of this emotional trial there occurred yet another event of which we may be certain while remaining conjectural about its full impact. On April 18, 1363, less than a year after Bonaventura's death in childbirth, and when Catherine was sixteen, Nanna died. Nanna, the sister who "replaced" Catherine's dead twin Giovanna, must have been about fourteen years old. Of her Catherine's biographers have hardly a word to say. Yet a simple chronology shows that it was precisely after Nanna's death that Lapa's efforts to get Catherine to marry became extreme and that this only surviving daughter gained the strength to say no clearly. Why this silence, and the generally distant or obviously hostile relations between Catherine and her family? Seldom was Catherine able to divulge even to her most intimate confessors all the details of her extended adolescent crisis, and her direct words about family members or letters to them are few indeed. A key to understanding how Catherine steeled herself against the deep sense of personal guilt that came from living on when so many she loved were dying is to be found by skipping briefly to an episode that occurred seven years later, in October 1370.[28]

Lapa was gravely ill, and Catherine beseeched God for her mother's recovery. Her prayer is certainly importunate and surprisingly arrogant as well if one remembers that she addressed it directly to God:

> Father, this is not what you promised me: that all my family would be saved. Now my mother is dead without confession; therefore I pray you to return her to me. This I want, and I will not move from here until you have restored her to me.

She does not pray; she insists (*hoc volo et numquam recedam hinc nisi reddas eam michi*) that God live up to his end of the bargain and keep his promise, that he not "defraud" her. When, we may ask, did Catherine and God make this deal, this contract to exchange her worldly sacrifices for the salvation of "all" her family? The mentality here is not that of the mature, reflective Catherine but comes straight from her stubborn, theologically unsophisticated adolescence. Oppressed with personal guilt over her own survival and the deaths of her sisters, she achieved inner peace by conceiving in her mind a bargain for all eternity. She would be not a murderer but a savior: for her twin Giovanna, for her beloved Bonaventura, and for little Nanna. The price to be paid was great but not too great—a life of hard penance and solitude. And when her parents, who could not be parties to this special arrangement of hers, objected to her austerities and tried to marry her off, Catherine not only forgave them but contracted to save them as well. Once the pact was made, to yield anything to their entreaties would be to damn them forever, and she loved them too much to do that. By her agreement with God the rebellious and troubled Catherine suddenly gained total power over Giacomo and Lapa, power in the next world that enabled her to defeat them in all struggles on earth.[29]

Fortified by a personal contract with God, Catherine sallied forth to do battle against the family she loved so much that nothing would stop her from saving them. Calmly she met with the local priest, Tommaso della Fonte, who was also a relative and whom her parents had enlisted to help bring her to her senses, and persuaded him of the sincerity of her religious vows. He suggested that if she truly were serious she should cut off her blond hair—the one remaining symbol of prettiness belonging to an otherwise rather plain girl, and even this a false, bleached virtue. With "jubilation" Catherine took a pair of shears and chopped to the roots. Before returning home she donned a cap, perhaps in accordance with apostolic tradition and to hide at least temporarily her defiant gesture. As Catherine must have anticipated, Lapa immediately demanded to know the reason for this strange attire, and the girl, not wanting to lie outright, began muttering incomprehensibly. According to Raymond of Capua's account the infuriated Lapa tore off the cap, while another contemporary version has Catherine flinging it at her after a brief shouting match in which the ironically stupid mother threatened to pull out her daughter's hair. It hardly matters who pulled or flung what; Catherine's second war, "harsher than the first," had begun.[30]

Mother, father, and brothers all determined to teach the girl a lesson, to break her will and make her agree to do as they wanted. Their concern was discipline, not salvation. Raymond quotes them, a composite of words that appears to come from Catherine's recollections: "Vilest girl, you cut off your hair, but do you think perhaps that you are not going to do what we wish? Despite your not wanting it, your hair will grow back and even if your heart should break, you will be forced to take a husband; you will have no peace until you have done our will." They backed their words with action, taking away her separate room where she had spent hours in brooding meditation, nightly vigils, and secret self-flagellations in imitation of Christ's passion. Henceforth she would sleep in her brother Stefano's room and serve the family's needs day and night. Maybe a heavy dose of sewing, washing, and cooking would help her to see how foolish she was and encourage her to act as other girls her age did. They even found a nice young man for her and harped constantly that she should get to know him better.[31]

Catherine's response was a timeless one for a troubled adolescent who truly becomes a man or woman. She could not fight the physical forces brought to oppress her, but with sufficient mental effort she would change their meaning. Raymond of Capua, in several of his most astute paragraphs, explains how Catherine came to realize that a private room would be unnecessary if she could construct for herself an interior oratory. He recalls how poorly he had understood her advice to him when he had been burdened with worldly cares: "Build a cell in your mind, from which you can never escape." It was as an adolescent that Catherine built her mental fortress, and if in many ways she became its prisoner (as Raymond inadvertently but I believe correctly reveals), the oratory proved impenetrable to the world around her. In her mind her father represented Jesus, her mother Mary, her brothers and other relatives the apostles and disciples; to serve them became an occasion for spiritual joy and growth.[32]

Months went by until Catherine, strengthened and consoled by a vision of Saint Dominic that clarified her sense of direction, called her parents and brothers together. She spoke cautiously but with absolute determination. For a long time they had gone forward with their marital plans for her, even entering into formal dowry negotiations, while she had remained silent out of the respect that is owed to parents. But the time for silence was over. She had from her earliest years promised her virginity to Jesus and Mary, a vow made not capriciously but after long reflection. She continued:

> Now that by the grace of God I have reached an age of discretion and have more wisdom, know well that in me certain things are so firm that it would be easier to soften a rock than to tear them from my heart. It is useless for you to huff and puff, a waste of time, and therefore I advise you to blow on the wind any idea of marriage because there is no way I intend to accommodate you. I must obey God not men.

Her brothers and parents could find no words to answer the once taciturn and shy child who now spoke with such courageous wisdom, who seemed ready to leave her paternal household rather than break her vow. Her father Giacomo was the first to regain his composure. "God watch over you sweet daughter," he began; they did not understand "but now we know with certainty that you are moved not by the whims of youth but by the impulse of divine love . . . Do as you please and as the holy Spirit instructs you." Then he turned to his wife Lapa and to his sons and ordered them: "No one is to bother my sweet daughter; no one is to try in any way to impede her; let her serve her Bridegroom as she pleases and pray ceaselessly for us."[33]

Giacomo allowed Catherine to have her own room back, where she would be free to "flagellate herself as much as she wanted." She never had cared much for meat and now gave it up entirely, developing a repugnance for its very odor. So also with wine in even the smallest amounts and with anything cooked except bread. Thus from the age of sixteen or so she subsisted on bread, water, and raw vegetables. She wore only rough wool and exchanged her hairshirt, the dirtiness of which offended her, for an iron chain bound so tightly against her hips that it enflamed her skin. For three years she observed a self-imposed vow of total silence except for confession, and this she maintained even though she lived at home. With great difficulty she conquered fatigue and reduced her sleep to as little as thirty minutes every two days on a wooden board (perhaps a forgivable medieval exaggeration here, but the point is clear enough). Years later Raymond confessed that he would doze off as the animated Catherine talked on and on, and she would awaken him by demanding sharply whether she was speaking of God to a wall or to him. Three times a day she flagellated herself with an iron chain, once for her sins, again for the living, and then for the dead. Until she ultimately became too weak to continue this punishing routine, each beating lasted for one-and-one-half hours and blood ran from her shoulders to her feet. When for whatever reason she could not speak of God or do his work she became understandably weak and lifeless, but if her heart was in some task she appeared youthful, energetic, and jovial. These harsh austerities quickly began to take their toll. Her mother recalled that Catherine had been so healthy and strong that she could hoist the load of an ass (another overstatement) on her shoulder and carry it easily up two long flights of stairs to the attic of their home. Then the once sturdy girl within a short time lost half her body weight.[34]

Lapa recognized the change from its inception, heard her daughter beating herself with the iron chain, and cried out: "Daughter, I see you already dead; without a doubt you will kill yourself. Woe is me! Who has robbed me of my daughter?" Lapa became half-crazed, scratching herself and pulling out her hair as if her child in fact were dead at her feet. Notwithstanding Giacomo's orders to leave the girl in peace, the anguished mother tried to do what little she could to halt Catherine's apparent course of self-destruction. In order that her daughter not sleep on a wooden board, Lapa took the child into her own bed. But Catherine would wait until the distraught woman had fallen asleep and then sneak back to her own room to continue her spiritual disciplines; when Lapa found her out the girl hid a sharp stick of wood under the sheet so that even at her mother's side she could torment her body. This subterfuge too Lapa soon discovered but her will was no match for Catherine's; seeing that opposition only made her daughter more stubborn, Lapa decided to "close her eyes and let the girl sleep wherever she wanted."[35]

Catherine at this time was depressed and felt constantly assaulted by evil spirits; she cried a great deal and worried that she would not be able to maintain her vow of virginity against the pressures of her family unless she was allowed to join the Dominican Order. The particular Congregation she wished to join was the Sisters of Penance, commonly called the Mantellata for the long black mantle they wore over their usual Dominican white habit. It was a tertiary, or lay, group of women, nearly all widows who lived at home in the world rather than in the seclusion of a convent. Catherine's choice was somewhat unusual—the obvious path for a fourteenth-century Sienese girl in her circumstances being a nunnery—one that puzzled her biographers and to which we shall return shortly. Her mother too was distressed by the decision, and yet her husband's orders to let Catherine be meant that Lapa had to act discreetly. She proposed that she and Catherine go to the hot springs of nearby Vignoni. There, removed a bit from worldly cares, Catherine might reduce the severity of her austerities and feel less depressed; her rapport with her mother might improve.[36]

The bathing cure did not work at all. Under the pretense of obtaining its full effect Catherine edged toward the canals along which the hot sulfuric water flowed into the pool where other bathers stayed and there she scalded her body and inflicted more pain upon herself than she had at home with the iron chain. When others tried to prevent her from so doing, she simply bathed only at hours when no one else was in the water. Upon their return to Siena, Catherine immediately resumed her penitential routines and began pestering her mother daily to go to the Sisters of Penance and beg them not to refuse her admission. This Lapa finally did, but to her satisfaction and Catherine's dismay, the Sisters declined, saying that the vestition of a young virgin would be "inopportune."[37]

Then Catherine became ill with a high fever and boils (or more precisely, according to Raymond of Capua, small subcutaneous hemorrhages) all over her skin. She had some form of pox common among youths of her age, originating more from "exuberance" than from "exhaustion" and apparently not related directly to her austerities, with the possible exception of the boiling water "cure" she recently had undergone. Lapa stood vigil at her daughter's bedside, applying what remedies she could and trying to console her with soothing words. But Catherine saw her illness and her mother's concern as an ideal occasion to force Lapa to accede to her wishes and said over and over again: "If you wish me to get better, make it possible for me to join the Sisters of Penance. Otherwise I fear greatly that God and Saint Dominic, who are calling me to do their holy work, will make certain that you cannot have me anymore, neither in one habit nor the other."[38]

The frightened Lapa returned to beg the Sisters of Penance on Catherine's behalf, this time with an earnestness that we may well surmise had been absent on her previous visit. They still were apprehensive but agreed that if the girl was not too pretty, and in view of the ardent desire of *both* mother and daughter, they would consider the matter. "But if she is too pretty, as we have said already, we are afraid of falling into some scandal arising from the malignity of men, who now rule in this world; and in this case there is no way we can accept her." And Lapa responded, "Come have a look, and judge for yourself." Two, maybe four, of the wisest widows in the Congregation went with Lapa to Catherine's bedside. They found a girl who was plain anyway and now disfigured by pox, and with so fervid a desire to join them in the service of God that all were astounded. Everyone agreed that as soon as the child became well Lapa should bring her to the church of San Domenico to be formally vested as a Sister of Penance. Within only a few days Catherine fully recovered, and over the futile lastminute objections of her mother, received the black-over-white Mantellata habit.[39]

Catherine's choice raises a series of questions that go to the core of the present effort to understand the personality of this holy anorexic. Why did she choose to be a tertiary instead of taking the second orders for which her youthful virginity made her an appropriate candidate? Why did she choose to live as a layperson in the world when her intense need for privacy seemingly would have been fulfilled more easily in a cloister? Why does her mother loom so large in the entire story, so much so that in Raymond of Capua's version Catherine's decision appears to be merely a constant while the drama revolves around Lapa's conversion and slow acceptance of the inevitable? Raymond, of course, begins and ends with supernatural causation—Catherine's vision of Saint Dominic directed her to join the Sisters of Penance, and so it came to be. Other dutiful hagiographers have speculated that Catherine's profound humility made her feel unworthy of becoming a nun and so she joined the lesser ranks of Dominican tertiaries. However, nothing that we know of Catherine's personality and of her actions on earth at any stage of her life even remotely supports such a hypothesis. More plausible is the conclusion that Catherine chose to become a tertiary precisely so that she could be active in the world and exert her considerable talents to save the Church from its malaise, that from the outset her vocation was public and reforming rather than private and penitential. Reasonable though this explanation is, it is less than fully satisfactory because it assigns to Catherine a public role that at the time of her choice she appears not even to have contemplated and because it ignores the familial context of her adolescent decision.[40]

As a girl in her late teens Catherine decided to live at home, but in a Dominican habit complemented with a long black mantle showing that she was dedicated to a life of penance. Penance for what? And why join a congregation that, in Siena at least, was intended primarily for widows? If her choice was not merely capricious or spiteful, and I think there was more to it than that, the answer to these questions may be found by returning to the themes of death, survival, salvation, and redemption. Catherine lived when others had died and she believed that her graces in this world might ameliorate the just punishment of her loved ones in the next. Her task was yet more arduous, for she had contracted to save *all* her family; she would live among the very people for whose salvation she was joyously ready to perform any sacrifice. First among these was her mother, an obdurate, impatient sinner whom she loved dearly and who therefore had to bow totally to her daughter's will and beg the Sisters of Penance to let her child join them.[41]

Already we have seen that Catherine's conversion to radical asceticism came at the time of the deaths of her sisters Bonaventura and Nanna. Her later insistence that her mother not die when the state of her soul would have condemned her to eternal punishment conveys the further sense of a girl totally dedicated to the spiritual welfare of her family. Now let us consider Catherine's response to the death of her father. He became gravely ill some time in 1368, when Catherine was about twenty-one. More than anyone else in her family, he had tried to understand her strange behavior, and he alone truly had recognized her special needs and given them space. They spoke at length, and Catherine realized that he was ready to die, that he was at peace with himself. She prayed not for his recovery but that he should be spared his due time in purgatory so that he might join immediately the company of saints in heaven. The response Catherine received was legalistic in tone; while he certainly had been a good man and a loving father, Giacomo had lived too fully in the muck of worldly sin; the requirements of eternal justice meant that some price had to be paid. Catherine meditated upon this response and determined upon yet another contract with God. In exchange for her father's immediate place in heaven she would take on the burden of his just punishments right here on earth. This God granted, and at Giacomo's death in August 1368 Catherine received both the consolation of a vision showing him among the celestial beings and a sharp pain in her hip. The ache remained with her "continually" until the moment of her own death. But it was a price Catherine happily paid for the release of her beloved father from the torments of purgatory. More than a century later the humanist Giovanni Francesco Pico retold with awe the story of Catherine's superhuman dedication to the salvation of her family.[42]

The symbolism and the psychological transference shown here, coming as they do from the unintentional wisdom of her devoted biographers, reveal nonetheless a troubled young woman and a solution that extends beyond her particular time and place. Catherine's holy anorexia, as with the other aspects of her religious impulse, developed in a familial context. For the love she received from a belatedly understanding father and an all-too-worldly mother she felt obligated to be a good girl, so good and so special that her sacrifices in this world would save their souls in the next. To relieve herself of the burden of God's favor in allowing her to live when her sisters had died she became His humblest servant and dedicated herself totally to His work. She conquered the drives of appetite, sex, sleep, and all material comfort; and if her punishments quickly took their physical toll, her will shaped the meaning of what she was doing. To live at home as a tertiary allowed her to play out the drama of her life in the only context that really meant anything to her. And when her world did grow larger to include popes, kings, and queens, she wrote to them and understood them as family folk. She was "Mamma" to her disciples, and Pope Gregory she addressed as "Babbo." And when she scolded him for his irresolution she especially added that he was her *dolcissimo Babbo* ("sweetest Daddy"), just as any adolescent girl growing wise to the imperfections of her father would do.[43]

With Giacomo's death the Benincasa home as Catherine had known it in her youth came to an end. Her brothers suffered a series of misfortunes. In Siena in early September 1368 a revolt broke out against the government of Twelve and its supporters, including the Benincasas, and it was Catherine who saved her brothers from death or imprisonment by leading them to a hiding place at the local hospital of Santa Maria. Several days later, after some order had been restored, they emerged and paid a fine of 100 gold florins to "remain at peace." Brothers Bartolo and Benincasa again accepted calls to participate in town governance, but new political convulsions led them to flee permanently from Siena, and on October 14, 1370, they petitioned for citizenship in Florence. There, with a third brother, Stefano, they tried to build their fortune by expanding a dyeing shop they had established years earlier. Their chances in Florence may have been poor from the outset, for there was firm opposition to their citizenship, and a letter dated October 7, 1373, from the priors of the woolen guild and the gonfalons of justice of Florence to the Republic of Siena asked its aid in forcing Benincasa and Bartolo, along with the heirs of the deceased Stefano, to pay debts totaling over 875 gold florins. By the fifteenth century the family had need of public charity, thus fulfilling Catherine's prayer that her brothers all be impoverished rather than realize the fruits of illicit monetary gains. The gulf between Catherine's asceticism and her brothers' worldliness was unbridgeable; her few letters to them are brief, formal, even icy, and scolding. If her holiness ultimately rescued their souls, Catherine never had the consolation of a vision revealing it to her.[44]

With Lapa she had a bit more success, at least in exterior form, and her mother eventually took the habit of the Sisters of Penance, thus following explicitly her daughter's path. But their spirits remained very different. When she was absent from Siena Catherine would write to her mother occasionally, but the letters, at least those portions we have, cannot have brought Lapa much consolation. They gave little news of what she was doing nor did they ask about those left behind in Siena. Instead, they uniformly urged Lapa to learn to be more patient, to abandon more completely worldly concerns, to think only of God. No hints of remorse came through on Catherine's part over how totally she had broken her mother's will and gone her own way. She could express tender affection for her mother's spiritual welfare, but never for her earthly tribulation. Lapa apparently had complained of Catherine's long absence, to which her daughter responded:

> You know that it becomes me to follow the will of God; and I know that you wish that I follow it. His will was that I should depart [from Siena to Avignon], a departure not without mystery nor without very useful results. It was his will that I remain and not the will of man; whoever says the contrary is a liar and is not truthful . . . You, like a good and sweet mother, should be happy, and not disconsolate, to bear every burden for the honor of God and your health and mine. Remember what you did for temporal goods when your sons left you to seek worldly riches; now you find the quest for life eternal so tiring that you say you will be reduced to nothingness if I do not answer you quickly. All this happens to you because you love more that part of me which comes from you, that is your body from which you formed me, than the part I have taken from God. Lift, lift your heart and your affection a little to that sweet and holy cross where every burden is lightened. Wish to bear a little finite pain to escape the eternal punishment we deserve for our sins.

Only after this rebuke did Catherine assure her mother that she would be back soon and was delayed only because some members of her entourage had been sick. Even when she was in Siena, Catherine chose for weeks and months at a time to live not at home in Lapa's company but at the house of her dear friend Alessia, a widow a few years older than herself and also a Mantellata. Only months after her daughter had transferred to Rome in 1378 with an assemblage of more than two dozen disciples and friends did Lapa follow Catherine there, and during the three months of Catherine's terminal illness it was the dying daughter who prayed for her mother's soul, not the reversal that one might expect.[45]

On January 1, 1380, as Catherine meditated on Christ's circumcision and the preciousness of his every drop of blood, she determined to add to her austerities by drinking no water. The saint had been in a state of depression for some time. Pope Urban VI, in whom she had placed such hope after Gregory XI's death, turned out to be a stubborn, willful, unloving, even spiteful man, quite unsuited to the delicate task of keeping the Papacy in Rome and heading off the rapidly deepening schism within the Church. At first he had seemed to want Catherine's advice, but then he stopped listening to her, at best tolerating her idealism in ways that this shrewd woman quickly saw through. Some disciples gathered around her to launch a community of spiritual perfection that would support Urban VI and that by its example was to reform the world, but many others she held dear did not heed her call. They thought society was hopelessly corrupt, that the effort was doomed to failure, and so they remained in their private cells and attended to saving their own souls. Catherine of Sweden, also venerated as a saint, flatly refused to join Catherine's proposed mission to Queen Giovanna of Naples to persuade her to support Pope Urban. Her ambassadorial plans thwarted, Catherine instead wrote a volley of letters, but nothing moved the Queen from her wicked life of private vice and public opposition to the Papacy. Even her beloved friend and confessor Raymond feared so much for his bodily welfare that he lingered in Genoa, refusing to continue on to Avignon and face the glories of martyrdom to which Catherine urged him. And in Rome itself mobs gathered to shout their hostility toward Urban and his followers, threatening them with physical harm. Visions of the Church in ruin tormented Catherine daily, all because Gregory XI had followed her advice and left France.

The logic of her life trapped Catherine and broke her emotionally. If in urging Gregory to return to Rome she had been doing God's will, it was impossible that the result now should be the Church's destruction. Therefore it must have been *her* will all along, an admission she never would allow. Desolate, she made a supreme sacrifice, for she must have known that the refusal to drink water would kill her. This time, however, she made no contract with God, did not exert her will or conclude with *hoc volo*. That God should save the Church she only could beg: "Here is my body which I acknowledge as coming from Thee and I now offer it to Thee; may it be an anvil for Thy beatings, to atone for their sins." After a total physical collapse on January 29, 1380, during which Catherine probably suffered convulsions and then may have gone into a coma, she finally ended her complete hunger strike. But the punishment had its effect upon her already debilitated body and exactly three months later she died. Her final days were filled with the agonies of great pain, tormenting devils, self-doubts, and fear for the Church's future. Yet she was serene, trusting that no matter how gloomy the world's prospects, soon she would be united in eternity with her bridegroom.[46]

The accomplishments that led Catherine Benincasa to become known as *the* Saint Catherine of Siena, co-patron with Francis of Assisi of all Italy and a Doctor of the Church with the same official status as Thomas Aquinas—miraculous healing of plague victims, prodigious charity, tireless exhortation of churchmen to return to Christianity's true precepts, constant peacemaking efforts ranging from Avignon to Pisa, Lucca, and Florence, authorship of *The Dialogue of Divine Providence*—obviously are not within the primary focus of the present study. It is my firm hope and conviction that an effort to understand in a historical and psychological context the person who did so much in no way detracts from an appreciation of her efforts in themselves. Concerning her personality, I offer the following summary, supported where possible by materials discussed in this chapter.

Catherine's infancy left her with an enormous capacity for faith and with a very strong need for autonomy. She recalled consciously neither the joys of being a favored child at her mother's breast nor the pains of its denial during the frightening days of the Black Death and then the abandonment she must have experienced when Lapa became pregnant once more and had to devote her attention to the new Nanna. But these infant experiences had a potential impact on her personality; this impact became actual during Catherine's adolescence when her mother, who thoroughly misunderstood her and stubbornly refused to let her go her own way, tried to bring Catherine to obedience by making filial devotion the price owed for past love. Catherine indeed did love her mother deeply, and she did feel obligated to pay back all her worldly debts, to be free of them as she would be free of all earthly things, else she could not truly be autonomous. The solution to the dilemma of balancing her great faith/dependency against her drive for free will/autonomy, and to the burden of surviving in the place of her three dead sisters, came through sacrifice, penance, and God. She became totally His servant, and therefore refused to serve men on earth, even while she humbly attended to their worldly needs and obeyed their commands. From the three-year moratorium of silence and fasting at home which she imposed on herself when she was sixteen she emerged convinced that she had achieved a direct and personal relationship with God. Once she had persuaded herself of the reality of this favored position she was ready to take on the world. Through prayers that sounded more like market transactions, including words such as "defrauded" and "established terms," she believed she had rescued her father from purgatory and her mother from hell. However much was owed, she had repaid it fully.

Her anorexia did not in itself determine the path of her religious expression, nor the reverse. Rather, the entirety of her active and seeking asceticism developed out of a personality forged in a familial context that Catherine never abandoned. The stages of her loss of appetite closely paralleled the turning points in her family relations, points that in turn coincided with advances in her total conquest of self. She had been a robust, happy, obedient child; then her two sisters died and Catherine restricted her diet to bread, water, and raw vegetables. Her actions at this time, including also flagellation, efforts to overcome fatigue, and absolute silence, probably remained under her fully conscious control. Yet she felt that her penances never were severe enough and that she was an unworthy sinner who had not tamed her unruly flesh. Her soul continued to be tormented by demons, and she felt in no position to save even herself much less the family she loved. Following the death of her father, however, she experienced a surge of confidence about the special nature of her rapport with God. Consoled by a vision revealing to her that by taking on earthly tribulation she had earned him an immediate place in heaven, Catherine experienced mystical union and believed she wore a bridal ring placed directly on her finger by Jesus and Mary. At the same time, and now beyond her conscious control, she lost her appetite and stopped eating even bread; no longer did she need to sleep. So fully confident was she that she had conquered her body that when her mother became gravely ill Catherine did not beg but virtually warned God to keep his part of their supernatural contract and restore Lapa's health.

Catherine then turned her efforts to saving the Church by returning the Papacy to Rome and launching a crusade. At first she seemed to experience some success, just as she had in saving her family. Gregory XI, whom she consistently addressed as *dolcissimo Babbo*, had the same sort of admiration and awe of Catherine's special holiness that her father Giacomo had expressed, and when he did in fact leave Avignon Catherine's triumph of will seemed complete. Growing beyond the role of adoring daughter, she felt emboldened enough to gather a band of disciples around her and become their "Mamma." She valued her spiritual experiences enough to take time out to dictate them to a train of secretaries and she gave advice freely to kings and queens, whether or not they asked for it. At this time she entered an eating/vomiting pattern typical of acute anorexia.

With the election of Urban VI her efforts at Church reform came to a dismal end. The Avignon papacy gave way to the yet more scandalous Great Schism, and even some of her disciples refused to answer their "Mamma's" call to join her at Rome in establishing a community of religious perfection. Exhausted by her austerities and broken emotionally by her failure to reform the Church, Catherine's will to live gave way to an active readiness for death. She contributed directly to that outcome by not drinking water for nearly a month. The self-imposed dehydration had its effect, and Catherine entered her deathbed. She lingered on for three months, suffering greatly and experiencing only brief periods of full lucidity. During this time her adolescent uncertainties returned, and she was tormented by fear that all her work had been for naught. In semidelirious states she shouted out "Vainglory no, but the true glory and praise of God, yes," denying to herself a truth revealed by the very passion with which she refused it. In the end she had committed the sin of vainglory and had starved herself to death. It had been her will, not His, that had triumphed all these years and that now lay vanquished.[47]

CHAPTER

3

THE CLOISTER

SAINT Catherine Benincasa of Siena's choice to live as an ascetic penitent in the world was unusual for a youthful virgin. More often, the adolescent holy anorexic of medieval and early modern Italy decided to enter a convent and lead a life of intensely private spirituality. Yet the world of the cloister, however restrictive its confines may seem to us, for these young women was alive with excitement. The apparent routine of regular devotions, prayers, communal meals, and meditation, along with a steady regimen of work and chores, provided an important framework of emotional and physical stability. Within this framework the Church calendar's endless variety of liturgy and celebration, the eagerly anticipated visits by confessors, superiors, and bishops, the petty jealousies and deep rivalries of a group of people dedicated to minute examination of conscience, the rites of initiation and passage, the loves and hates of the sisters for each other— these filled each day with unknown adventure.

The idea of the convent as a dreary, repressive place, as a subordinate variation of the religious cloister for men, is firmly and effectively refuted by the anthropologist Ida Magli. Writing more than a decade ago, and examining medieval Christian female monasticism in the light of Claude Lévi-Strauss's theoretical formulations on "primitive" religions, Magli offered a viewpoint rich in its suggestiveness, one that may serve to pose some important questions for the present effort to explore the dimensions of holy anorexia. For Christian women, absolute exclusion from sacerdotal functions shaped and channeled their religiosity. When they entered the Church in a formal role, it was as virgin or widow, a distinction that remained with them forever. Since she could not exercise priestly offices, the virgin or widow was unable to save herself much less anyone else, a position of helplessness analogous to her economic subalternation in the world. Whereas for a man the cloister was a refusal of his culture, his earthly power and riches, a place to do battle against his instincts, for a woman monastic profession was simultaneously a way of rebelling against her social condition and "a positive road to recapturing her individual reality and self-sufficiency." Enclosure allowed a woman to refuse her destiny as a "functionary of man and his culture" and to experiment with the elation of "true autonomy" in the context of an institution recognized as valid by the society. "Like a child who obstinately repeats his play so that it becomes real, within monastic discipline a woman becomes master of the cultural rules of which she has been a passive object and thereby discovers her original potential in all its significance."[1]

In Chapter 1 I tried to show that the female anorexic behavior pattern involves not only a refusal or inability to eat but also a wider psychological dimension in which a seemingly obedient and submissive girl (but one who herself feels thoroughly defiant) rebels against the world around her in a desperate effort to establish a sense of self. Generally this "world" is her family; her parents both symbolize and *are* the primary obstacles to her self-expression, even if their intentions are superficially the opposite. For a young man, on the other hand, there are ample ways to achieve autonomy, to be like his father, whether at the university or as a tradesman, whether as a soldier or a priest, and western European culture is rich with celebration to approve his self-determination. A male may be defeated in his struggle for mastery, but when this happens the defeat is public, external, visible, outward. There may be negative consequences, even severe emotional trauma, but usually not the typical anorexic behavior pattern. A girl had fewer avenues; indeed, until fairly recently with the possible exception of certain noble women, the only path was from parental domination to submission before a husband. Western culture reproves any deviation from this pattern in ways distinctly unfavorable and psychologically guilt-ridden for women. Spinster not bachelor, whore not philanderer, prostitute not john (everyman): such gender-split words convey images of a deep historical reality which tolerates or only smirkingly disapproves the same self-expression in men that it condemns in women, especially sexual expression and the refusal to be bound by marital vows.

The medieval Italian girl striving for autonomy, not unlike the modern American, British, or Japanese girl faced with the same dilemma, sometimes shifted the contest from an outer world in which she faced seemingly sure defeat to an inner struggle to achieve mastery over herself, over her bodily urges. In this sense the anorexic response is timeless. And at least temporarily, it is a real and powerful victory over the only thing western (or westernized) society allows a teenage girl to conquer—herself. But victory leads to self-destruction, and this violates the culture's belief that all its healthy members must exhibit a will to live. In the twentieth century such "deviant" cases are turned over for cure to the physicians, gods of scientific rationality, with very mixed results. In earlier times similar behavior called for the intervention of priests, male guardians of a patriarchal theology that understood woman as Eve in all her wickedness, also with very mixed results. Many were the witches, a few the saints, an unknowable number the "cured" who gave up their destructive autonomy and submitted to a husband or led lackluster single lives, and another unknown number those who starved themselves to death anonymously.

The girl who recognized early that a convent would be the best place in which to realize her need for self-mastery appears frequently in saints' *vitae*. A pattern of "recovered" holy anorexia emerges that may be summarized quickly: a superficially obedient but deeply strong-willed child is brought up in great religiosity, usually by her mother; in her early teens her father takes over and presses her to marry; she resists and comes to display the classic anorexic syndrome; ultimately she runs away to a convent, or her father dies, or his will in some way is broken dramatically; during her novitiate and for several years thereafter, she is deeply depressed, tormented by demonic visions, and still *unable* to eat; gradually, usually by her late twenties or early thirties, she "recovers" and becomes active in the affairs of the convent, often being elected its head; she learns to fast rigorously but in a fully self-controlled way and devils make room for more reassuring presentiments; throughout, her relations with her confessors are fraught with ambiguity and even occasionally with outright hostility, for these men interfere with her desire to experience God directly and personally as a fully autonomous individual; with time the other sisters, who at first were antagonistic, become her main source of worldly consolation.

This is the historical pattern, one not all that difficult to document. Beneath it lies a psychological set of circumstances, not so easily cited in time and place with quotations from the sources but no less real, or at least so I am convinced. The holy anorexic who ultimately recovers is a deeply loved infant. Always sure of the nurture and sensuous affection of her mother, she imbibes a capacity for faith that withstands any and all contrary challenges. When her human relations prove to be fleeting, ephemeral, shallow, and incapable, she turns instinctively (an instinct less genetic than learned in infancy) to her God of infinite love. There follows weaning, the denial of nurture, and then the imposition of authority—the thwarting of her pleasure, of her will. More often than not her father becomes significant at this stage. Denied the refuge of her mother's body, the child senses—long before she can understand—that this "refuge" is the possession of her powerful father. It is he (or even more inexplicably for the girl, as in the case of Catherine of Siena, her mother) who suddenly inverts her world and changes the reward of her seeking from pleasure to pain. Initially, for two decades or even more, she will find pleasure by treasuring pain, and gradually she substitutes as her love object the omnipotent Patriarch for the weaker earthly authority who set her upon this course in the first place. She desires to love and to be loved, and expresses her readiness for love by suffering, just as she suffered as a child.

To know for sure that she had sacrificed enough never came easily to the holy anorexic, and so physical beating and self-denial became simultaneously symbolic and effectual means of knowledge. Her catechism, the stories she heard, the paintings she gazed at, the stern punishments imposed by her confessor—all these told her that suffering was the way to salvation, to eternal love. And she believed the message fully. Cruel, inhuman, undeserved martyrdoms long past—whether Sebastian's arrows, Lucy's eyes, Agatha's breasts, or Christ's crucifixion—became real and present, truly a way to transcend the test of her father. Many of her acts had a ritualistic, imitative, repetitive quality; but what the outside world might observe, or in the case of a conventual routine impose, as a discipline became for the saint a liberating transformation of family contest into eternal triumph.

Both the "typical" pattern and some intricate extensions of it are exhaustively detailed in the writings of Veronica Giuliani. Not once, but on five different occasions, her confessors ordered her to write her autobiography; for thirty-three years, again at their orders because she hated to write and did so only poorly and with great effort, she kept a diary. While these documents certainly reflect the literary conventions and rhetoric of hagiography, they also are filled with spontaneous statements about herself. This outpouring, amounting to over 22,000 manuscript pages in her own script and unquestionably of her authorship, is supplemented by the firsthand accounts of dozens of nuns and confessors who testified during her beatification proceedings. Church officials were thoroughly skeptical about Sister Veronica's spiritual manifestations, and for years they had kept her under the closest scrutiny and devised harsh punishments to test her. The orders to write and rewrite her autobiography and to keep a diary were not commonplace, and may have reflected concern less with recording a saint for posterity than with gathering evidence about a living heretic. Her own words, along with the evidence given by people around her, tell eloquently of the trials that faced a strong woman who would be the master of her destiny. Her first autobiography displeased a later confessor and he made her write another, this time including only those events that honored God. Fortunately for the historical record, however, none of Veronica's confessors ever figured out whether she was a saint or a witch; they kept everything, and so we learn that Veronica had been a very head-strong and naughty little girl.[2]

Born on December 27, 1660, the infant who would become Saint Veronica was baptised the next day with the name Orsola, the youngest and as it turned out the last child of Francesco Giuliani, a gonfalonier of the little town of Mercatello-sul-Metauro in the Marche region of central Italy, and Benedetta Mancini, a gentlewoman noted for her piety. Orsola had six older sisters, two of whom died in infancy and three of whom preceded her in entering a convent. Thus only one child followed the usual path of a secular life, although little is known of her and in fact she may have died young; there is no mention of any male children and at least one witness recalled positively that Veronica had no brothers. From her earliest days Orsola was a difficult child, yet her mother doted upon her and assigned religious significance to everything she did. The baby sometimes "sweetly" but "obstinately" refused to breastfeed, or so her older sisters recalled. Their mother was much concerned until she realized that this happened only on Wednesday, Friday, or Saturday, the traditional Christian fast days. On these days Orsola sat by happily as her mother disgorged her breasts by giving suck to a needy infant. The family apparently read saints' *vitae* regularly and so it is likely that they were familiar with various versions of heroic breastfeeding tales, which appear in dozens of lives. Our concern is less with the story's veracity, or with any of several perfectly natural explanations focusing on the *mother's* psyche that might be invoked here, than with what its repetition meant to Orsola as she grew up. Again and again in her autobiographies she protests how much everyone around her loved her despite her mischievous ways, her clumsy breaking of things, her bullying attitudes. Even as an adult Veronica feared that little Orsola never deserved all this affection, never earned it, and yet desperately needed it, still needed it. The love that Orsola received from man Veronica repaid through her self-sacrificing love of God.[3]

In the opening pages of her first autobiography, written when she was in her early thirties, Veronica tells how Orsola was taken with the theme of religious suffering:

> When I was about three years old, hearing the lives of certain martyr saints being read, there came in me a desire to suffer . . . [I put] my hand in a firepot, with the idea of wanting to burn like the martyr saints did . . . I do not remember well; but I think that at that point I did not even feel the fire because I was so beside myself with joy . . . Everyone in the house cried, but I do not recall shedding a tear.

Then she adds that "at this tender age I do not think I had a particular light of God. I did these things because I heard that the martyr saints did them." In her second autobiography, the one that her confessor ordered her to make sure included only events that glorified God, written seven years later when Sister Veronica was forty, she tells the same basic story but makes no comment on whether she had God's light. Instead, she recalls that the pain was excruciating but that she said to herself: "If I can, with this hand I too want to burn for the love of God." In the fifth version, written when she was sixty years old, Abbess Veronica pleads that her memory is fading and she is senile. Only with the inspiration of Virgin Mary can she recall, and the whole manuscript is written with Mary as the narrator and Orsola referred to as "you" (*tu*, familiar form). About this incident she writes: "You suffered great pain, but you laughed at it."[4]

The incident itself apparently occurred on Christmas 1663, just two days before Orsola's third birthday. We may well envision the whole family gathered together around the fireplace as her father, or more likely her mother, celebrated the holy occasion by reading the exciting tales of early Christian martyrs. It is not improbable that the impulsive Orsola, who quite rightly in her first autobiography recognizes that she could not have understood her action, thrust her hand into the fire. Immediately she became the center of attention, too frightened and hurt even to cry, but sending her parents and sisters into alarmed wailing and ruining the festival day. Such things happened often to Orsola, and everyone loved her all the more. The equation pain/suffering=pleasure/love would be repeated throughout her childhood and then in magnified form at the convent.[5]

Inspired by hearing the *vita* of Rose of Lima (who in turn was a conscious imitator of Catherine of Siena) wherein it is told that little Rose punished herself by closing a heavy trunk lid on her finger, yet too afraid to do the same purposely to herself, Orsola for a time "played around" by putting her fingers in the space between the front door and doorjamb of her house. One day a giant (black, in some versions) dog appeared and her sister ran to slam the door shut, catching one of Orsola's fingers. Seeing the enormous amount of blood flowing from the wound, her sister screamed that she had killed poor Orsolina; the surgeon came quickly and dressed her finger with eggwhite. Through all this the child suffered silently, wishing only that she could have gone without medication, just like Rose of Lima. "But these things were mere notions, without any understanding," adds Veronica in her first autobiography.[6]

As a little girl Orsola's dolls were images of the Madonna and child. She would run wildly about the garden looking for her baby Jesus, and Veronica remembers her mother and sisters saying: "What is this? Are you crazy?" Before coming to the table to eat she would stand before an icon of Mary with child and beg, "give me your little son; my Jesus, come, I don't want to eat without you." Anything she received, a new dress or a necklace, she placed before Jesus and wanted to share with him. In order to nurse her baby she pulled down from the wall a small painting of him at Mary's breast, clutched the icon, unbuttoned her dress, and truly felt Jesus turn from his mother to her. The description in her third autobiography is especially vivid:

> I began to undress. That done, I took off the little corset I had and said: "My Jesus, leave those breasts. Come take milk here from me." And I offered my breast. He detached from that of the Virgin and attached to mine. Oh God! I cannot find words to tell how I felt at that moment and I do not even recall its effects, what it caused in me. At that moment the Babe seemed not painted, but in flesh.

I went often to this image and said before it: "Remember, beautiful Babe, that I breastfed you, just like your Mother did." Now I remember that for a few days, here, in this breast, I had a great burning, as if it were on fire. But I understood nothing.

Several times when she piled up chairs and climbed to reach a favorite image, one and all came crashing down. Undaunted by a bruised and scraped head, she turned to Jesus and said: "See what I did to come to you." Whenever child beggars appeared at the door she would take them by the hand and insist that they join her in saying a Hail Mary. To those who did she gave part of her meal, hugged and kissed them, and invited them to play. But occasionally an obstinate urchin refused, and Veronica remembers shoving one down the stairs, slapping another, and shouting at several as she pushed them roughly out the door.[7]

Orsola's constant exuberance, along with a good measure of cuts, bruises, fights, and broken objects, caused the entire household to revolve around the antics of this littlest child. Yet she was wont to sneak off and do things that no one could see or know about. She would find a remote place and enact penances: walking on her knees, licking the ground with her tongue to make crosses, standing with arms outstretched for long periods. Once her mother caught her trying to flagellate herself with an apronstring tied into knots; Donna Mancini just laughed, but Veronica remembers turning red as a beet "because I wanted no one to see me." "I did all sorts of things, but without the light of God, because I did not understand what I was doing. I only watched that no one would know," she added even in her second autobiography.[8]

Certainly she had no lack of imagination. Her favorite pair of new shoes, that she would let no one even touch, she remembers tossing out the window to a passing pilgrim who begged alms. Orsola had nothing at hand to give and so she threw him one of the shoes. At first he walked off contentedly but then he returned to ask for the other—one being of no use to him—and the child gave it up too. When this shoe landed on a high ledge above the door the mysterious pilgrim grew into a giant and reached it easily. Years later Veronica had a vision of Jesus carrying the very same pair of footwear. What young Orsola actually did with her prized possession we cannot know; our concern, rather, is with a pattern of childish behavior, and misbehavior, that in reality seems quite ordinary but that mother, older sisters, and ultimately Orsola herself saw as a series of religious prodigies.[9]

The fortuitous circumstance of Veronica Giuliani's five auto-biographies, in addition to their rich self-analysis, allows us to confront at least partially the difficulty of using hagiographical accounts in a historical context. Close comparison of the several texts suggests strongly that Veronica's protests that she was a naughty child reflect precisely what she felt about herself, not the tampering of some confessor or zealous supporter. In her mother's eyes little Orsola was obedient, special, generous, inspired by God. Veronica's self-appraisal is that she was secretive, a brat and a bully, stubborn, and an imitator, even an impostor. "All the damages that happened in the house, I was the cause of." It took Veronica many years of soul-searching, characterized by long periods of depression, anorexia, and misdirected asceticism, to resolve these clashing images of her childhood.[10]

Whatever chance there may have been that Orsola might have worked out in some other way her hopeless task of being as good as her mother thought she was ended with the pious Benedetta Mancini's death. Orsola was just six at the time, and her recollection comes from her first autobiography, since in the second she never mentions the death at all. (Apparently she or her confessor saw nothing about it that glorified God.) Her mother had loved her the most, Veronica remembers, "and always kept me at her side, day and night." Orsolina cried desperately, could not even get dressed because she sobbed so much, and would not go to bed at night. In her last days Benedetta had called her five daughters to her bedside, blessed them, and to each had recommended one of the five wounds of Christ crucified. To Orsola she had assigned his wounded side, the symbol of love. In her third autobiography (actually written one year before the second, and clearly not at all satisfactory to her confessor) she claims to remember well the death vigil and especially how, standing on a stool by her mother as the priest consecrated the host for the last time, she tried with all her might to take it, but could not reach. In adding this detail Veronica consciously intends to show her early devotion to the eucharist, but at a deeper level she may be expressing the desire .she felt as a six-year-old to save her mother from death, to eat herself the fatal wafer.[11]

After Benedetta died Orsola's upbringing was left temporarily to her older sisters, while her father Francesco took off for Piacenza to seek wider horizons in which to try his talents. Veronica recalls that he returned about a year later, when she was seven; she believed that he loved her very much and wanted to take her away with him. He promised her all sorts of wonderful presents if she would go with him. "But it was not possible that I would wish to go without all my other sisters. So I stayed with them, and my father left again." Faced with the "not possible" choice of abandoning her family in order not to abandon her father, Orsola stayed at the home she knew so well. In Mercatello she went around the narrow streets setting up devotional altars, dragging pieces of furniture from the house to do so. She wanted all her sisters to join her, but they were too busy, and as Veronica remembers: "I did these things with no sentiment; they were childish." "My life was to eat, drink and sleep; I worked very little." Apparently her sisters spoiled her even more than their mother had. Orsola constantly interrupted them when they were reading or saying prayers, pestering them with capricious tricks and trying to cajole them to go out with her to decorate her street altars.

> And this I did not only when I was little but also when I was big. To one this trick, to another a different one. I don't know what it was; I think it came from the good will of my sisters because the more I crossed them the more they liked me; not only them but everyone in the house. I was stubborn and if I wanted something I would not quiet down until I won. I was the smallest, but I wanted to command everyone and I wanted everything done my way; and in effect everyone gave in to me.[12]

From her third autobiography, and from testimony by nuns who lived with her for many years and said that Veronica had told them these things, we learn just what a brat Orsola had been. When her sisters refused to leave their work to come to pray at her altars she would go into a tantrum, take a cane, and start pounding on the furniture. One time she grabbed away the lacework they were doing and threw it to the ground. Nor did she behave any better with strangers. When she encountered a potmaker who she had heard had been leading a wicked life she "punished" him by sticking her fingers in the wet clay pans he had set out to dry. Veronica recalls one of the few occasions when she did stay quietly, and her sisters saying: "It is a miracle that Orsola is still!" "This they said because they knew it would not last. I never sat in one place."[13]

When she was nine years old Orsola's father summoned her and all her sisters to Piacenza. He now had a prestigious and lucrative position as Treasurer of the Customs House, elegant quarters, and a prospective stepmother for his daughters. Veronica in all her writings never mentions directly this rival for her father's affection, except for an allusion to his scandalous delay in actually marrying (if he ever did) the woman who now shared his bed, nor in any convincing way why within a few years he sent all his daughters back to Mercatello. Her reticence may be due in part, especially in her later autobiographies, to the dictates of her confessors; nevertheless, Veronica's writings reveal her profound emotional shock in losing her pious mother, being abandoned by her father, and then finally being reunited with him only to find that he had taken in a lover.[14]

Although the Giulianis had been among the better-off families of Mercatello nothing could have prepared Orsola and her sisters for what awaited them in the courtly city of Piacenza. As soon as they arrived their father ordered them to buy new clothes and to dress in accord with his high station; he provided them with servants and maids-in-waiting. Veronica recalls that she enjoyed all the luxury, and then she adds a very revealing self-delusion. "My father wanted me to be even more adorned than the others; so, often he brought me one vanity or another. He wanted me so much! When he was home, he always wanted me at his side. With everything I was thrilled." It well may be that Ser Giuliani favored Orsola with special presents, and there is every reason to accept Veronica's statement that he let her go around building and decorating little altars whenever she wanted, but it is inconceivable that he kept her at his side as he went about his official duties or attended to his lover. She was attributing to her father, I believe, her own rejected desires.[15]

Orsola's wish to become a nun grew strong, and she sensed that her will soon would come into conflict with her father's worldly intentions. Francesco Giuliani apparently allowed three of his older daughters to continue in their preparations for the conventual life—indeed, helped pack them off—but to Orsola he said that she must marry and that "as long as he lived he never wanted me to abandon him." The wording here is from Veronica's first autobiography which, for all its grammatical awkwardness, describes quite clearly how Orsola found herself trapped. The father she loves abandons her for three years and now has a rival for his affection right in the house; then he tells Orsola to give up her own ambitions so as not to abandon him. Not surprisingly, Veronica recalls being greatly saddened by the impossible choice and, we may add, one imposed by her father Francesco just as he had several years earlier when he first offered to take her, but not her sisters, to Piacenza. She became silent, hoping that he would change his mind, but his opposition only increased.[16]

The time came for Orsola to prepare for her first communion, but she felt herself unworthy, thought of herself as "so naughty" (*tanto cattiva* in the original and ambiguous as to whether her sense of guilt went beyond "naughty" to "bad") that she dared not ask her confessor to be admitted to this rite. Yet she envied deeply her sisters who received communion regularly, a grace she felt surely would strengthen and console her during her emotionally difficult battle with Ser Giuliani. Finally she summoned enough courage to propose to her confessor that he mention casually to her father that she might be ready for communion, but that he should not reveal that this idea in any way came from her. Apparently Orsola had found exactly the right person for her needs and she placed great confidence in this "saintly man," who proceeded to pass along to her in secret the hairshirt and flagellum she so desired. (In her third autobiography, however, Veronica admits that she stole the hairshirt of one of her sisters.) After two mornings of confession and examination he permitted her to receive her first communion and begin a penitential routine.[17]

For his part, Orsola's father tried to parade before her the joys of the world. Frequently he brought home prospective suitors, and he and they promised her riches and luxury; the very idea made Orsola "nauseous." She broke down in tears and vowed never again to come out of her room if they were there, but the next day and the next they were back; out of obedience she greeted them, and then sat in stony silence. Her father wept and assured her that he would do anything to make her happy, only that she not become a nun. Orsola answered: "If you want to make me happy, I want no other favor from you except that you place me in a convent. All my desires are there." At other times she spoke even more harshly, saying: "Do whatever you want, I will be a nun; and you will see. It is impossible to change me." Then Francesco tried another ploy, agreeing at least hypothetically, but with the stipulation that she not join the same convent as her three sisters. Veronica recalls very well how once before he had put this test of separation to her, and she uses some of the same words she did to describe his offer several years earlier to take her alone to Piacenza with him. "This he said on purpose, because he knew how much I loved my sisters and they me; he thought it would be impossible that I could stay without them."[18]

Yet Orsola rapidly was developing the strength to break even these bonds of familial love, replacing them with *mutual* possessiveness in God. "I am no longer yours; I belong entirely to my God," she told her father, and in her prayers she began, "My Jesus, I am all yours and you are all mine!" And Jesus responded, "I am for you and you entirely for me." Much of this is merely formulaic for the ordinarily devout Christian, but as we saw in the case of Catherine of Siena, for the holy anorexic possession *by* God and *of* God is crucial in solving the earthly dilemma of achieving total autonomy. The young girl becomes the arbiter of a direct and personal relationship with God that offers not only salvation in the next world but liberation in this, liberation from family, siblings, even confessors—anyone or anything that would tell her against her will what to do, how to do it, or what its value. Such self-assurance, however, does not come easily or without the sacrifice of conquering all bodily desire.[19]

Notwithstanding her disgust at the premature efforts of her father to find her a husband, Orsola went through a time when she herself was much attracted by worldly vanities. The exact dates of this stage cannot be determined with certainty either from Veronica's own writings, in which the chronology is sometimes confused, or from other documents, which are largely silent on the matter. The best we can say is that Orsola went to Piacenza when she was nine and lived in that city for about four or five years until her father sent her back to Mercatello, giving secret instructions to her uncle there that he try to undermine her determination to become a nun. During her stay in Piacenza Orsola both engaged in a contest of wills against her father and did battle against her internal urges, as we shall see shortly from her own words. My conclusion is that the two battles occurred simultaneously and interactively rather than sequentially, that Orsola did not first establish her autonomy and then decide what to do with herself, but rather underwent the emotional trauma of fighting on both fronts at once and emerging less than fully successful in either contest. I suspect, moreover, that her father's decision was as much to *send* her to Mercatello as it was to *allow* her to go, and that she had very mixed feelings about being abandoned in this way.[20]

Veronica's first autobiography tells explicitly of her worldly flir-
tations: Orsola liked to be seen in public, admired for her prettiness and rich dress; with her cousin, something of a young rake,
she spent hours in the garden, her motive being to keep him from
occasions of sin but apparently much taken with the messages he
brought her from suitors, the flowers he presented, their "games
of all sorts." She protested her intention to wed Jesus, threw the
flowers out of the window, and with her astuteness beat him in
games (including fencing), but she continued to see him. Even her
charitable impulses she felt were "more for vanity than for love of
God," and often she took things secretly from the house to give
away and then let others pay the consequences. When her father
wrongly accused a servant of stealing a brass candelabrum Orsola
intervened to prevent her from being fired but never told that it
was she who had taken it. She terrorized the maids, watching and
criticizing everything they did, ordering them to do useless tasks,
even slapping them, insisting without giving reason that her father fire one of them, and then not confessing any of this because
she convinced herself that she had done very well to punish such
ungodly people. She was so brazen that no one could stand up to
her, and her weaker sisters fell into a contest to see who could
best satisfy her whims. Orsola was very pleased with herself.[21]

When she was thirteen she coaxed her father to take her in
masked attire during Carnival to the gaming tables. Another time
she dressed in men's clothes—a practice considered invitingly
sexy in seventeenth-century Piacenza—and got her sisters to do
the same. "With this transvestism I was enormously satisfied;
it made me noticed by more people." Later she reflected on this
offense to God and promised herself never to do it again; "but
think! afterwards I did it again many times, and always with the
same thoughts [satisfaction? remorse?]."[22]

It was at this point that Francesco Giuliani sent Orsola back to
Mercatello, along with her sisters. Perhaps he was fed up with this
incorrigible, spoiled child, or maybe he really thought that her
uncle, a stern disciplinarian, could do better, or he may have
wished to devote more of his energies to his new family. It hardly
seems likely that if he truly had wished above all else that Orsola
not become a nun and stay by his side as long as he lived, he could
have been so insensitive as to send her from the bustling world of
Piacenza back to the quiet environs of her childhood, with its
memories of her deeply religious mother and in the immediate

---

company of her three sisters who were preparing imminently to enter a convent. Veronica is absolutely silent on the return, ending one paragraph that recalls how she felt when receiving communion and starting another with a laconic: "we had already returned home."[23]

She notes immediately, however, that "they were placed" not in their own home but at the house of their "uncle" (actually their dead mother's cousin), his two sisters, and his niece. The women they loved as mothers and sisters. Their uncle, by contrast, was "very strange" and no one dared say anything to him. "I, who was the boldest, did not show I was afraid, but all the same I was. The only good thing was that when I did something he kept quiet. Because of him I was much troubled, but still I said nothing to anyone." Orsola became ill with a strange malady that no one, including her uncle who was a physician, could understand or cure. My guess is that it was at this time, when she was about fifteen, that she became anorexic, but the descriptions we have of her behavior are too vague to be certain. If so, the massively documented anorexic pattern which she displayed for five years beginning when she was about eighteen would constitute a relapse or second phase rather than the onset of this syndrome.[24]

In any event, when she was fifteen she underwent a major emotional crisis. Her three elder sisters entered a convent and suddenly Orsola was left alone. "It was a living death; because I loved them so much I thought I could not survive without them." After a time and with great effort, for no one would help her and she did not really yet know how to write, she sent a letter to her father:

> Most dearly beloved father,
> I think I heard that your Excellency notified my Uncle that he and the others should try to remove from my head the thought of becoming a nun. Now I come with my side to say, with heartfelt sincerity, that I am firmly decided to become a nun, and as soon as possible. If you wish to remarry, go ahead, because there is no point in waiting for me to change my mind. You know very well the affection I have for your Excellency and for my dear sisters. I have given up home and carnality. Already my sisters are in the monastery; and I think that for me also there remains no other desire. The only thing that consoles me is the wish to enter a monastery. And for the love of God, with whom I wish to marry, with good heart I shall leave house, possessions, father, and sisters and everything. Your Excellency, go right ahead and allow the person who is taking care of our possessions to get me permission to become

a nun as soon as possible. That is all I have to say. Let this
letter be the first and last that I write to you, and this is it for
always, until the hour comes that I so long for. Prostrate at the
feet of the cross, I ask Christ's benediction and yours, and I
salute you with all my heart.

Most affectionate, obedient daughter
Orsola Giuliani[25]

Ser Giuliani answered quickly, and gave Orsola his unreserved
permission to become a nun. He did so, Veronica remembers him
writing back, not because it was his choice but to please her. With
her father's response Orsola's mysterious illness vanished; the major battle seemed to be over, even though she became very disap-
pointed when her uncle still held back his permission because she
was too young. This sudden collapse of paternal opposition, superficially in response to a letter that hardly seems compelling,
puzzled the saint's hagiographers, but they had the self-assuring
answer that it was God's will. The present analysis looks for human causation and in this instance can offer only possibilities, not
answers. It is noteworthy that even in her third autobiography,
with its lengthy discussion of her adolescence, Veronica felt no
need to dwell on this victory; she saw it neither as a triumph of
God's will nor of her own, but as something that just happened. It
may be that Orsola for years had exaggerated greatly both her father's love for her and his opposition to her plans for her future,
that he might have preferred her to marry and had arranged for a
few prospective suitors to drop by, but that all along he had been
ready to let her decide. He may not have cared all that much one
way or another, especially since he had his own new life to lead.
Certainly the nature of their relationship, virtually all of which
we know only through Veronica's feelings, reasonably can be read
in this way. The real struggle may have been within Orsola herself,
and thus its transposition onto her father in Veronica's adult recollection becomes understandably faulty. That the battle was internal, however, in no way lessened the sense of guilt Orsola felt at
the surges of her worldly and bodily drives—indeed, it exacerbated it. Her triumph over largely imagined paternal orders was no
triumph at all and quickly left this teenage girl to face harder tests
by herself.[26]

Orsola would enter the heavily cloistered Capuchin convent at
Città di Castello (about 50 kilometers from her native Mercatello)
only on October 28, 1677, nearly two years after her father's permission had arrived and against the advice of her confessor, who

thought she never would be able to put up with the rigor and strict discipline of this particular order. The intervening time was filled with anxiety, torment, and self-doubt. She found her exercises in concentrated prayer "tedious" and often left them incomplete in order to get out and attend to her childish decoration of roadside altars. As with today's anorexics in the early stages of their illness, Orsola wanted to be constantly on the go, even though her relatives prohibited her from doing housework because they feared it would harm her and they laughed at her constant running "like a crazy person." In an hour she did what took anyone else a whole day. "I was hot-tempered by nature; any little thing annoyed me and seemed big, so that sometimes I stamped my feet like a horse and, believe me, I did it all out of meanness." She continued to find pleasure in worldly vanities but at the same time felt an internal remorse that left her without peace. Suitors followed her whenever she went out of the house, and even in the privacy of her room, everywhere, thoughts of young men haunted her. Her confessor urged Orsola to go to communion more frequently, but she feared she was too impure. No matter how hard she tried to wish the opposite, she enjoyed being so desired by men.[27]

Then the narrative breaks suddenly. "I BORE GREAT TRIBU-LATION FOR THE SINS I COMMITTED WITH THOSE SPIN-STERS [her cousins, her young friends, her uncle's sisters?] AND I DID NOT KNOW HOW TO CONFESS THEM." Exactly what the "sins" were we do not know but for five years Orsola could not bring herself to confess them. The special bold lettering she used in the original manuscript suggests that they weighed heavily on Veronica even many years later, and if she felt they were in fact mortal sins, it meant that for five years all her communions had been sacrileges. She cried day and night and prayed to be able to tell everything, but once at the feet of a confessor she became "DUMBSTRUCK" and "I was unable TO SPEAK." "I could not see myself dressed in this holy habit and I felt I was in God's disgrace." For Orsola life was a continual travail, and yet she said nothing to anyone. On this note Veronica ended her first autobiography, responding to her confessor's criticism that now she had no excuse for not spending more time on the task with the plea that she had a headache and could write no more.[28]

Upon her vestition Orsola chose her new name, Sister Veronica, but not so easily did she shed her unconfessed sins or the emotional legacy of her early years. The recollection is from a fragmentary autobiographical piece begun at the order of another of her confessors, Padre Bastianelli. When he saw the result apparently he decided that such behavior and sentiments hardly were appropriate for a good nun, much less a putative saint, and he instructed her to terminate the narrative at once even though she barely had finished recounting the first year of her novitiate. From this document we learn that Veronica felt "upside down" and that, seeing herself "incarcerated" in convent walls, she did not know how to calm her bodily urges. There were moments when she felt she was in paradise, but most of the time she reasoned that she was in a race against all the other novices to show who loved God the most. She was losing, and so despite all the sleepless nights spent crying over she knew not what, Veronica carried more water and chopped more wood than anyone else. Superficial obedience, however, did little to tame her spirit. She placed no confidence in her confessor and found the novice mistress to be "incompetent," nor was she at ease with any of the other nuns. The abbess was "indiscreet," and Veronica overheard her repeating to one of the sisters something she had told her in private. "At that moment I decided never to reveal anything to anyone. And so I did." In defiance of her superior's orders that she rest and not assist at Divine Offices, she hid outside the door and recited all the prayers anyway.[29]

For three months Veronica did not make a good confession. Rather, she went through the motions by telling some trivial defect or omission while keeping to herself the pressing temptations she felt all the time, and then she received communion in this sorry state. When Don Francesco Ripa realized the shallowness of her confession and urged her to deeper examination, Veronica shot back: "Father, what do you want that we should do, since we are always silent and cloistered, or to say it more clearly, imprisoned?" He kept after her with constant questions, but she only became more contrary and stubborn, carefully revealing nothing that was of any consequence to her.[30]

One of the other novices who had a particular hostility toward Veronica quickly got on the superior's good side and told her all sorts of things about Veronica. She felt persecuted and dreaded the public mortification that awaited her in the refectory; her stomach seemed to collapse at the internal violence and she became mute, not out of obedience or humility but to avoid more punishment. The abbess was temperamental anyway, and the whole community sometimes would "yell at her." Yet even this satisfaction Veronica did not have (and sorely missed) because as a novice

she had to observe silence. "All my days I was averse to mortification and I used all my ingenuity to avoid punishment as much as
possible." Thus she passed a "whole" year of her novitiate.[31]

Although the normal length of probation was one year Veronica
may have remained a novice for three years, or at least so she
wrote in her second autobiography. The official record drawn in
her canonization proceedings concedes that she continued to stay
in a special quarter reserved for novices for several years but claims
that she was professed as a nun after the usual time. Veronica's testimony, however, is unambiguous, and from her detailed account
of this period we can be fairly certain that she knew how long she
had been a novice, or at least had felt that she was being denied
full admission to the community. Certainly her overall comport-
ment, and by now she was deeply anorexic as well, makes it understandable that her superiors would have been reluctant to allow her to profess. During this time, and also in the next few
years, she was tormented by cunningly insidious apparitions (or
else things actually happened that she later recalled in this way,
perhaps at the suggestion of her confessor).

> One day I was alone in my cell and heard a knock at the door.
> I thought it was the novice mistress [Sister Teresa Ristori] and
> so I said to come in. Once she entered I felt so sick that I
> barely could pay attention to her words; the more she talked,
> the more it bored me . . . She began, "I want to tell you some-
> thing . . . but you must promise to tell no one, not the con-
> fessor extraordinary who is now with us nor the ordinary
> [confessor] nor any other creature . . ."

After much hemming and hawing Sister Ristori came out with
the tale:

> "You should know that last night in the infirmary the talk
> was only of you, and all the sisters are scandalized. They never
> thought of such a thing. I myself am embarrassed to tell you.
> It is said that between you and your [ordinary] confessor there
> is a friendship so intimate that even in your spiritual talks
> you reveal your intent to sin together. What else? It is also
> said that the thing has gone so far that you can thank God
> that the two of you have not been severely punished."

Sister Ristori then ordered Veronica to see her confessor no more,
indicating that in any event he was to be removed forthwith from
his post, and it was all her fault. Veronica boldly suggested that
she would go alone to the Bishop, Monsignor Sebastiani, and tell

everything and then let him be the judge, but this infuriated her superior who warned: "I tell you and I tell you again that you are not to speak with anyone; and as to the Bishop, God help you if any of this should reach his ears." Then Sister Ristori stormed out. Veronica was sorely troubled by all this, and only after much anguish did she decide to disobey her superior and confide in the confessor extraordinary. He was very disturbed by the entire situation and for a long time remained silent. Finally he suggested that Veronica ask Sister Ristori to furnish her with a list of the names of the sisters who were spreading such gossip, which was a bit delicate since Veronica was supposed to have kept silent about the whole thing, and thus they agreed that she should broach the subject in a very roundabout way. This Veronica tried to do, but instantly the novice mistress (who apparently had conferred with the extraordinary confessor) told her to rid herself of all this nonsense; there never had been any such talk. It was the devil who had taken Sister Ristori's appearance and come to her room, using his every wile to build this trap. Still, the ordinary confessor in question was assigned to other duties and never returned to the convent.[32]

On several occasions the devil took Veronica's form and went around to the other sisters saying bad things about the novice mistress; from them she quickly learned of the wicked talk and gave Veronica the silent treatment for days on end. The troubled novice begged to know what she had done, and only with extreme difficulty and after much time did she persuade her superior that evil apparitions were about. Demons regularly slapped Veronica in the head as she tried to pray, made her see the fires of hell in church, knocked her off ladders, bit and kicked her, tossed stones all over her room as she slept peacefully and made so much racket that the other sisters awoke and came running to investigate, hissed like serpents, clanked chains, and let off loud, smelly anal odors that caused one and all to evacuate her cell.[33]

Much of the time when Veronica was not confined to novitiate quarters she was in the infirmary, ordered there to try to change her diet and break her self-starvation routine. In virtually all other canonization proceedings, testimony concerning extreme fasting appears in the section on temperance. (The investigation and its results generally are arranged not chronologically but with separate chapters based on each of the three theological virtues—faith, hope, and charity—and four cardinal virtues—prudence, temperance, justice, and fortitude.) Even in cases where confessors ordered saints to eat, as happened to Catherine of Siena, the fact of not eating ultimately came to be viewed as a display of heroic temperance or else as a miracle if survival without adequate minimal nutrition was deemed to defy the laws of nature. In proceedings on Veronica's beatification and canonization, however, the Congregation of Sacred Rites placed much of the testimony on her refusal or inability to eat under the virtue of fortitude. To these high prelates at least, there was nothing heroic in her diet itself, only in her patience in putting up with the outrageous and misguided orders of her confessors and superiors. In a formal sense, then, even the Church recognized that Veronica's anorexia was not a matter of admirably rigorous fasting, something to be imitated or extolled or marveled at; rather, it was an affliction, one that Veronica turned into an occasion for spiritual growth only by her will and fortitude in accepting punishment from the insensitive, often cruel mortals around her who tried to break her will. Ultimately she won, at least in her mind, and only then did she recover and become able to engage in the more usual and self-controlled fasting practices of her strict order (which are duly reported in the appropriate section of her proceedings on temperance).[34]

From the direct testimony of six nuns and five clerics we can trace the outlines of Veronica's anorexia. Sister Hyacinthe, sixty-eight years of age when she gave her deposition in 1727 or 1729, would have been about Veronica's age when they both entered the Capuchin monastery at Città di Castello. Hyacinthe relates that the abbess was worried that Veronica's continuous fasting on bread and water would harm her health and leave her unable to do a full share of the manual labor required around the convent, thus making her a burden on the community. This despite the fact that the youthful Veronica did more work by far than any of the other sisters. So the abbess went to Monsignor Eustachi and got him to order that Veronica be placed "in prison in the infirmary." The order came while they were all at choir and the mother abbess "with great fury ordered her to leave, shouting—'To the infirmary, to the Infirmary'—and made her depart immediately." For fifty straight days she was kept under the constant guard of two nuns who watched that she ate all that she was told and did not gorge on the sly. The physician who was called in ordered her to eat soup and similar nourishment, but no matter how hard she tried she could not retain what she had been forced to eat; she vomited regularly. Veronica finally was released only when on the feast of

Saint Clare she managed to keep down one egg. Then she went right back to her bread-and-water diet. Hyacinthe stated that this continued for the next three years and that, although she could not confirm the fact directly, it was said that Veronica had eaten almost nothing for a long time before her hospitalization.[35]

Other testimonies put the total time of Veronica's extreme fast at five years, adding that for three-day stretches she ate nothing at all and that she *could* not eat. Also, she slept very sparingly and yet was highly active. Sister Florida Ceoli, who succeeded Veronica as abbess, added that Doctor Fabbri used to weigh the portions given to the patient before and after she ate in order to check precisely on her intake. He would then inform her superior and her confessor when they should order her under the firm obligation of religious obedience to eat more. On Fridays, said Sister Maria Constans Spanaciari, Veronica chewed the entire day on only five orange seeds, in memory of Christ's five wounds.[36]

On numerous occasions during this time one or more of the sisters saw Veronica sneak into the kitchen and gorge down food, even in the hours immediately before she was to receive holy communion or during canticle when perhaps she thought the others would not see her. Hyacinthe explains that this was the work of the devil, who wanted the sisters to think that Veronica was faking and only pretending not to be able to eat. Abbess Ceoli repeats the same story, albeit secondhand, but with all the authority of her office:

> In the time that she made her rigorous fast of five years, about which I testified the other time in my examination, but when I was not yet a Religious here, the sisters sometimes found Sister Veronica in the kitchen, the refectory, or the dispensary, where she ate everything there was, and what is more, other times they found her eating before the hour of Communion, and then they saw her come to communion with the others. From this there derived great confusion and backbiting to the discredit of this Servant of God, but later it became clear, that in effect what appeared under the aspect of Sister Veronica was the Devil.[37]

This testimony caused the Promoter of the Faith, whose task during these proceedings is to guard the Church against heretics, quacks, lunatics, or other such potential embarrassments in its bosom who may be put forward by overzealous believers, to raise some pointed questions. Abbess Ceoli, however, defended her interpretation to the Promoter's satisfaction, stating that Father

Bald' Antonio Capelletti, then confessor for the monastery, had investigated the entire matter thoroughly (as had Monsignor Eustachi, added Father Crivelli in his deposition) and concluded that Veronica was at canticle while the apparition was in the kitchen. Moreover, Sisters Diomira, Liduina, and Vittoria, who were excused from communal exercises because they were supposed to be ill in the infirmary, once happened to be hanging around the kitchen and when they saw what they took to be Veronica stuffing down food they "flew" straight away to denounce her to the abbess, only to see the real Veronica attentively singing prayers with the others. Besides, the same sort of thing had happened at least once to Saint Mary Magdalen de' Pazzi (another holy anorexic, whose *vita* will be considered in due course), indicating that this was a timeworn deception in Lucifer's arsenal of tricks. We recognize here, of course, a description of the repetitive binge-eating/vomiting pattern typical of acute anorexic behavior.[38]

So also, in evaluating the response by physicians, priests, and superiors to Veronica's anorexia we may recognize in the particulars of late seventeenth century religious beliefs and practices nothing less than a behavior modification program worthy of many a twentieth-century hospital *équipe*. Today's anorexic may be threatened, cajoled, force fed, loved, promised, punished—holding back or allowing friends, television, *freedom* in exchange for weight gain measured in grams. Analogously, the treatment meted out to Veronica Giuliani, however sadistic and revolting its details may seem to us, consistently aimed to break her will and make her do what the experts thought was best for her.

Whereas during her early novitiate Veronica had tried to avoid castigation, willfully had disobeyed, and carefully had revealed nothing to anyone, she ultimately overcame her anorexic behavior pattern only by seeking ever more severe punishment, by carrying obedience to such extremes that it became a purely internal test, and by telling everything to everyone, over and over again. No matter what people around her made her do, she came to believe to the depths of her soul that God was directly at work in giving her opportunities to suffer for him, and this was exactly what she had wanted for herself all along.[39]

Abbess Ceoli, who at that time had been assigned to the kitchen, recalls preparing food for all the sisters with her usual careful attention to cleanliness. But somehow when Veronica's plate reached her in the refectory it was covered with cat vomit, as was her place setting; Veronica, seeing an opportunity for self-abasement and further triumph over bodily desires, suddenly regained her appetite and ate with gusto. Other times her *minestra* was contaminated with "pieces of rodents, clumps of hair and similar refuse," and then too she ate willingly, as she did when a fat leech crawled around in her soup spurting out blood. To this list the testimonies of Sisters Maria Joanna Maggio, Maria Constans Spanaciari, and Maria Maddalena Boscaini added dead mice, bugs, and various worms.[40]

Veronica may have been less than perfect in cleaning her room, or else the extraordinary confessor, Father Giovanni Maria Crivelli, S.J., just may have been feeling mean or in the mood to experiment. The story of his orders is repeated in several depositions, but since he testified willingly to it himself, we shall let him speak first:

[Among "innumerable" obediences] one was that she should remove herself to a dark cell in the infirmary and stay there until I ordered her to leave, and on her knees to lick with her own tongue the entire pavement, and then also to lick, standing on her feet, the walls of the cell [readers who have not tried this should consider the added difficulty, as Father Crivelli did, of reaching the bottom of the wall while on one's feet], and to consider herself unworthy of staying in it. She followed my orders with such relish and contentment that she even swallowed the spiderwebs, and the spiders themselves, gathering them up with her tongue as she licked the walls . . . I told her this was too much, that my intention was not to make her swallow the spiders and their webs, that in fact it displeased me that she had done so because she could have harmed herself. And she answered that I had done well, done her a great favor, and she stayed two months or more in that cell without ever leaving except to come to prayer or other communal functions of the monastery, until I finally ordered her to return to her usual cell.[41]

Sister Boscaini adds the innocently revealing details that Father Crivelli was "well aware of the delicacy" of Veronica, that the cell had no window or other light source, and that on other previous occasions he had ordered Veronica to clean various public rooms of the convent with her tongue. Then she directly contradicts the Jesuit and says that it was he who ordered Veronica to swallow anything that "stuck" to her tongue and afterward, as a further experiment in patriarchal discipline, chastised her for having done so. It was he who left her in the black cell although he knew full well that every night there she was harshly beaten by demons who tried to get her to disobey and flee. Even in later years when she was abbess, Father Crivelli gave Veronica lessons in humility by ordering the lowliest tertiary in the convent to command her to clean out the chicken coop, and on many occasions he had the other nuns ostracize Veronica by making her get on her knees outside of the choir, "like an excommunicant."[42]

Another of Veronica's many confessors, Canon Carsidoni, commanded her to go to the kitchen and throw herself in the fire. This he did only so that he could have firsthand experience of the virtue of obedience in the good sister, and once he realized that she was fully ready to do so, he had her called back and castigated her for trying to carry out an irrational order. Father Bald' Antonio, who it may be recalled had helped with the investigation of binge-eating devils who took Veronica's form, must have decided that a little more humility would be good for Veronica's spiritual growth. He ordered Abbess Ceoli, who at that time was a novice, to command Sister Veronica to get on her knees and then to kick her in the mouth. Florida had no choice but to obey under pain of sin; she tried to kick only very gently but some invisible hand made her use full force and Veronica humbly received a grossly swollen lip with blood spurting forth. Another novice—it is not clear whether under orders or because she was angry—punched Veronica so hard that blood flowed, and this too the patient nun saw as a divine favor. Other confessors gave orders that at least brought her some physical comfort; for example, Father Capelletti, as she was recovering from a broken leg, commanded her to prove her faith by getting out of her wheelchair and walking without a limp. Similarly she was cured "for obedience" of sciatica and dropsy.[43]

Perhaps more difficult for Veronica to accept, at least so her diary reveals, were the many, many times when her confessors refused to allow her to receive communion, not that she had committed any sin but simply to make it clear to her who had the power to dispense God's saving graces, who could deny at *his* whim the body of *her* bridegroom. When she was in her mid-thirties Veronica received in her hands, feet, and breast the wounds of Christ. This most exquisite sign of God's favor, one that to Veronica was the crowning moment of her life, the Church treated for the next twenty-nine years until she was autopsied as an embarrassment and a possible or even probable fake. Orders came from Rome that she was to write or speak of the wounds to no one except her confessors, the bishop, and by letter to her natal sisters at the convent in Mercatello. In short, she never was allowed to confide in any of the women with whom she was to live daily for the next three decades. Suspicious that the wounds were self-inflicted, her confessors ordered her to wear thick mittens bound tightly and sealed at her wrists. This went on for years, along with continued application of excruciatingly painful burning ointments, long after it became clear that nothing worked to heal the wounds or stop the bleeding. In her lifetime Veronica never had the satisfaction of full acceptance by her worldly brothers and sisters that she was in God's grace and not an agent of Satan.[44]

Notwithstanding these crude efforts at behavior modification, and beginning probably when she was in her mid-twenties, Veronica gradually emerged from the most severe phase of her anorexia. In the mid-1690s she suffered a relapse of sorts, and some of the above testimony refers to these years rather than to the darker days of the early 1680s, but for the later fast she had clerical permission. Less often was she tormented by demons; she slept a bit more or at least did not stand night after night without end in compulsive prayer. She did her share of chores and more, but with time allowed her younger and stronger sisters to help in the heavier work. Writing her autobiographies and keeping her diary were burdens, especially since she kept telling what she actually felt and thereby frequently offended the sensibilities of the very confessors who had ordered her to do so, but these tasks apparently helped her to understand herself better. Even when she continued to think in terms of a "race" to be the holiest of all the holy nuns, as in her letters to her sisters in Mercatello, the metaphor was more clearly as Saint Paul intended in his epistle to the Philippians and in his second missive to Timothy, less filled with a desperate need to be the winner. She came to welcome orders from her superiors and confessors because to obey them, no matter how absurd or trivial their commands, was in itself a good deed, one requiring no further examination of conscience. After 1698 she set aside the dozen or so differently styled chains and sharply studded flagellating instruments she had used to beat her flesh, the heavy wooden yoke she had borne on her shoulders, and the large rock under which she had pressed her tongue. As to her diet, she adhered strictly, and fully, to the spartan but not unhealthy regimen set out for everyone in her order: no meat and only two small meals daily except Sunday; for lunch a soup of legumes and one egg, occasionally a piece of fruit or, instead of the egg, on

Wednesdays, Fridays, Saturdays during Lent, and in the time from All Saints to Christmas and between Ascension Day and Pentecost perhaps a bit of salted or fresh fish, less than three ounces. Supper consisted year-round of bread-soup for those who still were hungry; the others had to eat at least a little salad and a morsel of bread or else either a few grapes, or two chestnuts or walnuts, or an apple or a root vegetable. The water they drank at meals might be lightly tempered with wine. When Veronica was ill, as with any Capuchin nun, she would receive a little meat and a small amount of undiluted wine, and this too she accepted when the doctor ordered it. In eating, as in all matters of bodily comfort and denial, she did precisely what the rules said to do; it became a matter of her will to do no more and no less, to accept without question everything concerning this world so that nothing could distract her from total concentration on the Savior.[45]

Her wise, moderate, outwardly calm and passive course came to be recognized by the other sisters. She was appointed for many years to be novice mistress, the very post she had so despised during her time of trial. Although she herself experienced the crown of thorns, mystical marriage with Jesus, and stigmata, she carefully warned the young women under her charge against seeking such extreme signs of supernatural grace. According to one testimony she specifically refused to let them read or use any of the guidebooks to harsh asceticism and deep mysticism that circulated widely at this time and almost certainly were in the convent's library. Although Veronica had been inspired greatly by the heroic sacrifices of Catherine of Siena, Rose of Lima, Mary Magdalen de' Pazzi, and others of their kind, as a teacher she realized how easily this path might lead an unsuspecting girl to the self-destructive and misguided exercise of her own will. It was far better to accept the rules, the time-tested norms of controlled prayer and penitential asceticism, safer, for a woman at least, to trust in the passive Mary than to imitate the crucified Christ, and let God's will be done in his way as he saw fit.[46]

On April 5, 1716 she was elected abbess, despite the consternation of high prelates in Rome who had blocked the appointment for fifteen years and who remained very skeptical about her; to this position she was reelected continuously and unanimously until her death in 1727. Whenever she had to reprove one of the nuns for some misdeed or omission she did so with utmost kindness and compassion, never calling her sister's defect to the attention of the community as a whole. If an example had to be made of someone she always chose to find the error publicly only in her own action, leaving the others to examine their consciences privately. Seldom did the sisters run to her with tales of sins committed by one or another among them because Abbess Veronica always already knew of the infraction. For the most part reprimand was not even necessary since Veronica's behavior was in itself such an inspiring—and yet reachable—model to follow. Her will, and like most superiors she knew how to wield authority, somehow seemed to be inherent in God's will, indistinguishable and intrinsic, without effort or interpretation. Her mystical experiences continued and even grew in intensity, yet she also had the energy and practical wisdom to have a new and efficient plumbing system installed at the convent. By her will she once had been dangerously ill and now by her will she was healthy. Ultimately the world of the convent proved to be exactly the right place for this remarkably strong woman to forge for herself a useful and constructive life on earth, just as she had felt all along.[47]

IN SELECTING the life of Orsola (Sister Veronica) Giuliani for extensive analysis of the "recovered" holy anorexic I gave primacy to quality of evidence rather than to historical chronology. Actually, as will be discussed in Chapter 6 on the decline of holy anorexia, she lived at a time when the model had lost its innovative, compelling quality. Some of the seemingly bizarre punishments she imposed on herself had become hackneyed by the late seventeenth century. She merely imitated, admittedly with a vengeance, what she had read in the more challenging *vitae* of her holy predecessors. Moreover, I have set aside some important historical issues, for example the special role of Jesuits as guardians of Catholic Reformation doctrinal purity and the fears of Jansenism raised explicitly in her canonization proceedings, in order to concentrate on the psychohistorical pattern. While the model itself is not timeless or unchanging, and certainly its actuality in any given woman's behavior is highly variable, the very specification of a type or model, in this instance that of the recovered holy anorexic, requires that we focus first on its structure before analyzing its history over time.

I also wanted to provide readers, without taxing them with a translation of all 22,000 pages of her writings, with evidence drawn as much as possible from a holy anorexic herself. That is another reason for choosing Veronica, not because she is especially important or influential in the normal sense that historians tend to take as biographical subjects people whose actions presumably altered the course of events. Nor would I assert that she is a particularly useful case for examining male clerical responses toward self-assertive female religiosity. Many of the other *vitae* I shall consider, more briefly, in due course better serve such purposes. At least one of Veronica's confessors—the Jesuit who ordered her to lick spiders from the walls—was a lunatic. Among the supernatural graces listed in her canonization proceedings is Veronica's correct prediction that Father Crivelli would become demented for the remainder of his life and experience only one brief moment of lucidity just before his death. Most confessors were not pathological.

All this is meant not as an apology or a caveat but rather as an invitation to consider the following conclusions. A certain degree of speculation and historical guesswork is necessary. Veronica grew up in a deeply religious household dominated by her mother's self-sacrificing piety. The woman was unhappy with her married state and instilled in her daughters, four of whom became nuns, a permanent aversion to marriage and sex. There was little love between husband and wife; Donna Benedetta devoted all her affection to her children, especially to Orsola, who was the youngest. She practiced love by punishing herself and instructed her daughters to do likewise. These lessons began even at the breast, as her mother denied Veronica nourishment on fast days and instead gave suck in charity to other needy infants. She compensated for this denial with her caresses and her adoring belief that little Orsola was a holy child. As her baby grew she filled Veronica with wondrous stories of heroic virgins who macerated their bodies. At a conscious level, as she herself recognized in her autobiographies, Veronica understood none of this, but the impact upon her emotional development was profound. She remained fixated with oral gratification and punishment, providing it to her dolls as a five-year-old and denying it to herself as a teenager. As a nun she punished her tongue by laying a heavy stone upon it, by licking insects, by swallowing cat vomit, by compulsive fasting—but nothing worked to eradicate her obsession with her mouth and its desires. When she finally achieved greater psychological stability at the age of thirty or so, it was by integrating into her psyche a dependency upon the comforts of the Blessed Virgin Mary as mother and nurturer. For Sister Veronica, Mary was not merely an abstract symbol of goodness but a real and present source of infinite and undenying love. By her death, Donna Benedetta had punished her daughters by abandoning them forever; they turned ultimately to the mother of God who never had known the flesh, who never would die, who lived eternally with her son Jesus at her breast.

In the years before she reached this solution, Veronica battled with only marginal success to find expression for the fierce bodily and emotional urges that tormented her. Her father did not love her, although she tried desperately to capture his affection with her rough-and-tumble, tomboyish antics. She would be the son he always wanted and that her sickly, pious mother had not provided. Her effort failed, and he turned to another woman who gave him the sexual pleasures forbidden to a daughter; finally he abandoned Veronica completely and denied her even the triumph of defeating his will by giving in instantly to her formal request for permission to become a nun.

The convent she entered at the age of seventeen, never to exit, was in the center of town but totally closed to the world outside. The glassless windows of each cell all looked out only onto each other across an interior courtyard. Attendance at the adjacent church was behind a heavy grill that allowed no one to see in or out. In this prison, as she herself called it, Veronica's fantasies exploded. Prodding confessors put into her head sins she may have dreamed of but surely never had acted out, and the nuns filled her whole body with the devil. She totally lost her sense of self. Having failed at being a boy, having rejected motherhood, and having chosen by entering a different convent to give up the companionship of her natal sisters, she faced only herself. Judging herself to be a fraud, a "disgrace" to her holy habit, Sister Veronica entered a phase of compulsive, ascetic masochism and holy anorexia. Her self-mortifications became functionally autonomous, beyond her conscious control. Only after a decade of effort to understand herself, and especially with the therapeutic effect of writing her autobiographies, did she overcome her obsession with the male-dominant image of Christ crucified and lay to rest her inner passions. This she accomplished by settling upon (regressing to) the more controlled love/sacrifice reward system her mother had first taught her and that was carefully spelled out by the rules of her strict order, with their emphasis on unquestioning, childlike obedience. Her prison became a haven and its inmates her sisters.

WIVES AND MOTHERS

T HE RISE of mendicancy in the thirteenth century opened new
avenues of religious expression for Italian women. To be sure,
one might better refer here to a reopening. Jesus had called to
himself not only poor fishermen but also fallen women such as
Mary Magdalen and had condoned even explicitly sensuous gestures, as when the prostitute with her tears washed his feet and
then dried them with her hair. The Samaritan woman who gave
him water lived with a man out of wedlock, and even a wife's adultery was not beyond Jesus' forgiveness. In the early centuries
women had been active in church affairs, and their numbers loom
large among those remembered for having sacrificed their very
lives. But beginning in the fifth century, supported by the pessi-
mistic theology of Augustine and given reality by the Church's
thorough involvement in the male-dominated institutions of the
secular world, there was a revival of the antiwoman doctrines of
Saint Paul, the Hellenized Jew who had brought to his Christianity many of the negative images of femininity found in both those
traditions. Notwithstanding a superficial reverence for some early
female martyrs (who over time had become more important as bits
of wonder-working bone than as personages), the well-established
Benedictine houses for women, and the unbroken veneration of
Mary, Christianity in the centuries from Augustine to Francis
condemned women to subordinate and dependent paths to individual salvation. Neither martyrdom nor virgin birth could serve
as practical spiritual examples for medieval women to follow, and
even the conventual life, when it was not as corrupt as the world
outside, was available only to a few.[1]

Women who were married, who had paid the marriage debt and

known the flesh, could reach God only through the intermediary of a male priesthood, a situation not unlike their dependency at home and in the marketplace. A few simply ran away from it all and took up lives as recluses, hermits, or anonymous vagabonds, and several of these did become approved objects of veneration within the Christian fold. By the late twelfth century, however, at least on the Italian peninsula where Cistercian reforms had made less headway than in France and along the Rhine, a deeply pious married woman was much more likely to be remembered as a heretic than as a saint.[2]

Among the new mendicant orders of the thirteenth century it was the Franciscans who appealed most directly to married women. The Dominicans, it is true, also tried to attract women, and it was this order that carried out papal efforts to bring varyingly heterodox beguinages under firmer control and direction. The misogyny embedded in the Dominican Saint Thomas Aquinas's life and doctrine, however, was far from unique and crystallized the deep suspicion of church intellectuals that a woman who had engaged in sexual intercourse was a living danger to male salvation and could never be trusted to forge for herself an intense relationship with God. Franciscans were hardly proto-feminists and they too placed all women, and especially those who had been married, under close tutelage. Yet the example of Francis himself, like Jesus before him, so clearly displayed compassion for women and a calm immunity to their potent sexuality that at least in the early years, again as had happened in the primitive church, a female might join more freely in new modes of piety. It is in the Franciscan tradition that one finds the easy innocence of intimate male-female work for a common cause such as the founder had with Clare of Assisi and her sisters and cousins, or later in Rome with the matron Giacomina di Settesoli.[3]

The wife and mother who turned to radical piety, more often after her husband's death but occasionally earlier, faced enormous practical as well as emotional trials. Long periods of extreme fasting, characterized in many cases by an inability to eat, were common. In considering these *vitae* in the context of the present study of holy anorexia, it is worth emphasizing that the pattern does not fit the current-day medical definition of anorexia nervosa. Most of these women were older than twenty-five, and several probably already had undergone menopause. They had had years of experience, with varying degrees of satisfaction and adjustment, in sexual activity. Many showed signs of personality

---

traits or disorders that today's physician would classify easily, but not as anorexia nervosa. I include them here because my purpose in exploring the dimensions of holy anorexia is not to place a modern label on a very different past but rather to examine that past both for its own sake and for whatever light it may shed on the present. If, as I propose, holy anorexia—broadly defined to include all historically relevant types of self-starvation by pious women—has existed for centuries in western European society and is but one aspect of the struggle by females striving for autonomy in a patriarchal culture, then it may be that the more narrowly and rigidly defined interpersonal models for understanding and treating anorexia nervosa in our time might usefully be reexamined, or at least their limitations and present-mindedness better understood. The many parallels between holy anorexia on the one hand and anorexia nervosa on the other allow us to see both in a different way, but it bears repeating that they are not the same thing.

The essential features of holy anorexia among wives and mothers are revealed in the *vitae* of three thirteenth-century women: Umiliana de' Cerchi, Margaret of Cortona, and Angela of Foligno. For Umiliana de' Cerchi we have a *vita* written two years after her death by Friar Vito da Cortona, who probably encountered her regularly at the church of Santa Croce and who took down the "testimony" of many women who had known her personally. Margaret of Cortona's life comes to us from Friar Giunta Bevegnati, one of her confessors; it is constructed largely as a dialogue between Margaret and Jesus, with the savior speaking in the first person. The *Libro di Angela da Foligno*, dictated by her to her confessor, Friar Arnaldo, is a work of fundamental importance in the literature of Christian mysticism. It also contains a deeply insightful analysis of her very human feelings as she tried to move ever closer to total immersion in God, and it is the basic source for the extremely sparse biographical information we have about her. In none of the three cases, however, is there anything approaching the volume of documentation available for Veronica Giuliani, itself a rather unusual case in this regard, nor were these women public figures on the scale of Catherine of Siena. As a result, we must make do with less certainty about some dates and events, less detail especially on childhood and adolescence, and much caution about the degree to which the ideas expressed are partly those of the male confessor rather than the holy woman herself. Still, the insights and personal revelations are many, and we do know that all three *vitae* were read eagerly and widely re-told, indicating at least that the struggles and longings presented in them variously fascinated or inspired medieval people.[4]

Within a few years of her death in 1246, some forty biographical accounts were written about Umiliana de' Cerchi, both in Latin and in the emerging vernacular. In essence all of these rely on Friar Vito's *vita*, as well as on a supplement recounting her miraculous intercessions that Hippolytus Fiorentinus wrote in 1252. Before proceeding to the life itself, Friar Vito listed by name the three confessors and thirty witnesses whose testimony he gathered. Every one of the thirty was female and all but two of them were lay people; among these were two of Umiliana's sisters, the wives of three of her brothers, her mother-in-law, her dead husband's older brother's wife, her nurse, and three family servants. Round-ing out the list were thirteen married Florentine women, two wid-ows, a recluse, and a single girl. As we shall see shortly, Umiliana's religious aspirations were fiercely opposed by her husband, her fa-ther, and several other male relatives. Thus the presence of so many female relations in the list of witnesses, along with varyingly fleeting references to their activities when Umiliana was still alive, suggest a gender split in the Cerchi family, and possibly in other patrician Florentine families as well. The men, deeply in-volved in the world of business, continued to support the Emperor against the Papacy or vacillated between the two forces, while the women, perhaps against the wishes of their husbands and fa-thers, moved into the Franciscan orbit, still a new and relatively powerless, idealistic movement. Umiliana's charitable activities when she was alive, like her wonder-working relics, made her a focal point among pious women. That Franciscan hagiographers quickly channeled and shaped these popular female impulses and then used them to strengthen their own foothold in the city and in their drive for domination in the sphere of organized religiosity in no way denies Umiliana's importance as an individual, nor does it lessen the significance of efforts by the women around her to express themselves in a mutually supportive sisterhood.[5]

She was born in December 1219 into the patrician household of Ulivieri Cerchi, a family well established in the countryside also, especially in the nearby Mugello region. It is likely that Umiliana was still a child when her mother died. Ulivieri must have remar-ried fairly soon, this time to Ermellina di Cambio, a member of the Benizi family that included Saint Philip, a founder of the Ser-vite Order. Altogether there probably were seventeen children,

---

eleven boys and six girls, but we do not know for sure how many were of each marriage, how many survived to adulthood, or whether any were older than Umiliana. Later biographies say that she never engaged in childish play, but the earliest sources do not emphasize this hagiographical convention or anything else concrete about her formative years.[6]

They begin: "Being in her sixteenth year, she was consigned in marriage by her parents, and almost filled with God, a month after joining her husband she began to spurn worldly pomp and ornamentation, and did not wear makeup; and the fine dresses she wore out of respect for her husband were not pleasing to her but a torment." During the first year of her conversion, apparently from a usual childhood and early adolescence rather than from any noteworthy wickedness, Umiliana was much consoled and encouraged by her husband's older brother's wife, Ravenna, who also lived with them. Together the two pious women went about Florence distributing alms, visiting the infirm, clothing the naked, and bringing food to convents. Umiliana's husband, a rich cloth manufacturer and moneylender, did not take kindly to his wife's new spirituality; he and others in his family, young and old, heaped verbal abuse upon her regularly and, it would seem, actually beat her.[7]

Umiliana resorted to secretiveness. Many times she gathered bits of bread from the table as her husband was eating and tucked them into her corset to give later to the poor. The sheets in the house she cut down to the minimum size needed to cover the mattresses and so also she trimmed the scarlet petticoat her husband had bought her, which she then carefully restitched at the sides and hem so that no one would notice her charity. After she had sold so many of her husband's belongings that she could not take more without being detected, she sewed with her own noble hands to have more to give. She held back part of the family's food supplies and evaded their censure by cooking secretly and silently at night so that at dawn she and her sister-in-law would be ready to bring meals to poor people at the hospice of San Gallo. Depending upon the recipients, Umiliana also knew how to prepare even the most exquisite culinary delights for sick clerics. For herself, however, she was content with much more ordinary, even "vile," fare.[8]

Although Umiliana suffered painful illnesses she never complained, and it did not upset her when her children were sick or died. On such occasions she was not very solicitous about them and simply would say that it was a blessing that they could pass away in their immaculate state, carrying with them their virginity. Exactly how many children she bore we do not know, but at the time of her husband's death when she was twenty or twenty-one she had two surviving daughters. Her relationship with them, while not so obviously strained as that with her husband, must have been ambivalent. A later account says that she loved her children not like other mothers with earthly love and natural affection but with holy and celestial charity. From her contemporaries we learn that when she returned to her father's house, in itself not especially uncommon for a young widow, her daughters continued to live with her husband's family. Such a separation of mother from daughters was most unusual. Umiliana's child-supervision rights apparently were very restricted; nevertheless, during one of their visits her daughter Regale fell, suffered a concussion of some sort, and was unconscious for a time. The girl had tripped coming into her mother's room, and now in Umiliana's arms she was cold to the touch and had no pulse.

> Dazed by the sudden death [Umiliana thought] of her daughter, because of the scandal she feared among her relatives, she took refuge in an image of the Madonna and prostrating herself with great reverence and many tears she said: "My beneficent love have mercy on me; take away this tribulation, and the scandal that because of me would befall my family."

The hagiographer's point here is to document the child's miraculous recovery, but at the same time he reveals a mother perceived by her relatives to be unfit, a mother who may well have internalized their judgment. A lawsuit by the Cerchis to get back Umiliana's dowry, even though she had been married for five years and borne children who survived and lived with her in-laws, gives more mundane evidence that something was very wrong here. During the last years of her life, when she was secluded in a tower, the greatest temptations against Umiliana's efforts at concentrated prayer were diabolic apparitions of visits by her innocent daughters. Yet her love for children is touchingly represented in the story of her effort to clutch a vision of a dove, symbol of the Holy Spirit, so that she could give it to her little nephew.[9]

So also a later hagiographer comments with greater psychological insight than he probably intended on Umiliana's married life: "God, wishing to call her to a higher grade of perfection, liberated her from the company, in fact from the slavery of that man, taking away his life with a severe illness." She spent the first ten months of her widowhood in her husband's home, caring for her children

---

and devoting ever more time to prayer and good works. Regularly she invited poor people to join her and the girls for meals. Then her father called her home, or else her dead husband's family threw her out—it is not clear exactly what happened—and with great sadness she obeyed and abandoned her daughters. My sense is that her relatives on both sides saw her behavior as bizarre, not holy, and that even the intervention of her sister-in-law Ravenna could not prevent the expulsion and isolation of this helpless widow. Immediately her father pressed her to remarry, but Umiliana refused, withdrawing to her room and the consolations of the Blessed Virgin. All night long a lamp burned by her night table as she prayed before a draped image of Mary and envisioned the flames of the Holy Spirit rising from her bedspread. Not even her father's threat to wall her up permanently in her cell changed Umiliana's mind about marriage. With the advice of Friar Michele degli Alberti she decided to become a third-order Franciscan sister of penance.[10]

Ulivieri Cerchi, however, had other plans, and in this instance his pecuniary interests dovetailed nicely with Saint Paul's warnings, duly included by Umiliana's later biographers, about what to do with young widows:

> Do not accept young widows because if their natural desires get stronger than their dedication to Christ, they want to marry again, and then people condemn them for being unfaithful to their original promise. Besides, they learn how to be idle and go round from house to house; and then, not merely idle, they learn to be gossips and meddlers in other people's affairs, and to chatter when they would be better keeping quiet. I think it is best for young widows to marry again and have children and a home to look after, and not give the enemy any chance to raise a scandal about them; there are already some who have left us to follow Satan.

Umiliana was now twenty-two. Her father and his sons were getting nowhere in their efforts to marry her off for a second time, and so they called in her mother's sister, perhaps the same Luciana who ultimately joined the witnesses to Umiliana's sanctity, to speak with her. The matron went through the usual litany about how young women have blood that boils quickly and how their human frailty is more easily under pressure to stray, to which had to be added the danger of the maximum liberty of widowhood. Then Umiliana responded: "Know well dear aunt that I have a most noble husband, over whom I will never cry nor from whose

dominion will I be left in perpetual widowhood." One earthly
husband had been more than enough for Umiliana, and now she
was married to Jesus Christ. Fortified by celestial visions, when
her relatives pressured, threatened, or harangued her about getting
married, as well as when they beat her, she laughed and invited
them to set up the prospective suitor on one side of the room and
a roaring fire on the other; then between the two positions she
would choose what she wished.[11]

The frustrated Ulivieri gave up and determined instead to rob
his daughter of her just patrimony. One day before an assembly of
communal judges he called Umiliana and explained to her that
since he had to litigate against her dead husband's family in order
to get back the dowry he had given, she would have to sign over
her power of attorney to him. She did so upon condition that she
would not be called to testify in the proceedings, only to learn
that her father already had won the case and then kept the dowry
for himself. "I did not believe that my father wished to defraud me
. . . but now I see that there is no good on earth when a father
cheats his own daughter. From now on you will have me in your
house no longer as a daughter but as a maidservant."[12]

Umiliana felt great remorse over the fact that she could not
consecrate her virginity to God, and now that she had no worldly
possessions to give in charity, the only thing left was herself. "I
give you totally my soul and my body," she began her orations.
Friar Vito records that she wished to join the Poor Clares at Mon-
ticelli, but for reasons that are unclear, and here one may speculate that she was judged to be too ill or unstable, instead she remained at home. Although she longed to run off to the woods and
live in complete solitude, Umiliana remained shut up in the family tower, her prison she called it, just a few yards from the bustling Piazza Signoria. Even from this cell her father tried unsuccessfully to evict her so that he could make room for her cousin
Galgano's family. Here she observed total silence; when she went
to church each morning to confess and to receive communion she
kept her eyes half closed and toward the ground so as not to see
vain objects. Once, as a horse nearly ran her over, she looked up
and saw its male rider, an offense to her chastity that so depressed
her that she prayed fervently to be made permanently blind.[13]

In her cell Umiliana slept very little, cried incessantly (after a
long spell during which she was totally unable to cry), and fought
diabolic torments. Hers were not only the usual array of serpents
letting off foul odors, noisy wild beasts, and nude cadavers but the

very desires closest to her heart. She was tempted to break her vow of silence by visions of her daughters dead in their crib, her good sister-in-law Ravenna calling to her, a holy abbot begging bread, the Madonna and child reaching out toward her. She suffered psychosomatic pains in her kidneys and shoulders so severe that for fifteen days her teeth locked and she could not chew any food. Her brothers thought she was suffering from an epileptic fit and pried her mouth open with a knife. She suffered sharp uterine pains, like labor contractions, and also stomach aches with frequent vomiting of blood. Even when she could eat Umiliana fasted on bread and water for five forty-day cycles each year as well as every Monday, Wednesday, Friday, and Saturday. Her life was "one continual fast," and eventually her confessor felt obliged to prohibit her from such strenuous austerity. Even then her maid Precilia regularly returned for her food tray and found it hardly touched. Frequently she ate nothing at all for three-day stretches when she was in ecstasy, and these meals she gave to the poor. Until her confessor ordered her to desist, she also flagellated herself until the blood ran and wore a hairshirt of goatskin with rough cords made from horsehair.[14]

These austerities took their toll—her limbs were "denuded of flesh, like a skeleton, and her body was similar to a drum filled with flatulence." In January 1246 the stomach pains that had plagued her for years grew acute, and she became mortally ill, bleeding from her nostrils and coughing up blood. Her nurse and spiritual companion, Gilsa, tended Umiliana as well as she could, but by March the dying saint became paralyzed on one side and for forty-two days she ate nothing. On Saturday, May 19, 1246, at the age of twenty-seven, Umiliana de' Cerchi died. At her express wish, none of her relatives stood vigil during her final hours. But her friend Gilsa instantly spread the news of Umiliana's death, causing crowds of people, mostly women both rich and poor, to gather and carry her in triumph to Santa Croce, where what remained after these seekers of wonder-working relics tore apart her vestments and flesh and then decapitated her body, was buried near the pulpit.[15]

THE NEXT thirteenth-century holy anorexic whose *vita* merits examination in some detail is Margaret of Cortona. Although she never married, Margaret shared her lover's bed for nine years and bore a son by him. That she had known the flesh, rather than the technicality of being an unwed mother, was but one of an inter-related set of forces that drove her to ever more severe levels of penitential asceticism. Her psyche, her humanity, are abundantly laid bare in her confessor's biography, much of which is a compilation of her spiritual experiences as she related them to him.

Margaret probably was born around 1247 in the hamlet of Laviano (in the present-day commune of Castiglione del Lago) near the shore of Lake Trasimeno on the Tuscany-Umbria border. Her father, presumably Tancredi di Bartolomeo, was a tenant farmer of modest means. We do not know her mother's name, only the likelihood that the apparently devout woman died when Margaret was still a child. Years later the Virgin Mary appeared to Margaret and reassured her that her prayers had been answered and that her mother, after having done penance in purgatory for ten years, was now in paradise. Her mother's piety was not extraordinary, however, at least to judge from what Christ said in a spiritual dialogue with Margaret after she had prayed in the way she had learned from childhood: "Daughter, your mother did not teach you well, because you must pray for everyone, and it is your general prayer that pleases me." Margaret's brother, Bartolo, who outlived her, was a Franciscan tertiary active in joining crusading missions to the Holy Land. Both children, and possibly a sister named Adriana, thus were faced at an early age with the loss of their mother. Tancredi soon remarried, and legend has it that her stepmother was cold and hostile toward Margaret.[16]

She was a stunningly attractive girl—and even years of harsh austerities could not mask entirely her natural beauty—with manners far more refined than her peasant origin would suggest. When she was fifteen she fell in love with a rich young nobleman from Montepulciano, by tradition Arsenio del Monte Santa Maria (or dei Pecora). The difference between them in social status caused his family to reject any possibility of marriage. Nevertheless, Margaret accepted his invitation to come live with him, and at the age of sixteen one night she left home by herself in a tiny boat to cross the marshes and take up residence as Arsenio's mistress. Although she was troubled by the irregularity of her position, and her beauty and enormous popularity among the Montepulciani only increased his family's hostility toward her, Margaret acted fully the part of the wealthy wife. She enjoyed being paid homage by the townsfolk, wearing dresses richer than anyone else's, the gold ringlets in her hair, facial makeup, and charging around the crowded streets on her adorned steed. Her fame would spread all the way back to the peasants of Laviano, who would envy and admire her as they remained stooped over their fields.[17]

After a while Margaret tired of such ostentation, or perhaps the adulation she received became tinged with mockery, and she began to spend more time alone at Arsenio's country villa at Palazzi. There she conceived a son. After her conversion she recalled these years in a spiritual exchange with Jesus: "Remember also that when you still loved worldly things and lived in the darkness of sin, I your master and doctor of truth gave you such maternal compassion toward the poor and the afflicted and roused in you such delight in solitary and remote places that you went around saying in your fervor, 'Oh, how sweet it would be to pray here, and with what solemnity and devotion one could sing the praises of God and do redeeming penance, in tranquility and certainty.'"[18]

Whatever her yearnings and internal tribulations, they were not sufficient in themselves to jolt Margaret to a new path. Then one day, as she waited at home for Arsenio to return from a hunting expedition in the nearby woods of Petrignano, she was alarmed to see his dog return alone, baying and then pulling at her dress. Margaret followed the animal to an oak tree. Under its branches she came upon her lover's body, covered with blood. Arsenio's killing left Margaret with a practical problem: whether it was the work of unknown assassins or the just punishment of God, she herself was in danger. She could expect nothing from his family and so, suddenly reduced to the status of an impoverished unwed mother with a young son to care for, she returned home to Laviano, dressed in black, crying, and filled with shame.[19]

Her stepmother had not forgiven Margaret's escape nine years earlier, and certainly not her ill-won prosperity with Arsenio, and at his new wife's instigation Tancredi refused to let his daughter and grandson set foot in the house. As she sat under a fig tree in the backyard Margaret felt tempted to accept her destiny. What alternative was there for a twenty-five-year-old mother with an illegitimate child, rejected by her father, yet still very attractive, except prostitution? The devil tried to trick her by reassuring her that she had nothing to feel guilty about since it was not she who had refused to marry and that given "the beauty of your body you should be able to find love with important and carnal men." But Margaret resisted this temptation and instead determined to go with her little boy to the city of Cortona, there to place herself under the guiding mercy of the Franciscans.[20] Dressed as a penitent and with her child in tow, Margaret appeared at the gates of

Cortona, most likely some time in 1272, to seek refuge at the Moscari family's palace. There Donna Marinaria and her daughter-in-law Raniera, who may have had advance word about the misfortunes of the deceased Arsenio's lover and who were active with the Franciscans in doing charitable work, took them in. In exchange for room and board, Margaret assisted the pious sisters by doing chores around the house and joined them in ministering to the poor people of Cortona. The Moscatis accompanied Margaret to the Convent of San Francesco, where she sought vestition as a penitential tertiary. Notwithstanding this noble introduction, however, the friars refused "because at that time they doubted her perseverance, both because she was too pretty and because she was too young." Margaret then went to work as a midwife, and her services came to be much in demand among Cortona's patrician women, for many of whose children she stood as godmother. For a time, more as expiation than out of necessity, on her way to church she went from door to door as a beggar, but then she came to understand how "inopportune" such behavior was for a proper lady, and instead she went directly to mass or else stayed in her room at home with her son.

Throughout, she remained determined to overcome the hesitations of her spiritual advisers and to forge for herself a path of sanctity. When some of her noble friends jokingly reproached her—"What ever will become of you, they said, Margaret you are so vain!"—she replied: "There will come a time when you will call me saint, because saint I will be; and you will come to visit me with pilgrim's staff and mendicant sacks hanging from your shoulders." It was not only a negative amending for sins past but also a positive drive for outstanding holiness (here innocently confessed by Margaret in a way so frankly heterodox that it is surprising that her biographer in his enthusiasm let it slip through) that carried this woman to the self-destruction of her body.[21]

After three years and "much insistence" on her part the Franciscans finally accepted Margaret as a tertiary. In order to be free to devote all her time to God she sent her son to a tutor in Arezzo and in due course he too joined the order as a friar. Occasionally she included the lad, whose religiosity was dutiful but not extraordinary, in her prayers, but from her earthly life Margaret cut him out completely. Rumors had spread among townspeople hostile to the penitent and her son that in desperation after she had abandoned him he had drowned himself in a well in Arezzo. Whether this evil gossip reached Margaret's ears we cannot be certain but for whatever reason, when her son's tutor came to bring news of him and to get paid, Margaret was so absorbed in prayer that she made no acknowledgment, even when asked repeatedly to do so by the friars around her, and let the teacher leave in a very agitated state, shouting and cursing as he made his exit. From her room in the Moscati palace she moved to a more isolated adjacent cell. There she remained for thirteen years, able to go about town regularly on charitable missions and yet free to engage in spiritual exercises in complete solitude. Her talents as a fundraiser and organizer soon became evident in her founding of a confraternity and establishment of a hospital in 1278, still functioning in Cortona as the Ospedale di S. Maria della Misericordia, dedicated especially to the care of poor mothers and their children.[22]

It was among these people that Margaret became renowned for the exceptional humility with which she shouted out publicly her sins, moving her listeners to weep as she also discovered their defects and suffered with them for their misdeeds. Among her audience of penitents were not only humble people but also priests and even a visiting inquisitor. A story emerged, possibly a true one, that Dante Aligheri himself came before Margaret on February 2, 1289, to accuse himself of pusillanimity, and some scholars hold that he later represented Margaret as Lucia, the psychopomp who encouraged him to embark on his journey to Hell (*Inferno* 2.97). Whatever the factual basis of this matter, it symbolizes well the charismatic qualities of such a woman.[23]

She determined to return once more to Laviano and there to seek public forgiveness during Sunday mass. With a cord tied around her neck in place of the jewelry she once had worn, she made peace with her father, and to a local gossip who charged her with false humility she gave her cloak, her shawl, and her meal; then, upon returning to Cortona, Margaret begged money to pay off all the gossip's debts. Had her confessor not refused to allow it, she also intended to go back to Montepulciano, but he worried that such self-abasement might in itself become an occasion for vainglory and that it would be imprudent to allow a young female of such fervid impulses to go on a long journey. Her wish was to be led around blindfolded by a woman who should cry out: " 'Here is Margaret, dear citizens! Here is she who once carried herself with such airs, and with her vanity and bad example did so much harm to the souls in this town!' Thus I will be deemed crazy by those before whom I boasted with my words and my looks."[24]

Even her biography, according to a perceptive modern analysis,

was constructed largely from autobiographical confessions written down by her Franciscan spiritual advisers and read to the faithful while Margaret was still alive and active among them. One
Sunday, as Friar Giunta was preaching during mass, "as if beyond
herself and out of her mind" Margaret "began to cry out in front of
everyone, asking if I knew anything of Christ crucified and where
had I put the Master." Because prayers should not be interrupted
with such commotion, and to console his wailing penitent and
the assembled worshipers who also had fallen into tears, the friar
shouted out that God would not hide His presence from anyone
who ardently sought Him, and that He would return shortly. At
this Margaret became deadly pale and took a seat in front of all the
people. Another time, on Good Friday, she emerged from her cell
"with her head shaved, almost intoxicated, like a mother who has
lost her son" and went around the streets of Cortona screaming in
a loud voice. Inspired by compassion or curiosity, men left their
work and women their children to come to the Oratory of the
Convent of San Francesco to see Margaret meditate on the crucifixion. They were moved to tears as they found her suffering
such atrocious internal pain that she seemed about to die. Her
teeth chattered as she writhed like a worm or a snake and turned
ashen in color, her pulse dropping and her body temperature falling as she became speechless, blind, and totally insensitive to the
world.[25]

At least one passage in which Jesus spoke to Margaret—words
that may well have originated with her rather than her confessor—
suggests a paranoid element in her thinking:

> You must live in continuous fear because you find yourself
> among enemies, in full battle. Therefore, behave yourself as if
> you are alone and crossing a hostile and cruel land where you
> may be kidnapped, wounded, robbed, and killed; watch closely
> on all sides; never put down your weapons, nor abandon your-
> self in sleep, nor trust in anyone until you have reached the
> friendly land.

Spiritual dialogues of this sort also might be interpreted as color-
ful but hardly extraordinary variations on the timeless Christian
exhortation to shut out the world and prepare for eternity, yet in
the case of Margaret of Cortona I think there is more. Her desire
to do public penance, to return to the earthly places of her sinfulness, her outbursts in church and on the streets, her autobiography, and then, possibly, her joining the audiences assembled to

listen to its intimate details, suggest a form of *santa pazza* still
very much linked to the living world. Margaret intended to be
holy, indeed, predicted during the early years of her stay in Cortona that in the end she would be venerated as a saint. A saint necessarily lives both in the spirit and in the flesh. Her public behavior reveals a woman tormented by a world around her that was
simultaneously an enemy of her soul and the theater in which her
bodily self moved about on its missions of charity and her psyche
bared itself in humiliating confession—the very actions to which
people responded in ways that reassured Margaret, here in this
world, that her path of holiness was true.[26]

An analogous ambivalence characterizes Margaret's secluded
life in her solitary cell. She would conquer her flesh as once she
had indulged it, but to truly achieve complete victory over her
bodily desires would have been to eradicate her link to the past,
thus depriving her conversion from sinner to saint of its full unity
and meaning. Even in the wicked days of her life with Arsenio,
God had intervened with moments of light, just as now in the
years of her holiness the devil plunged her into times of darkness,
even when she was near death. The motif of inverted values,
where the new makes little sense except in active contrast to the
old, and where both the body and the spirit take on added meaning when their desires are in active conflict, is amply displayed in
Margaret of Cortona's private austerities, especially her diet.[27]

Upon her conversion Margaret had decided to offer her body to
God as a sacrifice, and it was with this intent that she flagellated
herself with a knotted rope and slapped and punched herself with
such force that her naturally pale skin turned black and blue with
bruises. At first she abstained from meat but continued to use animal fats in preparing her meals, and only later did she limit her
condiments to a bit of olive oil. At that time, however, she was
actively working as a midwife and, so as not to bother her patients' families with preparing special meals for her, she would
eat whatever was served for everyone, including meat, but only
sparingly. At the Moscati palace she was able to be more strict,
and there she abstained from eggs or cheese except during Lent,
when she ate these items but gave up fish. Often she would forget
to cook anything at all. One day her son must have complained
about this spartan regimen, to which his mother replied: "My
son, when you come home if you find the food still uncooked, eat
it as is, and in silence; because there is no point in my being both-

ered with you for such a small matter during time reserved for singing the praises of God."[28]

About the time that she moved from her room in the palace to a more solitary adjacent cell she also increased the rigors of her fast, eating only vegetables with no condiments and shortly thereafter no cooked food except a little bread. Thus her regular diet for years consisted of bread, nuts, raw vegetables, and water—all in small quantities eaten at 3:00 P.M. and 6:00 P.M. At God's command, she never ate in the presence of others. "In order to be more light-headed and allow her soul more easily to be fervent," Margaret made no exception for feast days, a rather clear indication that she realized and actively sought the obvious side effects of rigorous fasting. Not surprisingly, her diet weakened her so much that she had difficulty walking and had to spend more time in her cell. There she was tormented by demons in the forms of nude women and men, serpents, and beasts who paraded before her the worldly lust she once had enjoyed and tried to entice her with plates of delicate aromatic foods.[29]

Margaret's confessors came to realize the dangers, spiritual as well as physical, of what she was doing and intervened. She was dismayed that her hard mortifications were not destroying her natural beauty as rapidly as she wished, and so she went to Friar Giunta and said, "have pity and allow me to redouble my rampage against this odious body, as I have wished for so long; not even your prohibition should impede the impulse of my free will. I assure you, that even though I would do so gladly, I will not wound myself mortally." The friar was very dubious about granting such a dangerous and unspecified penance to a woman well known to him for her extreme behavior, and he decided to question her further about exactly what she intended. Margaret then confessed that she secretly had bought a razor and meant to cut her nose and upper lip "because with the beauty of my face I did harm to many souls. Therefore, wishing to do justice upon myself, by myself, for this offense to God and to transform the beauty of my body into ugliness, I pray you to permit me without delay to offer to Christ the King this sacrifice which I propose." Friar Giunta absolutely refused, pointing out to Margaret that such an action might lead to hemorrhaging or other complications and then adding to this practical advice the warning that if she disobeyed him he would no longer hear her confessions and that none of his Franciscan brothers would care for her or guide her.[30]

The ambience in which Margaret sought spiritual perfection through harsh austerity was one that offered considerable support for such a path. Under the influence of male ascetic mystics such as Jacopone da Todi, her contemporary, the Spiritual Franciscans actively lauded the virtues of extreme self-mortification, for men as well as for women. But Margaret's severity was too much even for these strict friars, who feared that she would bring about her own death, and in various ways they urged or ordered her to stop. Apparently she internalized their advice enough that in her dialogues with Jesus he too concurred, telling her that while he appreciated her efforts to macerate her body he did not want her so reduced by fasting and fever that she could not go to mass. For days Margaret had been unable to arise from the plank on the ground on which she rested, so weakened was she by her abstinence, but the divine consolation of her talk with Jesus greatly encouraged her, and the next morning she hurried off to church as if she had not been sick at all.[31]

On another occasion we find Margaret confessing to an episode of binge eating, one that suggests as well significant tensions between male friars and the religious females of Cortona over this saint in their midst. Several pious townswomen had come to reprimand her for being too severe with her body and had brought along a plate of cooked figs which they insisted in God's name that she eat. Since she had promised Jesus to take at least a little food from time to time, while concentrating on meditation not on eating, there was nothing intrinsically wrong here. But instead of retiring to her cell with the plate to eat alone as she had vowed, Margaret went out and joined the women, apparently stuffing herself and not thinking very much about God. Quickly she felt the burden of this sin and wept inconsolably until Jesus appeared. At first he scolded her for "giving faith so easily to the words of women who told you that with such abstinence you would become crazy," and only then did he go on to encourage her to listen exclusively to him and to the good Franciscan friars. The women also must have told Margaret to exchange her patched up veil for a new white one and to wash her filthy dress, because Jesus also explicitly countermanded this advice and assured Margaret that, whatever the opinions of townswomen, the friars who had put up with the stink of her sin years earlier would not be offended now by her smelly clothes.[32]

Margaret's own doubts about what she was doing she expressed in the guise of diabolic visitations. Already the fame of her sanc-

tity caused people to come to see her and try to touch her, Lucifer
began, so did not her continued austerities now that surely she
was among the saved reveal a strain of vainglory? Another time
the devil calmly reasoned with her that it should be sufficient for
her to follow the general rules on fasting observed by all Franciscans, because of course they were destined to go to heaven. "So
what are you doing in this cell, where you are ruining your soul
and your body?" But she resisted this sophistry, telling the devil
that God had taught her a special penitential routine and had
"promised me life eternal if I persevere." The pact was hard to
keep, however, for at times Margaret, not unlike modern anorexics, was indeed weak and hungry. Once it was the cooked figs, another time a woman who brought her a dish of cauliflower that
she ate only to find that it sat so heavily on her stomach that she
was unable to pray all night—but always God forgave her, promising her that if her abstinence became so extreme that it truly debilitated her body excessively, he would allow her a richer diet,
only however when she would come to lose all sense of taste. Her
stomach in fact became so weak that wine and food tasted to her
like earth. For days on end, as when she repeated her eight-day
general confession, she was *unable* to eat.

Friar Giunta had pity and called in a physician, but Margaret
refused to take any medicine and tearfully cried that "she wanted
to see her body debilitated, infected, devoured by worms." She
was sure her stomach was only pretending to be ill and she called
it a "dark traitor." When the friar tried on his own to coax her to
eat more he received this reply:

> Dear Father, I have no intention of making a peace pact be-
> tween my body and my soul, and neither do I intend to hold
> back. Therefore, allow me to tame my body by not altering
> my diet; I will not stop for the rest of my life, until there is no
> more life left. You should not think that [my body] is so mor-
> tified and weak as it seems; it acts this way so that I should
> not demand the debt it contracted in the world, when it liked
> pleasure. Let it be enough, my Father, let it be enough, that in
> these Easter holidays I condition vegetables with oil, to obey
> your orders, which I did not wish to do.

Then in a soliloquy Margaret goes on:

> Oh my body, why do you not help me to serve my creator and
> redeemer? Why are you not as quick to obey as you were to
> disobey His commands? Do not lament, do not cry; do not

pretend to be half dead. You will bear the weight that I place on your shoulders, all of it, just as at one time you bore it to displease our Creator . . . I not only wish to abstain from bodily food but I wish to die a thousand times a day, were it possible, in this mortal life of mine.[34]

Worn out by years of active warfare against her body, Margaret longed for death and the seat in paradise which a vision had shown prepared for her. "I want to die of starvation to satiate the poor," she told her confessor. And to Jesus she expressed her readiness for even the most atrocious death because unlike him, who had died to atone for original sin, she had sinned by her willful action. Now by his grace her body had become a "vessel of purity," and the time was appropriate to render it to him. But she was tormented by an apparition of a ferocious devil who told her, "God will never forgive you or show the mercy you expect because with your fasting you have committed suicide." Apparently many Cortonesi, and a few friars as well, had similar thoughts, because in a more reassuring vision Jesus advised Margaret to avoid any further conversation with secular people, and as she was near death he added that he was gravely offended by the busybody clerics who did not understand the real nature of her sickness and were trying to get her to eat.[35]

Friar Giunta, seeing Margaret's body destroyed by fasting, tears, vigils, flagellation, hairshirts, and myriad illnesses, "feared that by her continued refusal to take nourishment" she was indeed shortening her life, and he ordered her to eat food appropriate for a sick person, with only the exception that the eating not damage her soul. This possible exception allowed Margaret a final chance to express God's will as she understood it through direct communication with Jesus, and against the men who claimed spiritual direction over her.

When you interrogate your confessor and ask him if he knows if you have offended me in any way, it is necessary that he not show instantly that he is so sure of himself, but that he consider carefully and examine attentively your acts and your words . . . Because you are my vessel and my bride and your purity must be watched over with perpetual integrity.

On February 22, 1297, Margaret of Cortona died, wasted in body but with joy beaming from her angelic face.[36]

CONCERNING the details of Angela of Foligno's life we know almost nothing. The date of her death, January 4, 1309, is well documented but virtually all other "facts" about her, and these are few indeed, must be deduced or implied from her writings. These in turn make only occasional and often elliptical references to her daily life in Foligno, either before or after her conversion. While hagiographers over the centuries have embellished greatly the little that is known, or simply invented a life that they felt might accompany nicely her mysticism, nothing in these elaborations contributes to the present effort to understand holy anorexia. The reason we stop to consider Angela is found not in her *vita* but in the enormous vitality and clarity with which she explains *why* she took up the way of the cross. Hers was a decision based on love, God's love for her and hers for him. Everything she came to do was because of this love affair (and her writings justify using precisely this term) with the crucified Jesus—the penances, the joys, the despair, the certainty of being loved. Along with Francesca Romana and Catherine of Genoa, whose experiences will be considered in the following chapters, Angela of Foligno stands out and stands for a major aspect in the motivation that drove some married women to holy anorexia. Few were as articulate as she in describing the inner dynamic of her spiritual quest, and so it matters less that its external circumstances are obscure—unimportant, she would have said.[37]

Sometime in 1291 Angela came to nearby Assisi with a group of pilgrims. As she sat on the ground at the entrance to the upper basilica of the church of San Francesco she began to cry out in a loud voice: "Unknown Love, why? why do you abandon me?" Angela could say nothing else and kept wailing the same phrase over and over again. She shouted incomprehensibly that she wanted to die, and so overwhelmed was she with grief at being left alone that all her joints collapsed. Her fellow pilgrims gathered around and "watched over her as if to protect her," especially one holy man from Puglia whom Angela had persuaded to give away all his worldly possessions to the poor and together with her to make a vow of absolute poverty. Friar Arnaldo, who was a relative of Angela's as well as her confessor and principal personal counselor, stood by and observed everything, but he took no action. Other friars who knew them both had come to investigate Angela's scandalous behavior, and Friar Arnaldo was just too embarrassed to do anything. Wounded in his disgraced pride and for shame, he

kept his distance, watching with growing discomfort and indigna-
tion. Even after she had quieted down, the friar could not speak
calmly. He warned her "in the future never to set foot in Assisi,
seeing that she was struck by crises of this sort, and I told her
companions not to bring her ever again."[38]

Only later, probably in 1292 when he returned to Foligno, did
Friar Arnaldo determine to try to find out more about Angela's
spiritual crisis at the church entry in Assisi. He was a very bright
but obviously troubled young man, one whose own religious
searchings apparently brought him to be excommunicated as a
rebel fugitive and listed among the heretical *Fraticelli* in France
who were condemned by Pope John XXII in his Bull of 1317. Friar
Arnaldo suspected that Angela's shocking behavior resulted from
her being possessed by some evil spirit, and so he intended to take
careful notes on everything she said in response to his "thousand"
questions. Probably the two spoke in an emerging Umbrian dia-
lect, and he then tried to transpose her grammar from first person
to third and write down a Latin version. He intended then to bring
this compilation to some wise and holy person who might shed
light on the whole matter. Angela had not yet reached the stage of
"clear and perfect certainty" about her saintly path that she later
achieved, and so she agreed to this form of trial, insisting only
that the friar not reveal her thoughts and experiences to anyone
who would know her personally.[39]

Quickly, however, Angela's fervor convinced Friar Arnaldo that
his method was "like trying to sift flour with a coarse sieve that
caught only the gross and let slip through all the precious and
fine." He stopped asking so many questions, transposing the grammar, or adding anything of his own and instead tried desperately
to keep up with Angela's flow of words. She scolded him about the
results when he read them back to her for her approval, saying
that his rendition was "dry and without gusto," admitting the accuracy of the text but complaining that it was "obscure" and that
he had gotten the less important details right while missing entirely her most precious thoughts. Friar Arnaldo struggled to
write more quickly, yet he felt it was already a miracle that he had
managed to put her ideas down in at least a fairly organized way,
admittedly in truncated and shortened form. To do his best he had
to have his mind at peace, and therefore he began to go to confession before their meetings so that he would not be distracted by
thoughts of his own sins. This helped a bit, and sometimes he felt

divinely inspired; still, the physical circumstances were awkward. Friar Arnaldo feared the judgments of his brothers, who criticized him for sitting so close to Angela in church, but he had to do this to be sure of hearing her words properly. The backbiting of the friars who were "against him" caused his immediate superior and his provincial head to explicitly prohibit him from continuing the redaction, and they did not wish even to consider the holiness of what he was writing. For a while one of his friends had to take over as scribe. At times he resorted to stuffing scraps of paper into his prayer book and scribbling down as best he could in the dimly lit church when the others were not watching too closely, convinced more than ever that these were the words of a saint and that a little disorder or incompleteness would be understood whereas tampering or adding his own ideas would be unpardonable.[40]

It is impossible to be certain today that we are reading an exact Latin translation of Angela of Foligno's very words, without any additions or changes. Questions exist about the time, the internal sequencing, even the authorship of parts of the work, and no critical edition exists on the scale available for Catherine of Siena. Although such an endeavor would be welcome, it is beyond the scope of the present study and therefore I shall rely on the best scholarly editions (Doncoeur, Ferré, and Castiglione-Humani), as well as upon their judgment about what is Angela's. Whatever the full circumstances, we can be certain that, historically, a mystical work of fundamental importance, one translated into every major European language, has been read and retold in varying versions for centuries by believers who accepted that it recounted at first hand the experience of a married mother who abandoned everything for God.[41]

Angela's call to special holiness had come several years earlier, most probably in 1285 when she was in her mid to late thirties and a housewife with several children. Hers had been a mundane existence—whether in fact she had been unfaithful to her husband, as some scholars conclude, hardly merits expending research effort upon—neither especially sinful nor pious beyond the routine devotions of ordinary Christians. Then quite suddenly a great sense of eternal damnation came over her, and in bitter tears she made a total confession before Friar Arnaldo. In a series of steps or stages, the self-imposition of increasingly harsh penances allowed her to see some hope for her salvation in God's mercy. Yet for Angela these early years were filled with pain and anguish because she did not feel God's love. The obligation to engage in sexual intercourse, as well as her other family ties, blocked her path.

> In this period I lived with my husband: how bitter it was for me when an injustice was launched against me or I was wronged! Still I accepted everything patiently, as well as I could. Then it came about, with God's permission, that my mother, who had been a great impediment to me, died. Her death was followed by my husband's and in a short time by my children's. Because I had begun the way of the cross and had begged God to be freed from every worldly tie, I found consolation in their deaths; I felt that in the future, God having conceded me these graces, my heart always would remain united with his and the heart of God always united with mine.[42]

While some of Angela's modern biographers have been taken aback by the starkness of these words and have tried to explain them away by citing a later passage that mentions grief over the deaths of her mother and children (but not over her husband's demise), my sense is that this woman meant exactly what she said. Her family opposed her spiritual quest, both actively by their words and deeds and passively by their very existence. She could not progress further in her total love of God while they remained, and so she was glad when they died. However, the union with God that she hoped soon would follow continued to elude her. She increased her mortifications and experienced some consolation in concentrated prayer and in brief visions of the Blessed Virgin and John the Baptist, but at the same time strange and uncontrollable impulses overcame her and she herself began to think she was insane or possessed.[43]

In order to remain at prayer she wished not to need to eat, and only with effort did she realize that this desire was a demonic trick. After she sold the last of her possessions, a country house she prized highly, Angela went through a phase of screaming every time she heard the name of God. Whenever she saw any representation of Christ's passion she would become feverish and fall ill. Her companion tried to keep her away from such images, but still the people around Foligno started saying she was possessed by demons, and "I felt great shame and admitted that without doubt I must be sick and demoniac." At times she walked about the streets with her eyes so on fire that her companion worried that people would think them both insane. The incident at the church in Assisi, triggered, Friar Arnaldo ultimately learned, by the departure of the Holy Spirit from Angela after this consolation had accompanied her pilgrimage, was by no means unique, nor was it to be her last experience of spiritual emptiness.[44]

For two years beginning in 1294 Angela underwent a period of aridity. She felt abandoned by God and was unable to confess. As she was washing some lettuce leaves the devil teased her about whether God intended equally "dignified" duties for her in the hereafter. This intrusion came as Angela was reflecting that she deserved to be put in hell, there to go around gathering dung; she was disturbed that such a trivial demonic reference to the womanly chores she was doing here on earth should make her so sad and cause her to doubt her efforts at self-deprecation and acceptance of anything her Love willed. On another occasion, as she considered the impossibility of ever fully sharing Christ's passion, she felt so depressed she thought she might die. "Still I have not recovered and I feel I have lost my joy forever; I have lost the vigor with which I usually was cheerful and from that moment on I have not been able to be happy." Demons filled her head with visions of her soul being strung upside down so that all her virtues turned to vices; in anger, pain, tears, desperation she punched herself so hard that her head and body were covered with bruises, and still the torture continued. Human vices, even ones she never had known before, tormented every member of her body. Even when these desires may have shifted away from her "intimate parts" to places where she felt the pain less, so on fire was she that until Friar Arnaldo prohibited it, she used natural fire to extinguish the internal burning. During this long crisis, and to a lesser degree afterwards as well, Arnaldo tells us that she was unable to eat or ate only very little.[45]

Angela of Foligno wanted to die. She first felt this desire strongly immediately after her return from Assisi in 1291 and then again about a year later. As her spiritual understanding deepened, her wish changed from instant death to a drawn-out, physically painful and tormented ending, one in which she would experience all the sufferings of the world in her every limb and organ. Her Love had sacrificed, and so would she. Often the act of receiving communion awakened in her a longing for martyrdom. Only around 1296, more than a decade after her initial conversion and after she had reached the final step on her way to the cross, did an active yearning for death torment her less. Angela continued to want to die, but the desire became more passive; no longer did she need to

seek God or strain to know his will because God was within her
and would manifest his intention in whatever way he chose.[46]

So also at this time Angela came to reduce the rigor of her austerities. Earlier she had undertaken a detailed examination of
each part of her body, judging the sin member by member and assigning to each its due penance. She and her companion one Holy
Thursday had gone to the local hospital of San Feliciano to wash
the feet of sick women and the hands of the men who were there.
One leper they tended had flesh so putrified and rotten that pieces
peeled off into the wash basin they were using. Angela then proceeded to drink this mixture, it giving her almost the sensation of
receiving communion, and when a bit of flesh got stuck in her
throat she tried to swallow it too until against her will she choked
it out. Only gradually did her body promise to obey her soul and
profess to be its servant. She felt herself to be party to a one-sided,
open-ended, incalculable pact with God, communicated to her in
a dialogue with Christ crucified. "You need do for me only what I
did for you. It is not you who suffers for my fault but I who suffer
for yours; I without hope of receiving any benefit from you, you
with hope of receiving a gift without end." There was no limit to
how much she owed, to how long and harsh her mortifications deserved to be. Once she realized the impossibility of ever doing
enough and became less depressed, Angela attenuated her penitential practices at least somewhat, and while she never indulged
her bodily sensations with softness or concern, she took reasonable care of her physical being. Even her anorexia abated. When
she felt hungry she would interrupt her prayer to ask God's permission to eat, and this he would grant, sometimes immediately,
other times making her wait a while.[47]

Angela's mystical experiences increasingly centered on one
event: the crucifixion. Whereas earlier she had swooned even
upon seeing a painting that depicted the passion, she now came to
be immune to such icons, preferring not to gaze upon them because they failed so utterly to convey the imagery in her own
mind. For Angela there was nothing symbolic, remote, mysterious, vicarious, or theological about the crucifixion. God, a man,
had made the supreme sacrifice directly and personally for her and
his act of love was alive, right here and now. Her visions convey a
vivid realism, expressed by a woman with an exact knowledge of
the physique of a thirty-three-year-old man, now dead. Christ's
blood was still fresh and flowed red from his wounds; his limbs
appeared dislocated by the relentless tension and his muscles and

bone joints were distorted. Still, on his skin she discerned no tears or breaks. More even than the open puncture wounds, it was this bodily disfigurement caused by muscular stress during hanging that illuminated Angela's soul and allowed her to penetrate the full meaning of his passion. As she contemplated, she too felt waves of pain through her body. Friar Arnaldo recounts that on one Holy Saturday Angela during a mystical rapture was in her Love's tomb:

> at first she kissed Christ's breast and saw that he lay dead, with his eyes closed; then she kissed his mouth from which a sweet perfume emanated, impossible to describe. After a brief pause she drew her cheek to Christ's and Christ placed his hand on her other cheek, clutching her to him. In that moment she heard these words: "Before I was laid in this tomb I held you this tightly to me."[48]

With deceptive facility, we moderns might read into Angela's necrophilic experiences the suppressed, repressed, oppressed, and expressed sexual fantasies of a menopausal widow. More to the point, however, is how Angela herself understood her feelings, admittedly with the advice and prodding of Friar Arnaldo and other male clerics. The reader may recall that Catherine of Siena's prayers for her mother's recovery from a grave illness were expressed in contractual terms more appropriate for a business deal than a miracle. But no one would infer from this that subliminally she wished to be a banker or a merchant. Rather, she spoke in the language of her time, class, place, and familial experience. Similarly, Angela's life as a widowed woman who had engaged in sexual intercourse and knew how the male body, alive and dead, felt in her arms and under her fingers prepared her to relive the crucifixion in the explicit way she did. For her God's love was fundamental; not only might it redeem her in the hereafter but it was real, living, and present in her, in the town of Foligno as she went about the streets or meditated in her cell. And of course she expressed this love in the only way she and her listeners could understand. God's love was total and therefore ipso facto both spiritual and physical, sometimes indescribably sensuous.[49]

Throughout the *Book*, Angela returned to the theme of love. Her path of holiness, even more clearly than in the other lives we have considered thus far, was not one of negative expiation but rather a choice by a woman who loved and was loved. The lovers spoke:

JESUS:
I give you a love of me that will make your soul always on fire
for me, a love so ardent that if a person says something bad
about you, you will take it as a compliment . . . I love you so
much that I am totally unable to remember your faults; my
eyes do not see them; in you I have hidden a great treasure.

ANGELA:
My soul felt that all this was true, and I no longer doubted
anything. I felt and I saw the eyes of God as he watched, and
in those eyes my soul experienced such happiness that no
man, not even one of those saints who is up above if he were
to descend, could have spoken to me about happiness and
made me understand better.

JESUS:
I want you in this life to hunger for me, and desire me, and
languish for me.

ANGELA:
Never on this earth has a mother embraced her son, nor has
any other human creature been able to embrace with a love
that nears the immense love with which God embraces the
soul. He grasps it to himself with such sweetness and with
such heat that I think anyone who has not had the experience
cannot understand.[50]

A loyal following of lay people and clerics gathered around Angela and tried to understand, hoping to further their own spiritual
growth by sharing in hers. For a time she nurtured them, although
she never accepted the role of "Mamma" in the way that Catherine
of Siena later did. In dictating the *Book* Angela had begun only
with great hesitation about the meaning of her internal experiences, and there is every reason to accept that she shared Friar
Arnaldo's suspicion that she might be possessed. But as her confidence grew she continued to "publicize" her way to the cross so
that, for a time at least, we must conclude that she actively sought
a public role. Her efforts to mediate conflicts within the Franciscan fold between Spirituals and Conventuals, as well as her attacks on the Brethren of the Free Spirit, also suggest a political, this-worldly concern on her part. Yet she never was entirely
comfortable with this role, and after 1300, with the departure
of Friar Arnaldo, the style and content of her message changed
drastically.[51]

Her letters to her spiritual children became dry and formal, almost businesslike, in sharp contrast to the emotionally charged, flowing, sometimes theologically obscure and heterodox qualities of the first part of the *Book*. Some of the change undoubtedly is to be attributed to Friar Arnaldo's absence from the scene, and yet much remains that belongs to Angela. Her love affair with Christ crucified not only was hard for her to explain but came to be something that in her mind she *should not* share, even vicariously, with others. "Experience teaches," she wrote, again grasping for human metaphors to express her spirit, "that the husband who loves his wife in the secret of his heart cannot stand to share her with anyone." Angela felt her heart at one with Christ's and they kept no "secrets" from each other. Faced with the lesser spirituality of her Franciscan brethren, who spent a lot of time just plain bickering over doctrinal points that she found trivial, Angela warned them against love, called even "good" love of God the most dangerous force on earth. "Until one is able to live in a state of perfect love, every love should be held suspect," she wrote, knowing full well that at least in Foligno she alone had achieved perfect love.[52]

Despite her efforts to shed her followers and make them more self-reliant, they continued to pester her. Years earlier she had railed against those who studied the Bible but did not feel God. Now she warned her clerical devotees that she was a woman without truth whose words should be held suspect. "At this moment I do not feel like writing," she continued, "but I am constrained to do so by the many letters you send me." She proceeded to give them a lesson on pride, the root of all human vices, she called it. Then she scolded them for going through the motions of prayer in a mechanical fashion with their minds on other things and for getting so bogged down on rules for fasting that they lost sight of the larger purpose—unity with the God of Love. Shortly before her death in 1309 she explicitly challenged the male-appropriated cleric's right to judge his fellow creatures. It was fine for him to abhor sin, yet "I say only that you should not judge a sinner, because you do not know the judgment of God."[53]

About her own path Angela felt absolutely certain, and she had lived in this certainty for over a decade. Even if the whole world were to tell her something contrary to what God had revealed to her, she would pay no attention. Against the backdrop of this confidence, which is expressed throughout her writings from 1296 on, her final public confession may appear puzzling. She wished to go through Foligno completely naked, carrying dead fish and hunks of rotting meat around her neck and saying:

> Come see this worthless woman, full of malice and pretence, receptacle of every vice and evil. I observed Lent by staying blocked up in my cell to attract people's esteem, and said to all those who invited me: "I do not eat meat or fish." But in reality I was gluttonous and full of greed, an epicure and a toper . . . Do not believe me any more, do not adore this idol any more because in this idol lives the devil. All the words I spoke were the diabolic words of a cheat; pray that for God's justice this idol should fall and smash in pieces so that all my deceiving and false works will become unveiled. [54]

Hagiographers have seen in this confession either a relapse to Angela's earlier depressive state or simply an exaggerated sense of humility not so uncommon for a saint. While these elements certainly are present, it seems to me that the confession becomes fully intelligible only when placed in the wider context of Angela of Foligno's efforts to liberate herself from the world of patriarchal Franciscan religiosity. She served as a counselor and spiritual mother, yet the key word here is "served," and Angela intended to serve no one and nothing but God. To be sure, her dilemma was complex and her behavior ambivalent. Friar Arnaldo had been a necessary companion early in her quest for spiritual perfection, and the idolization by other Franciscans and lay people in later years certainly reassured her that her path was true. Yet Angela, in ways only hinted at by Margaret of Cortona and absent entirely in Umiliana de' Cerchi, achieved total autonomy in her spirituality. In the end, no priest or friar stood as gatekeeper to her salvation or shared in her unity with the God of Love.

The emotional cost of her tortured achievement had been great. As she herself confessed, she was a malicious person and filled with the devil. To drive out her inner demons she whipped and burned herself. Yet no amount of verbal self-abuse and physical punishment entirely calmed her aggressive tendencies. Whereas in the case of Veronica Giuliani we know of childhood circumstances that may possibly contribute to an explanation of her later self-destructiveness—the death of her mother, her father's withdrawal of his love—for Angela of Foligno no evidence exists on her early years. And yet there is the adult rage, the overt anger against her family, the world, herself. So also with Umiliana and Margaret—wives and mothers who wished to kill. Umiliana was indeed an unfit mother, and just maybe she did try to harm her daughter Regale as she feared others would suspect. Margaret's lack of concern for her son's welfare and whereabouts shocked her confessor and was plainly negligent; Angela was glad when her family died. Even when the impulse to hurt expressed itself only in fantasy, the psychological import remained. These women identified with the suffering of Jesus on the cross both as victim and as aggressor. In their bodies they shared with all humankind the guilt of original sin, the responsibility for demanding the death of the Redeemer. In their souls they shared with their Bridegroom the exquisite pleasure of making the ultimate sacrifice and of finally laying their anger to rest. Thus they declared unremitting war against their bodies, carrying their ascetic masochism to levels unknown among virginal holy anorexics and thereby narrowly escaping the schizophrenic depths against which they battled.

CHAPTER

5

HISTORICAL
DIMENSIONS: ASCENT

BEFORE tracing the historical development of holy anorexia
from its beginnings in the early thirteenth century until its
transformation during the Catholic Reformation, let us review
briefly the psychological dimensions explored in the preceding
three chapters. Whether anorexia leads to death, as in Catherine
of Siena's case, or the girl recovers, as with Veronica Giuliani, or
it is part of a later and perhaps more complex response, as with
Umiliana de' Cerchi, Margaret of Cortona, and Angela of Foligno,
certain traits are common to all holy anorexics. Their childhood,
insofar as we are able to know it, provides them with a great capacity for faith. In their infancy doting parents, especially mothers, cue them to feel special, chosen above all others to be loved.
The circumstances of early oral gratification in themselves are
not that extraordinary—Veronica's mother's charity in wet nursing some neighboring child or Catherine's breastfeeding and weaning cycle probably served the mother's emotional needs more than
her daughter's, and in any event were fairly commonplace—and so
also the little girls' earliest religious impulses seem reasonable
enough: a childish belief in the fanciful, magical, wondrous stories
told of heros past and present. They are of cheerful disposition,
very outgoing, perhaps a bit boisterous and domineering in ways
more usual for a little boy than a girl but still well within the
bounds of acceptable and even endearing behavior, especially for a
youngest or favored child. Among the 261 holy women under
study we have reliable information about siblings for 120 of them;
of these 120 fully 73 were the youngest child, and among these, 47
percent were well known for their compulsive fasting, whereas for

the total population of female Italian saints since 1200 the corresponding figure is only 26 percent.[1]

Holy anorexia in adolescence and adulthood, however, does *not*
represent psychological regression to an infantile stage of oral
contentment, a subliminal retreat to the safety of the womb as it
were. There can be no retreat because that path invariably is
blocked by painful experiences associated with the quest for autonomy, for a sense of self. Where such regression does ultimately
occur, as we saw with Veronica Giuliani, it is part of a path toward
recovery from the most self-destructive manifestations of holy
anorexia. Often a death in the family seems to have been crucial.
The pious and trusting little girl loses someone she loves deeply;
her dependency is shattered and her faith is tested. Ultimately she
passes the test and visualizes her dead mother, father, brother, or
sister in heaven, or in purgatory and in need of human sacrifice
and prayer. Yet the world of base physical urges and desires remains; it is her body, the girl decides with no small amount of
pressure from catechism lessons only she takes literally and seriously, that brings death, that brought the death of her loved one. It
is not any single zone—oral, anal, or genital—that she becomes
fixated upon, but her entire body, all of which is hopelessly corrupt and impedes not only her own salvation but that of the
people she loves.

The drive to destruction of her body—for the flesh cannot be
tamed and therefore must be obliterated—is especially prominent
among holy anorexics who have been married, but it is present in
all of them. Since virgins and pious widows do not engage in sexual intercourse, food is the only thing that enters the bodies of
these anorexics by their own volition, or because they are pressed
to accede to the orders of their confessors. Over this invasion of
their bodies these women retain but one choice—whether to
bring a bowl to their lips or a fork to their mouths—and they
choose to say no. Food is food, not an incorporated phallic symbol,
but it is no less sexual for being food. It sustains the body, corrupt
life on earth, and thereby kills the soul, life everlasting. Death,
the enemy that stole her loved one and ominously threatens her,
must be defeated, and the surest way to triumph over the fear of
death is to die willingly. For some—Veronica Giuliani and Angela
of Foligno are the clearest examples we have examined thus far—
bodily desires eventually do die, and then a soul liberated from
the flesh may nonetheless remain its temporal prisoner until

nature runs its course, although not without setbacks and relapses of doubt. For others, such as Catherine of Siena and Umiliana de' Cerchi, the battle ends only with total annihilation of the flesh and death. Either way, autonomy demands freedom from the shackles of sexual desire, hunger, and weariness.

Early in her saintly career the holy anorexic fully commands the war against her body and therefore suffers deeply at every defeat, whether it is a plate of food she gobbles down or a disturbing flagellation by nude devils and wild beasts. Then with varying degrees of success the holy radical begins to feel victorious in her contest, and she surrenders active control over the battle to the depths of her psyche or to established conventual norms. Changes in hormonal balance, fueled by the psychic effect of sustained mental prayer, suppress the life-preserving needs for nourishment and rest. Lowered body temperature, insensitivity to external heat or cold, slowed pulse rate, general inanition, and unresponsiveness to pain all occur frequently in the hagiographical accounts; they portray the expected outcomes of extreme self-starvation.

Just as critical as the course of this war against bodily urges, wherein the quest for autonomy is purely internal, is the contest for freedom from the patriarchy that attempts to impose itself between the holy anorexic and her God. The authority figure may in fact be female, as for a time it was during Catherine of Siena's battle against her mother or when Veronica Giuliani fought her abbess, but always in the official church it is a male priest who dispenses the saving body of Christ. The holy anorexic rebels against passive, vicarious, dependent Christianity; her piety centers intensely and personally upon Jesus and his crucifixion, and she actively seeks an intimate, physical union with God. Once she convinces herself that her spiritual bridegroom communicates directly with her and she thereby achieves true autonomy, the commands of earthly men become trivial. Her total dependence upon God's will, ultimately hailed as heroically virtuous by the very patriarchy she is rebelling against, legitimizes her defiance and places her in a position of enormous strength. For in her actions on earth the "will of God" to which she yields is a force she alone interprets and arbitrates. The wedding ring that Jesus placed on Catherine of Siena's finger, and later her stigmata, could be seen only by Catherine, a circumstance that led her followers not to suspect a fake but to be all the more convinced of the truth of their "Mamma's" special relationship with God. Her will is to do God's will, and she alone claims to know God's will,

I

Holy anorexics often began to fast in response to the terrors of hell that awaited gluttons, here depicted at the center right.

2
Large crowds gathered at the funerals of holy women.

3
Clare of Assisi prays in aid of her sister Agnes as male members of the
family pull the girl by the hair and unsuccessfully try to drag her away
from her holy mission.

4
Margaret of Cortona emerges from her tiny cell and accepts the advice
of townswomen to change her filthy dress.

5

A portrait of Catherine of Siena by one of her contemporaries. The saint
allows a devotee to kiss her hand, betraying the sin of vainglory that
troubled her throughout her life.

14
At the age of eleven, Mary Magdalen de' Pazzi spent entire nights
flagellating herself.

15
Mary Magdalen de' Pazzi sits on the floor to eat the morsel of bread she
has begged from the other sisters.

16
Devils tempt Mary Magdalen de' Pazzi to break her diet of bread and water by opening the pantry cabinets and displaying before her the delicacies they store.

17
To combat fierce temptations against her chastity, Mary Magdalen lies naked on a bed of sharp branches and splinters in the convent's woodshed. Her flagellum is in the foreground.

J.M.J.

Alli 20: Marzo 1695:

Per fare l'obbedienza
scrivo tutto quello
che ho auto sopra
il punto di cibarmi
di pane et Aqua
questa inspiratione
è quasi come comando
auto da S Dio fù
à punto alli 20
Marzo stiedi con
questo desiderio di
rimetermi à quanto
il sig: mi chiedeua
sino alli 8: di
settembre pure del 1695:

18

Veronica Giuliani's diary entry for March 20, 1695, in which, for obedience, she reveals the details of her latest superhuman fast.

an assertion not quickly or easily allowed by suspicious male clerics anxious to defend their powers against female interlopers. Only a very few women had the stamina and charisma to sustain such a claim, and even among these holy anorexics there is no reason to suggest that they intended in a careful and planned way to appropriate male prerogatives (a statement that would have to be modified were we to expand our scope to include anorexic heretics). Intentions aside, however, holy anorexics did in fact break out of the established boundaries within which a male hierarchy confined female piety, and thereby established newer and wider avenues for religious expression by women more generally. Although recovered anorexics usually led satisfying personal lives, it was more often their sisters who starved themselves to death without ever reaching psychological equilibrium and absolute certainty about their autonomy, who spearheaded advances in women's religiosity.

The reader who has stayed with me through the preceding chapters may have a number of questions that have not been addressed thus far. Are there male holy anorexics, and what about them? Are there anorexics before the thirteenth century, and what about the desert ascetics of early Christianity? What of the female saints who were not anorexic, maybe even pleasantly plump, such as Catherine of Bologna? In short, I have tried to set forth three psychological types, each illustrated by historical personages, but thus far I have not placed holy anorexia in its historical setting. With this task I now proceed.

Very few cases of holy anorexia can be asserted before the thirteenth century, if for no other reason than because the documentation is inadequate. The anorexic behavior syndrome necessarily involves not only a refusal to eat, which is claimed in many heroic tales, but also a personality crisis over autonomy, which the early legends do not discuss. The prototype for these early stories is the temptation of Jesus in the wilderness, when he fasted for forty days and forty nights. But the point of the Gospel message is his refusal to be tempted by Satan, a point that rests on Jesus' being *hungry*, something that female holy anorexics seldom admit to feeling. For Jesus, as for the men (and a few women) who removed themselves to the desert or other harsh places, fasting was a controlled penance undertaken to cleanse the body of impurities and to steel the spirit for the battle to defend the faith. Holy anorexics, by contrast, were ordered by religious authorities to eat but claimed they were unable to do so. They believed their bodies could not be purified and actively sought to destroy them. Fasting in preparation for celebration is common in all religions, but no matter how rigorous the self-denial involved, its scope always is limited, its purpose clear. Anorexic behavior, whether of the thirteenth-century holy variety or the twentieth-century secular type, whatever its stated goal at the outset (saintliness or slimness), clearly has no stopping point, no agreed upon termination, no event to look forward to.[2]

A reading of the New Testament reveals little justification or precedent for holy anorexia. Indeed, injunctions against excessive fasting and indifference to strict Jewish dietary laws abound. Unlike the establishment Pharisees or the radical followers of John the Baptist, Jesus' disciples did not fast, and in two accounts Jesus himself is charged with being a glutton and a winebibber. When his disciples were hungry and broke the Sabbath by plucking ears of corn, Jesus freely defended them. In an important passage he explicitly denied the contaminating power of food or of eating with "unclean" hands, saying that what enters the mouth goes to the belly and exits into the privy, leaving the heart untouched. Thus all foods are clean, and at least according to Luke, in Paradise the faithful disciples would join Jesus at table to eat and drink. Until that day, while doing their evangelical work, the disciples were enjoined to partake of food exactly like everyone else.[3]

Just as the gospels are uniform in negating fasting as a path to holiness, so also the letters of Paul, whose blinding conversion did not eradicate entirely the rich legacy of his Jewish heritage and Greek learning, ultimately rejected the notion that there was virtue in severe abstemiousness. Upon his conversion Saul ate and drank nothing for three days, but this fast was temporary. Later, in writing to the Romans, Paul condemned dietary legalism in no uncertain terms: "People range from those who believe they may eat any sort of meat to those whose faith is so weak they dare not eat anything except vegetables." The context is an exhortation not to be too quick to judge others, but the point remains that here and elsewhere Paul does not see food regulation and fasting as intrinsically good or evil. Again in his letter to the Colossians he warns against false asceticism, and in many passages he charges women with being especially "silly" and prone to engage in religious fads.[4]

For the western world at least, the ascetic impulse has its historical antecedents less in Judeo-Christian beliefs than in ancient Greece and the East. It may be seen clearly in the Pythagoreans, whose dualism laid the basis for later justification of bodily mortification as a means of liberating the soul from the body, and whose ideas probably had a direct impact on early Christian ascetics. Euripides, in plays such as *The Bacchantes* and *Hippolytus*, dramatized the conflict between body and soul, developing the universal links of sexual drive and appetite. It was Plato who then expressed the dualistic basis of extreme asceticism in its fullest logical form. The human soul, he reasoned, is of divine origin and therefore destined to participate in the world to come. But this soul is trapped in the body, literally incarcerated in the world that is, a world incapable of betterment. Thus the body impedes the freedom of the soul, acting as its prison, and only by disengaging from the world of the senses can the religious spirit liberate itself to realize its divine potential. Aristotle's plea for reasoned moderation stopped well short of the final implications of Plato's thought and gave to temperance in the satisfaction of bodily desires a justification that impressed Thomas Aquinas centuries later, when the overweight Dominican found himself embattled by new outbreaks of this very old dualistic heresy. At the other extreme, Zoroastrians seemed almost to find virtue in gluttony; plainly dualistic, they believed fasting to be sinful because a body weakened by malnourishment would be unable to exercise vigorous piety, cultivate the land, and give birth to healthy offspring. Eating meat, they held, nourished not only the body but also the brain and made for greater rationality. In opposition to the followers of Mani, Zoroastrians explicitly condemned self-tortures such as flagellation, starvation, and exposure to extreme temperatures. Among the early Christian saints more than a few, knowingly or not, followed the extremes either of self-indulgence or self-denial to the point of heresy. But centuries of battle against Manicheans, Gnostics, Zoroastrians, neo-Pythagoreans, and other assorted dualists led Church Fathers to be as wary of extreme asceticism as of gluttony and to adopt a moderate stance on fasting, one that never offered a justification for holy anorexia.[5]

Fourth-century Christians faced a series of theological, constitutional, and ethical crises. In essence, their religion had been only one among many, its evangelical fervor outweighing its doctrinal clarity. Now Christianity became formalistic and conservative. Earlier toleration and even veneration of *vitae* justified more in pagan writings and dualist practice than in the New Testament gave way to codes and regulations appropriate for an established, official institution. No longer would the individualistic, even obsessive, asceticism of the desert monks of Syria, Palestine, and Egypt be encouraged. Even the *Lausiac History* and the *Life of Saint Pachomius*, which were of less practical importance in the development of Christian monasticism than the carefully measured rules set forth by Saints Basil and Jerome later in the century, tended to demystify the virtues of rigorous asceticism and to urge instead more controlled and formalized penitential practices. The ways of Candida (*Lausiac History* 57) are illustrative: "She abstained totally from the meat of warm-blooded animals, while on feast days she ate fish and vegetables seasoned with oil; she was always content with dry bread and water tempered with a bit of vinegar." Such a diet certainly was not epicurean, but its rigors were by no means life-threatening.[6]

Saint Gregory of Nyssa believed that the body was composed of two pairs of opposing elements, hot and cold, wet and dry. Both carnal indulgence and excessive mortification were likely to upset the balance of these elements and defeat the soul in its quest for perfection. Better for the novice to learn from an experienced teacher than to try to strike out on a new path, Gregory warned in the late fourth century. He found ample support in the epistles of Paul for his view that good Christians need both "spiritual food for the well-being of our souls" and "sensible food to strengthen our bodies." The goal of self-control should not be to make the body suffer but to provide for "the efficient working of the instruments of the soul."[7]

John Cassian, the early fifth-century writer whose *Cenobitic Institutions* forged the bridge between Eastern and Western monasticism, even more explicitly condemned excessive fasting. Gluttony was indeed the first of the eight principal vices he analyzed, noting that this sin manifested itself in three distinct ways: eating before the prescribed time for communal meals, satiating fully one's hunger, and seeking especially delicate and succulent food. But Cassian's remedy involved limited abstinence, extreme regularity about mealtimes, and a balanced diet. The early Fathers, he wrote, never abstained from bread, and the exemplary saints did not live on legumes, herbs, and fruits alone, nor did they lose sight of the absolute necessity of wise discretion about fasting. Truly holy people should not let their abstinence become known to others, lest they fall into vainglory. Better to take nourishment every day than to fast totally for long periods of time and then suddenly eat again. Ill-considered fasting not only interrupts spiritual activity, he noted, but causes physical prostration and consequent inability to concentrate on prayer. Catherine of Siena, like other holy anorexics, may have begun to fast only as Cassian suggested, but over her lifetime she managed to fall into every error he had warned against.[8]

The triumph of moderation became complete with Benedict of Norcia in the sixth century. After spending several years as a hermit in the rugged mountains of the Abruzzi in central Italy, Benedict ultimately established at Monte Cassino the rule that would spread throughout Western Christendom and become the standard for monastic life. His regulations on eating and drinking are eminently sensible. The main meal might be served either at noon or at mid-afternoon, according to the season; the brothers were to receive a pound weight of bread each day, with one-third kept back for supper where this meal was taken. No other rules on quantity of food were made, except for a commonsense warning that the abbot not allow surfeiting lest the monks be overtaken by indigestion. Two different dishes of cooked food were to be prepared for each meal, so that anyone who could not eat one might choose the other; in addition, fruit or young vegetables were allowed when available. Except for the very weak or sick among them, monks were not to eat the meat of four-footed animals, meaning that their mainstays were fowl and fish. The abbot might use his discretion to add more for brothers engaging in hard labor and to allot smaller portions to young children who needed less. Benedict thought it better to abstain from wine, but recognizing the "infirmity of the weak" he allowed his monks a pint of wine daily, more if required by the heat of summer or the pace of work. To observe Lent Benedict ruled only that each brother should offer to his abbot to forgo "somewhat of his food, drink, and sleep," the exact amount sacrificed being up to the individual. These then were the regulations, and although each abbot and abbess had sufficient authority to allow a more pleasant or more spartan diet, at no time or place did Western Christendom advocate or even allow self-starvation.[9]

At the dawn of the thirteenth century Italian women who came to be venerated as saints frequently rejected the established norms of Benedictine-style conventual life in favor of less sure and controlled, often highly individualistic holy careers. Even though many of them ate very little, they cannot be considered holy anorexics for reasons that perhaps will become clear if we examine briefly a couple of these *vitae*. So much legend surrounds many of these early lives that it is not always possible to reach even a reasonably informed judgment about what actually may have happened.

It is written, for example, that by the age of ten Bona of Pisa had left her mother to live alone in a small cell next to the nearby church of Saint Martin, where for three years she prayed and knitted, fasting three days each week on bread and water. When the Arno River overflowed its banks and threatened her city she offered her body as a sacrifice to God and as a call to her fellow Pisans to obey the Church. Three years later, at the instigation of her mother, Bona left with two other women to seek out her father, who apparently now lived in Palestine and whose sons by his first wife included the Patriarch of Jerusalem, a Master of the Order of Templars, and a Cavalier of the Hospitallers. She evaded the soldiers sent by her embarrassed father to capture her as she disembarked (for most probably Bona was an illegitimate child), and escaped to a cave, where she and her two companions lived with a wise hermit named Ubaldus. When the women tried to return to Pisa their ship was overtaken by Saracen pirates and Bona was brought in chains to a prison in Africa. There she nearly died of her injuries and suffered bleeding from the mouth and a high fever. At the age of eighteen she was ransomed and returned to her cell in Pisa, from whence she sallied forth as many as nine times on long, arduous pilgrimages across Europe to Compostela. When she was in Pisa citizens flocked to her for advice and because she had a special gift for curing headaches.[10]

Verdiana's story, while less filled with adventure, also contains fanciful elements. Even as a child she tortured her body with a tight iron band and a hairshirt; she slept on the cold floor and practiced "superhuman" fasts and vigils. She too went on pilgrimage to Compostela, but only once, and also to Rome. Then she returned to the rural town of Castelfiorentino, near Florence, where at her request she was walled into a tiny cell her neighbors built for her. For the next thirty-four years, until her death in 1242, no one ever saw her. Through a small window she confessed, received communion, and worked miracles. Verdiana ate only once a day and never consumed meat, eggs, cheese, or wine; even this meager repast she had to share for a length of time with two huge snakes which had entered her abode and had made a habit of supping with her. If for any reason the snakes found the food insufficient they would rear up and beat her with their tails until she was unable to get up. Despite her terror she told no one about them, except her confessor under oath of his silence, and when eventually one was killed and the other ran away, she mourned the loss of these friends sent by God. When she died the townsfolk carried her corpse in triumphal procession to church and there it remained for seventeen days while a proper tomb was prepared. People flocked from everywhere to view her body. To touch it was to be cured of leprosy, paralysis, battle wounds, and blindness; to invoke Verdiana's aid was to be immune to fire and to be freed from diabolic possession.[11]

In both these stories, as in others like them, the heroine negates society's expectations for her gender. Fighting Saracens or living with snakes may be admirable activities for young men, but they hardly constitute appropriate behavior for adolescent women. Bona and Verdiana came from humble backgrounds, from familial circumstances despised no less by peasants and the urban poor than by clerical elites of noble parentage. The descriptions of hard fasting are formulaic and conventional; they contain no history, no development or struggle against bodily urges. There is no hint that these women could not eat and, indeed, the stated diets are not life-threatening and the storytellers never claim that harsh austerities led to death. In a sense, then, the accounts are gender neutral. They portray an adventurous person, a loner who rejects the comforts of family and friends, one who defies established holy paths. There may have been many men and women who followed such a course, but surely only a small percentage can have come to the attention of a miracle-seeking public and then also withstood the skeptical testing of churchmen. The few who did served to legitimate the very practices they themselves eschewed. In a world of famine, inexplicable sickness and death, medicine and labor might be questioned. Stories of wild adventures and crazy self-punishments followed by the power to heal and to foretell the future were too infrequent to satisfy everyday needs but just common enough to offer some hope in a hopeless situation, when official church prayers would not do. The presence of Bona, Verdiana, and later one might add Gerardesca, Sperandea, and a few others of their type, among the roster of Italian female saints documents a popular need for antiheros who become heroic, but their lives do not suggest a model of holy anorexia.[12]

FOR THE first major holy anorexic on the Italian scene we turn to Clare of Assisi, companion of Saint Francis and founder of the

Poor Clares, the Order which to our own time is present throughout the Catholic world. Testimony on her diet comes from the
nuns who lived with her at San Damiano and appeared before
Bishop Bartholomew of Spoleto in November, 1253, within three
months of Clare's death, as he carried out an order from Pope Innocent IV to conduct an investigation of her life. Sister Pacifica of
Guelfuccio, who had known Clare from their childhood days in
Assisi and who may have joined her in running away from home
forty years earlier, was the first to speak. She said that the putative
saint for many years had eaten nothing at all on Mondays, Wednesdays, and Fridays. Even on other days she ate very little, so little
that she became gravely ill. Then Saint Francis himself and the
Bishop of Assisi ordered her to take at least an ounce and a half of
bread each day. Sister Benvenuta of Perugia testified next, and
when interrogated specifically about how she knew that Francis
had ordered Clare to eat, said she had been present when he gave
this command. The other sisters confirmed all this and added
other details about her special austerities during Lent and the
forty days before Christmas.[13]

Our concern is with Francis's command. We know that he too
was very abstemious, but it was he who ordered her to eat, not
vice versa. That Clare might have ordered Francis to change his
diet, or for that matter to alter any of his religious practices, was a
cultural impossibility. It was Clare and her sisters who were en-
closed in the convent walls of San Damiano that Francis had se-
lected for them, while he and his brothers took to the highways to
spread the message of Lady Poverty. At Francis's wish, he and his
followers might visit the Poor Clares to serve their spiritual and
temporal needs (until Gregory IX in 1230 forbade such visits unless licensed by him). In later years the Observant or Strict Clares
maintained that Franciscan friars were obligated to serve their
needs, but the plain meaning of Francis's practice won out—the
men chose whether to visit and serve, and no obligation to the
women existed. Thus even Saint Francis, quite properly known
for his gentle ways and concern for the weak, qualities considered
feminine and nurturing by his culture, could not transcend the
male-dominant role in his relationship with Clare. If their caloric
intake/body weight ratios had been identical, still she would have
been the anorexic and he not. He too severely damaged his health
with his self-punishing asceticism, but there was no one to order
him to eat, and a whole world in which to express his drive for
autonomy. For Clare and her sisters there was Francis to guide

them, then a male prelacy to order them, and finally only their own bodies to conquer.[14]

Clare ultimately recovered from the illness brought on by her not eating and, as with many other former anorexics, she exerted considerable talent and energy as a prioress. She too came to doubt the wisdom of severe austerity. In the rules she wrote for her order, Clare specified that Lenten restrictions were to be observed by the sisters every day of the year except Christmas. Exceptions were to be made, however, for the young, the weak, those serving outside monastery walls, and "in times of manifest necessity." The Lenten diet, it may be noted, was monotonous and sparse but not unhealthy. In a letter to Blessed Agnes of Prague, Clare even more explicitly backed away from her earlier excesses, displaying much the same experiential wisdom shown by present-day recovered anorexics.

> Since we do not have *a body of bronze, nor is ours the strength of granite*—indeed we are rather fragile and inclined toward every bodily infirmity—I pray you and beseech you in the name of the Lord, oh dearest one, to moderate with wise discretion the almost exaggerated and impossible austerity which I know you have embarked upon so that . . . your *sacrifice* always will be *seasoned with the salt* of prudence.[15]

Clare's innovative, living model of self-abasing female piety riveted the attention of thirteenth-century Italian people, and many were the women who followed her path, beginning with members of her own family. Initially her relatives had used force to try to drag her bodily away from the Benedictine house of refuge where Francis had placed her after she had run away from home on the night of Palm Sunday in 1212 to meet him at nearby Porziuncola. There he had cut off her hair and vested her in a sackcloth, and it was in this penitential garb that her friends and relatives found her a day or two later. Unable to move her by verbal threats, nor by pulling at her as she clung to an altarcloth, they left empty-handed.[16]

Sixteen days after Clare ran away, before her parents could have resigned themselves to losing their eldest daughter, her sister Agnes, age fifteen, left home and joined her. When the family learned of this latest outrage they gathered twelve "furious" men who rode to the new monastery where the two sisters were hiding and used a trick to gain entrance. They had given up on Clare and did not bother to speak to her, but to Agnes they shouted: "Why did you come to this place? Hurry up and come home with us right now." Agnes refused, saying she did not wish to be separated from her sister. Then one of the twelve jumped on her, punching her and dragging her away by the hair, while the others tried to carry her off. These "violent animals" dragged her down the side of the mountain on which the monastery was located, ripping her clothes and marking the way with her torn-out hair. Clare screamed at Agnes to continue resisting, and prayed for divine help. Suddenly Agnes's body became heavy, so heavy that all twelve men together were unable to lift her over a rivulet. Nearby peasants and vineworkers came to assist, but try as they might the weight was too much and they gave up. Laughingly they said: "She's been eating lead all night, no wonder she's so heavy." Her paternal uncle, Ser Monaldo, was beside himself with rage, but as he tried to crush her with a mortal blow his arm was overcome by an atrocious pain. With Agnes now lying almost dead on the ground, Clare finally arrived on the scene and implored the gang to leave the girl to her. Once the men left, with only the taste of bitterness over their failure, Agnes arose happily and embarked upon the holy path of her sister. In due course a third sister, Beatrice, joined them, and eventually even Clare's mother, Ortolana dei Fiumi, followed along.[17]

Clare's earliest biographer expresses vividly the powerful attraction of this woman's life. The fame of her sanctity quickly spread from hamlet to hamlet, he tells us, and women rushed from everywhere after "the sweet fragrance of her perfume." Virgins inspired by her example hastened to preserve their inborn gift for Christ; married women tried to live more chastely. Noble ladies abandoned their palaces to build themselves spartan monasteries and take up ashes and a hairshirt. Through these examples of strength "by the weaker sex" even young men came to despise the false pleasures of the flesh and joined the race for purity. Many married couples agreed upon pacts of mutual continence, husbands taking orders and wives removing themselves to monasteries. "Mothers brought daughters to Christ, daughters their mothers; sisters brought sisters and aunts their nieces." Innumerable virgins, inspired by Clare's reputation, even if they could not become nuns, tried to live at home in accordance with the spirit of her rule. So many were the converts that it seemed as if one of Isaiah's prophecies had come true: more numerous were those who chose a solitary life than those who had a husband.[18]

Of course this panegyric has no historical value as a precise numerical estimate of Clare's impact on ratios of married to unmarried women in mid-thirteenth-century Italy. What it does show is the emergence of a clear, attractive, fascinating model for female piety, one actively encouraged by Franciscan preachers. Clare left her feet bare, slept on the ground, mortified her body with a hairshirt, did not speak unless obliged by necessity or charity, never left her monastery, and voluntarily starved herself to the point of serious illness. In earlier centuries there had been heroically austere women, as there had been men, but these were loners, hermits, bizarre exceptions. Clare's destruction of her bodily desires, by contrast, was presented as an ideal to be emulated by all pious women. Holy anorexia might be practiced at home by young girls, or to the degree possible by married ladies who had legal obligations regarding the conjugal bed, by widows, by women of every class and circumstance.[19]

Among the women who came to be officially recognized for their exceptional holiness, Clare's new way had a profound impact. For many of these the historical record is very weak, and although what little is preserved for us does not deny a pattern of holy anorexia, the repetition of claims of prodigious fasting would not advance the present effort to examine historical change. Altogether, among forty-two thirteenth-century female Italian saints, seventeen were known for compulsive fasting and other extreme austerities (of whom four were of the pre-Clare reclusive, androgynous type), nine were not especially noteworthy for self-mortification, and documentation on the remaining sixteen is too poor to allow even a tentative conclusion. Most of the sixteen, however, are "names" associated with Clare as nuns at Assisi or nearby Franciscan convents, and it is hardly likely that they in fact deviated substantially from the Clare model.[20]

In the thirteenth-century contest between Franciscans and Dominicans for the hearts and minds of religious women, it is not surprising that the latter would venerate holy anorexics of their own. At least until Catherine of Siena, the Dominicans possessed no female saint of the stature and popularity of Clare. Nevertheless, Catherine's predecessors are of considerable historical interest. One of the earliest, Benvenuta Bojani, was born in the northern town of Cividale del Friuli (in the province of Udine) on May 14, 1255. She was the last of seven girls and much indulged by her parents, who made no effort to dissuade her from her early imitations of an ascetic life. Her father in particular favored her because of her extraordinary piety and he gladly allowed her to join the

Dominican tertiaries and to set about equaling Saint Dominic himself in the rigor and fervor of her vigils and mortifications.[21]

Her self-destructive tendencies are described in detail by her earliest biographer and confessor, Conrad of Castellerio. As a child she had spent long hours in a hidden corner of the family garden in prayer, and for five years, beginning when she was seven, Benvenuta each day recited 1,700 Hail Marys (the short form) and 700 Our Fathers. At the age of twelve she donned a hairshirt which she never removed for the next six-and-one-half years; around her ribs she wore an iron chain and her hips she wrapped tightly with a cord. Over the next two years, as her body filled out, the cord embedded itself in her skin, causing her great suffering.[22]

At around the time of her mother's death in 1271, the teenage Benvenuta added a series of active punishments to the passive torments she had undertaken at twelve. She rested her weary limbs on the bare ground, using a rock for a pillow. Even then she tried to concentrate on prayer, and if she felt overcome by sleep she would bathe her eyes with vinegar or sour juice. Three times each night she flagellated herself, anchoring the chain around her hips and then whipping her back. With these heavy and repeated blows she damaged her shoulders so severely that Dominic himself appeared to her in a vision and ordered her to consult with Father Conrad about what she was doing. She tried, but was so overcome with shame and self-loathing that she was unable to confess. Only after a second and sharper supernatural warning did Benvenuta return, this time with her face covered, to show the Father her ulcerated shoulders. He took the chain away and commanded her to obey his prudent advice.[23]

The young woman's fasting went well beyond any rule for Dominicans. During the several forty-day fasts she observed each year she alternated a day on bread and water with another when she ate only one item. Even at other times of the year she generally fasted for three days each week, often on bread and water. Then for a period of time she suffered diabolic molestations. Already, busybodies around town had been spreading vicious gossip about her, and now as she prayed in the garden she was tormented by a devil who took the form of a handsome youth. Another time he came to her room, enticing her to break her vow of virginity, but Benvenuta screamed and he disappeared. Thereafter the devil was more cunning and more frightening, appearing to her as a wandering friar who cast doubts on her confessor, as a cat, and as a serpent. Then an infuriated demon took to beating her, shoving her to the ground with such violence that blood ran from her mouth and punching her during the night so that she awoke with bruises on her hands and face.[24]

These tortures had their effect, and around 1275, at about the age of twenty-one, Benvenuta became seriously ill. Her whole body felt so weak that she was unable to stand without assistance. A year later she developed a severe hand tremor; she could not stay in bed because an asthmatic condition caused her to suffocate unless she sat upright. Then, immobilization in a chair led to bedsores that bled and caused excruciating pain whenever she moved. On top of all this her stomach changed and she became acutely nauseated at all earthly food. She was able to drink water, but anything she was coaxed or forced to eat by her servants she vomited within an hour. Her only nourishment was from an angel who at noon each day brought her heavenly food in a shining little vase and fed her with his fingers. This went on for five years, until her father's death in 1280. Shortly thereafter she asked to be carried to church, and there Saint Dominic appeared and took her by the hand saying: "Get up, oh daughter." She did and was cured of all her ailments. Her relatives wanted to be sure, and so they prepared her a heaping bowl of rice cooked in a rich almond sauce; this she ate happily and did not regurgitate.[25]

The timing of Benvenuta's penance and illness, which took an active turn in 1271 at her mother's death and ended nine years later when her father died, seems not to be purely coincidental. However, Father Conrad's biography tells us very little about the specifics of the parental relationship, and so we can only speculate. Benvenuta's father had dearly wanted a son, but at her birth he allegedly had said: "Very well! Since it is so, let her too be welcome (benvenuta)," thus naming her. Although at least two sons are mentioned in the account, what is striking is the portrayal of the father as such a helpful, loving, gentle man toward his youngest daughter.

Upon her mother's death, I suspect, the sixteen-year-old Benvenuta gave up any lingering thoughts of marriage. She did not make the obvious choice of entering a nunnery, because that would have meant abandoning her father. Instead, she stayed at home to do penance and say prayers for the release of souls from purgatory, her mother surely among these (and the account mentions this as a special concern of Benvenuta's). Her illness of five years captured fully her father's affection. Who else but he was the angel that kept her alive with daily feedings? When he died, her need to be sick ended, indeed, it had to end. She recovered fully, went to Bologna on a promised pilgrimage to Dominic's tomb, and returned not to her home but to the local Dominican convent.[26]

There she renewed a life of harsh austerity, prayed especially hard for her dear father, and led the nuns in envisioning and then resisting *collective* diabolic assaults as the dragons she saw and heard frightened them all. She exercised the gifts of clairvoyance, prophecy, and bilocation; in her visions and revelations she was present at the Last Supper, embraced Jesus as he was tied to the column to be whipped, and attended the crucifixion. Such experiences made her very depressed, and once again she became unable to sleep or to eat. At the age of thirty-seven she prayed to be allowed to die, before Father Conrad's imminent transfer to another post. Immediately she felt a sharp pain in her breast and within three days, as a multitude of people came to stand witness to a saint's death, she expired. In her last hours she was tormented by a demon who paraded before her the severe mortifications she had practiced for so long and tried to persuade her that in thus willfully shortening her life she had eternally damned herself. But a vision of Mary had warned Benvenuta that this would happen and so she died peacefully.[27]

It is upon such *vitae* that the Dominicans forged their model of holy anorexia, of women who destroyed themselves to save their families and who ultimately were canonized as glorious examples of heroic virtue. For Catherine of Siena the documentation allowed us to make a fuller analysis of her personality, but even in these less rich life stories, the pattern seems to hold.

As accounts of holy Dominican women proliferated in the late thirteenth and early fourteenth centuries, so also did a composite biography for this order emerge. In contrast to the Clare model— with its emphasis on sisterhood, obedience, quiet and retiring penance, and a steady regimen to tame bodily urges—the Dominican young woman was individualistic, even faintly heretical, outgoing and public. Her austerities were yet more extreme, a war replete with stunning victories and crashing defeats as the forces of good and evil fought over the ground of her body and soul. Joan of Orvieto, a tertiary who died at the age of forty-two in 1306, had long experience both with the pains of continuous stomach disorders accompanied by vomiting and the joys of celestial communion and miraculous recovery after receiving the host in this manner. She was a girl of humble origins, and her circumstances surely became precarious as her father died when she was three and her mother two years later. Joan responded to the taunts of her playmates by claiming an angel as her real mother. Her vivid imagination also may account in part for the repeated stories of men who followed her about in her teenage years and threatened her with impure gestures; in two instances God punished them with fatal illnesses. The evidence is ambiguous, however, and it must be allowed that such distressing encounters in fact may have troubled her adolescence. When her adopted family proposed a marriage for her, she ran away to a friend's house and took the Dominican habit. From that time on she led a life of sacrifice for others; everyone knew that the surest way to obtain the great power of Joan's prayer and penance was to do her a bad turn, for above all she loved her enemies.[28]

The theme of individual struggle and penance for the sins of others is revealed even more clearly in the *vita* of Agnes of Montepulciano, written by the same Raymond of Capua who composed Catherine of Siena's biography. Raymond did not know Agnes personally, and so he based his work on the testimony of nuns advanced in years who had known Agnes in their youth. These limitations forced Raymond to be more cautious and formulaic, less analytical and nuanced than in his treatment of Catherine. Agnes was a loner, happier by herself repeating her prayers than in the company of other children. Her parents did not take very seriously her exuberant chatter about the joys of a cloistered life. One day when she was about nine, as she walked alone from her outlying village of Gracciano toward the town of Montepulciano, Agnes was overtaken by a furious storm of large black crows that viciously attacked her. Somehow she escaped and returned home, whereupon she convinced her parents that this had been a diabolic attack meant to show them that their daughter's religious aspirations were not to be treated as "childish words." Persuaded of the Devil's (Agnes'?) pertinacity, they allowed her to enter the Dominican convent at Montepulciano, where she apparently became a nun at an extraordinarily young age.[29]

When she was only fifteen, shortly after transferring to a new foundation at Procena, she was elected abbess, a step that required a papal dispensation because of her youth. Here she redoubled her austerities, sleeping on the ground with a rock for a pillow, refusing all food but small amounts of hard bread, and drinking only a little water. She was very irritable, and if the nuns ever approached her while she was in prayer she would scream at them, calling them cruel enemies intent upon destroying her unity with her bridegroom. Raymond related one story that even he was at some loss to understand. After much fervent prayer to Mary, the Blessed Virgin let Agnes hold baby Jesus for a few hours. When Mary wanted the child back Agnes refused, and the two of them engaged in a fierce tug-of-war; although the real mother proved stronger, Agnes did manage to rip off a cross from the baby's neck, a relic still venerated by the faithful in Montepulciano. What interests us in this apocryphal tale is its familial implication: Agnes, the bride of Christ, engaged in a struggle for possession of her husband's body against her mother-in-law. The young saint knew what she wanted, and she did not easily allow anyone to get in her way.[30]

Eventually the physical effects of her harsh austerities caught up with her, however, and at about the age of thirty she became gravely ill. All her limbs were weak, and she suffered severe headaches. Agnes tried to resist all medical advice and even the express orders of her religious superiors, arguing that since the enemy was ready to use any treachery she had to give him no quarter. Only reluctantly did she finally yield, and even then she absolutely refused to eat the meat dishes her sisters prepared for her, changing them miraculously to fish. After her return to Montepulciano she relented yet further, eating chicken on occasion and going for lengthy treatments at the mineral baths of Chianciano. But her health was broken; none of the cures or medicines did much good, and in any event she welcomed her illness as the fulfillment of a revelation that this was to be her path toward spiritual perfection and final victory over her bodily urges. Her gift of prophecy caused her to be sought after as a peacemaker who might bring warring factions to see a just resolution of their conflicts, and often she was called upon for her powers as an exorcist. Agnes died on April 20, 1317, at about the age of forty-nine.[31]

Taken together, the *vitae* of Benvenuta, Joan, and Agnes offer a stark alternative to the lives of Clare and her Franciscan sisters. The outlines of collective differences between Dominicans and Franciscans may be derived from the percentages shown in table 1. The Poor Clares, centered near their founder in the Umbria and Marche regions, were especially prominent in the thirteenth and fifteenth centuries. Dominicans, by contrast, were likely to come from Tuscany or the northeast, that is, from Florence and Venice, centers of opposition to the Papacy. Their numbers grew in the fourteenth and early sixteenth centuries, times of trouble, earlier with the Avignon papacy and then with the Protestant Reformation. The composite Dominican was more likely to have had to deal with the death of her mother or father at an early age, or to have struggled against parents opposed to her religious vocation who tried to force her to marry. Overall, the quality of our information on Dominicans is better, a consequence of the greater scope for individualism offered in this order and in the humanist centers of northern Italy as well as of the dating of these *vitae*, but comparison with the Augustinian and other mendicant orders reveals differences independent of source quality. Dominicans, more often fortified in their youth by visions and other private, direct communications with God, went on to lead holy lives marked by substantially higher levels of austerity, mystical contemplation, fasting, reclusion, and fortitude in bearing painful illness. They displayed an anorexic behavior pattern more often set within a rich psychological portrait revealing an intense struggle for autonomy, from the male world around them and ultimately from their own bodies. They more often continued their self-starvation until death. Franciscan holy anorexics, at least the virgins among them, were more likely to recover eventually by accepting the primacy of obedience and by taking the nurturing Mary as their main source of comfort.

Although the primary centers of innovative female piety were in northern Italy, where the contest among mendicant orders was most closely intertwined with civic development, holy women from the south also appear occasionally on the roster of new saints. In general, the documentation on these women is weak, and even when their miracle working is abundantly described, less interest seems to have focused on their private lives. Thus it is difficult to analyze in depth a distinct pattern of holy anorexia for the region from Rome southward. However, the two cases we now consider—Francesca Romana and Eustochia of Messina—present issues that partially transcend questions of "typicality."

Francesca Bussa was born in 1384 in the Parione district of Rome, and upon her marriage at about the age of thirteen she moved to Trastevere, within easy walking distance of the papal fortress at Castel Sant' Angelo. Her noble family's fortunes, as well as those of her husband's clan, the Ponzianis, rose and fell with that of the "true" Pope during these years of the Great Schism, and several times she suffered directly the perils of war, witnessing the plundering of her palace and the temporary capture by

TABLE I   CHARACTERISTICS OF SAINTS IN DIFFERENT ORDERS

	No Order	Benedict	Francis	Dominic	Augustine	Other Mendicant	Post-Ref	Overall
Number of Cases	20	20	88 (29)	41 (26)	23	34	35	261
	(%)	(%)	(%)	(%)	(%)	(%)	(%)	(%)
Relationship with mother								
Hostile	15	20	13 (14)	29 (31)	0	26	23	18
Died early	15	10	10 (17)	17 (19)	17	18	9	13
Neutral	45	55	60 (48)	34 (23)	61	53	31	50
Supportive	25	15	17 (21)	20 (27)	22	3	37	19
Relationship with father								
Hostile	10	25	21 (48)	37 (39)	9	26	17	22
Died early	30	0	9 (10)	17 (23)	17	21	14	14
Neutral	40	70	60 (35)	29 (15)	57	47	32	49
Supportive	20	5	10 (7)	17 (23)	17	6	37	15
Regular nun (not tertiary)	0	90	68 (72)	42 (39)	57	56	89	61
Never left birthplace	35	25	33 (24)	42 (42)	48	53	23	36
Had childhood visions	5	15	7 (10)	27 (42)	13	18	11	13
Never married	55	90	77 (79)	81 (81)	78	85	89	80
Resisted marriage	15	10	19 (31)	27 (35)	9	27	11	18
Central aspects of holy reputation								
Asceticism	25	25	24 (48)	49 (65)	52	41	9	31
Reclusion	30	35	17 (28)	27 (23)	22	21	20	22
Contemplation/mysticism	20	35	22 (45)	42 (58)	26	38	17	28
Compulsive fasting	25	25	19 (38)	42 (58)	26	41	11	26
Fortitude in illness	25	40	25 (45)	51 (65)	9	35	31	31
Quality of documentation								
Weak	60	55	67	37	78	47	17	53
Moderate	20	20	18	34	18	12	40	23
Strong	20	25	15	29	4	41	43	24
Geographic distribution by place of childhood								

Tuscany	25	10	7 (7)	17 (27)	22	50	11	18
Umbria-Marche	20	15	31 (31)	5 (4)	31	3	0	17
Northeast	30	45	10 (14)	22 (23)	4	14	9	16
Northwest	15	0	3 (3)	15 (15)	4	12	20	9
Lombardy	0	10	11 (7)	12 (8)	30	6	31	14
South and elsewhere	10	20	38 (38)	29 (23)	9	15	29	26
Geographic distribution by place of adulthood								
Tuscany	15	10	5 (7)	22 (31)	26	55	9	18
Umbria-Marche	15	10	38 (45)	7 (8)	35	6	0	20
Northeast	30	45	9 (10)	29 (15)	9	9	5	16
Northwest	5	0	3 (0)	15 (15)	4	3	20	7
Lombardy	0	10	10 (3)	10 (8)	22	12	23	12
South and elsewhere	35	25	35 (35)	17 (23)	4	15	43	27
Family status (excluding 43 cases with missing information)								
Noble (urban or rural)	32	81	45 (48)	46 (44)	25	52	27	43
Urban (non-noble)	32	6	41 (38)	28 (28)	31	37	49	36
Rural (non-noble)	36	13	14 (14)	26 (28)	44	11	24	21
Holy anorexia pattern evident	30	50	32 (52)	56 (65)	52	47	23	39
Saint opposed by male authority figures	55	65	39 (69)	58 (65)	26	47	34	44
Century the saint died								
Thirteenth	15	30	25 (35)	10 (4)	13	12	0	16
Fourteenth	30	15	9 (7)	25 (27)	35	23	0	17
Fifteenth	10	25	31 (24)	10 (12)	31	14	5	19
Sixteenth	20	10	16 (10)	38 (41)	17	12	9	18
Seventeenth	0	10	2 (7)	5 (8)	4	9	9	5
Eighteenth	5	0	7 (14)	7 (4)	0	18		7
Nineteenth	10	5	9 (3)	0 (0)	0	6	54	12
Twentieth	10	5	1 (0)	5 (4)	0	6	23	6

Note: Figures in parentheses for Franciscans and Dominicans are derived from cases with moderate or strong documentation only.

Ladislaus of Naples of her eldest son. Through all these tribulations she was a model wife and mother, never disputing with her
husband, devoting herself to bringing up her children, and tire-
lessly caring for the sick and the poor. Francesca is the patron
saint of Rome, and dozens of popular accounts of her life written
over the centuries all confirm this portrait of the charitable, holy,
noble lady. Yet the original documents concerning her life—a biography by Giovanni Matteotti, her confessor during the last ten
years of her life, and the extremely important depositions taken
beginning in 1440, the year of her death, tell a more complex
story. Altogether four distinct hearings or *processi* were undertaken before Francesca's ultimate canonization in 1608; although
the Church placed greatest weight on the *processo* of 1451 because of its elaborate juridical formalities, our main interest is in
the more spontaneous testimonies of 1440.[32]

Francesca de' Ponziani died on March 9 of that year, and tradition has it that immediately a "rich chorus fortified by voices of
every sex and condition" arose to proclaim her sanctity. However,
recent work by Arnold Esch detailing the exact location of the
witnesses and the events they spoke of shows that her life had
been closely associated with a particular family network in Rome
and that only after her death did her cult rapidly diffuse so that
she became Francesca Romana, a "saint for all." Thus the earliest
testimonies tend to be from noble people who had known Francesca well.[33]

Donna Joanna, widow of Pietro Pistalonto and a resident of the
Parione district where the putative saint had been born, testified
that even in her cradle Francesca had been so modest that she
could not stand to be touched by her father or by any man. When
anyone tried to stroke or pat her naked body she wailed and
screamed. The testimony skips quickly to her adolescence, and it
is told that although she wished to become a nun, she was helpless to resist her father's choice that she marry Lorenzo Ponziani.
The consummation of the marriage, when she was but thirteen,
had an immediate and traumatic effect on the girl; no sooner had
the wedding celebration ended, than without warning she suddenly lost all her strength, became paralyzed and dumb, and was
totally unable to eat. Her baffled physicians and relatives concluded that she had been victimized by some evil spirit, and they
resorted to black magic. But she resisted all their ministrations
and hovered near death for almost a year. Then, on July 16, 1398,
the eve of the feast of Saint Alexis, a fifth-century saint whose

cult had become very popular in Rome beginning in the tenth century, a vision of the saint cured her of all traces of illness, and the next morning she joined her sister-in-law Vannozza in a life dedicated to public charity. There is a striking parallel here with Umiliana de' Cerchi, the Franciscan tertiary discussed in the preceding chapter, who also abhorred marriage and joined with her sister-in-law Ravenna in doing good deeds, but there is no evidence that Francesca or her confessors and admirers explicitly imitated the earlier saint. Nor was Francesca's husband as hostile as Umiliana's had been. Indeed, years later, at least according to Francesca's confessor, Lorenzo came to realize that his wife's strange illness had not been the work of a demon but rather a result of her broken heart over having been unable to conserve her virginity for God.[34]

Husband, family, and friends all were delighted to see Francesca's return to good health, and she seemed to be free even from the internal burdens that had weighed so heavily upon her. Cheerfully, she agreed to wear gowns befitting her noble station and in all other ways to fulfill her socially and legally defined duties. At the age of sixteen she gave birth to a son, Battista, and within five years to two other children, Evangelist and Agnes. Yet simultaneously she led a life of fierce self-punishment. From the age of fourteen onward, Francesca at all times wore a hairshirt under her silken dresses and regularly she scourged herself by fastening a tight iron band around her hips and another fitted with sharp metal studs that dug into her flesh. In her separate bedroom she flagellated herself until the blood ran. To guarantee that she would be chaste in spirit even while fulfilling her duty to allow her husband access to her body, she anticipated their sexual encounters by heating three-ounce portions of wax or pork fat and excoriating her vulva with molten droppings. Thus she made herself ready to enter his bed, stricken with excruciating pain made worse by even the slightest movement on her part. Upon returning to her own chamber she vomited and coughed up blood, so disgusted was she by the sexual act. While such grim details of Francesca's self-punishment hardly require further comment, we may ponder upon her husband's statement twenty years later, when his battle wounds and advancing age may have contributed to his willingness to give up claims to his wife's body, that he had never noticed that she had been engaging in such holy practices. For the remaining twelve years of their marriage they lived as brother and sister.[35]

By the age of seventeen or eighteen Francesca had reduced her food intake to only one meal each day, and this one spartan in the extreme: no fish, eggs, chicken, or anything sweet or delicate; only bitter legumes and beans not even flavored with oil. Occasionally, if her confessor insisted, she would pick at a baked apple in the evening. Her body temperature fell, her stomach shrank, she suffered constantly from constipation and sharp abdominal pains; yet she would drink no wine as her physicians advised. Only when ordered by her confessor to take a little wine did she do so, and then she vomited for three days. She slept only two hours each day, and even during these times she told of being tormented by dreams of men who carried giant cooked onions (a food she detested and that always nauseated her) and smeared them over her face and stuffed them in her mouth.[36]

Notwithstanding this severe regimen, when Francesca's mother-in-law died in 1401 her father-in-law insisted that she, rather than her older sister-in-law, take over as first lady of the palace. This Francesca did, and for the rest of her life she treated her servants kindly, as if they were younger brothers and sisters; never was she upset when she had to interrupt her meditations to attend to more mundane needs. A modern account captures well this "holy housewife" theme, even though the quotation itself is impossible to document from the original sources. "It is most laudable in a married woman to be devout," Francesca would say, "but she must never forget that she is a housewife. And sometimes she must leave God at the altar to find Him in her housekeeping."[37]

Attention to such duties did little to counter the extraordinary demonic assaults that troubled Francesca for years and that are captured for us in a rich series of fifteenth-century frescoes in the Monastery of the Oblates de' Specchi. Her devils took the forms of monkeys, lions, snakes, and assorted monstrosities, but far more insidious were the explicitly sexual demons that appeared to Francesca as nude men, women, and children engaging in every sort of physical play, especially sodomy. Often she became so frightened that she had to awaken her husband, as when a young devil tried to seduce her even as she lay beside Lorenzo and prayed. Once, when she was pregnant, a devil dragged her off by the hair, held her dangling over the balcony, and threatened to drop her onto the roadway below. To avoid any repetition of the incident, the next day she cut off all her magnificent locks. On another occasion it was her olfactory senses that first alerted her when the devil carried in a putrefying male corpse. Then he pressed her down onto the corpse and she could feel its flesh shedding away under her. Only after great struggle did she arise and wake up the household; although no one else could see the corpse they all recognized the horrid odor that pervaded the room and stuck to her clothes for days despite all their sanitary efforts. Francesca remained haunted by this macabre scene, and to the aversion she always had felt about the male touch was now added a vivid sense that all men smelled like corpses and that their odor had gotten inside her body. To fortify her spirit against such assaults she obtained a human skull and used it regularly as her drinking goblet, but her sister-in-law Vannozza, who did not comprehend fully Francesca's emotional needs, managed to steal away the skull. At this time Francesca was probably only in her late teens, and pregnant once again. Years later, in 1430 or 1431, after she and Lorenzo had agreed on mutual continence and Francesca's primary wifely obligation remained only to attend his sickbed, demons would pin her to a narrow plank suspended high in the air. Thus she was unable to answer his first beck and call, and this made him very upset. Again and again the devil locked her out on the terrace, punched her about, or hid things from her— anything to interfere with her nursing duties and cause Lorenzo to complain that he had to call her a hundred times before she finally came.[38]

In the history of holy anorexia Francesca de' Ponziani's *vita* is important for several reasons. She was a noble Roman associated with the traditional and prestigious Benedictine order rather than with the newer mendicants. By the mid-fifteenth century, then, the anorexic behavior pattern that for two centuries had flourished primarily among Dominicans and Franciscans active in northern Italian city-states came to be seen as virtuous even at the center of establishment Christianity. The social and cultural factors that had contributed so greatly to the spread of the Poor Clares and then to the popularity of Catherine of Siena's *vita* were not present in Rome or in areas further south, so that Francesca's story was neither widely imitated nor even diffused immediately as a role model. More important than her personhood among the faithful who accorded her such widespread veneration were the miracles attributed to her and the intercessions people believed she had made for them. Her popular image was that of a lady of prodigious charity who was also a loving wife and a devoted mother. In this respect, Francesca foreshadows the modern female saint, one known primarily for her good works. And yet the *vita* itself, developed from contemporary witnesses and the voluminous biography of her last confessor, owes much to the earlier *topos* of female sanctity achieved through self-destructive asceticism.

More clearly even than in the cases we have examined thus far, Francesca Bussa's story reveals the dilemma of a female driven to be autonomous. She was a woman favored by high birth, great wealth, a considerate husband (at least until his waning years), children, and a supportive family network. She had no father who attempted to steal her dowry or husband who abused her. She was the perfect candidate for the ideal condition that Jacob Burckhardt claims existed in Renaissance Italy: "we must keep before our minds the fact that women stood on a footing of perfect equality with men." She could have chosen education, and certainly she could have had great freedom to grant her sexual pleasures both within and outside of her marriage. But obviously Francesca's emotional needs were different. An inner turmoil, perhaps reflected as early as her infancy when she squirmed in inexpressible rage at the fondling and unwanted caresses of her father, surfaced from the moment that she was *taken* by Lorenzo in marriage. Her year-long illness, with its obvious psychological dimensions, ended only superficially. Outwardly she assumed the duties of wife and mother, but inwardly she never willingly gave her body to anyone. Her conscious efforts at self-maceration, her compulsive eating habits, her vivid and sexually charged dreams—all these reveal the emotional torment of a woman trapped by social and legal norms that made her a man's possession. Her capacity to withstand these pressures was quite remarkable; she is most unusual among married saints in her ability over many years to sustain an externally "normal" life as wife and mother while undergoing intense spiritual experiences that involved her day and night with everything from guardian angels to nude, horned devils. Women of less strength generally had to break with all familial obligations before they could concentrate fully on their personal quests for union with God. As we saw in the lives of Umiliana de' Cerchi, Margaret of Cortona, and Angela of Foligno, the struggle to break worldly ties was not easy, but how much more difficult was the path taken by Francesca Bussa de' Ponziani. Her holy anorexia freed her spirit even while it left her body dutifully attending to household chores.[39]

The other southern Italian *vita* that merits special attention is a life of Eustochia of Messina (Sicily). There is some controversy about the authorship of the work, but all agree that it was written by women, an important early example of nuns taking it upon themselves to write the history of one of their heroines. Within a year of Eustochia's death on January 20, 1485, Prioress Cecilia of the monastery of Santa Lucia in Foligno probably asked the putative saint's first companion, Iacoba Pollicino, to write a biography. Sister Iacoba almost certainly was not sufficiently literate to do so, and it is likely that she used an amanuensis, Sister Felicita di Perugia, to compose at least part of the *vita*; two sections were added, all before 1491, presumably by two other companions of Eustochia, Geronima Vaccari and Cecilia de Ansalono. The result is a work of considerable literary interest (even if Michele Catalano's claim that it has "an importance not inferior to Dante" seems exaggerated) both for its vibrant mixture of Sicilian and Tuscan dialects and for its use of a "female language" quite distinct from that characteristic of male hagiography. As we might expect, the authors lacked the sophistication of a Raymond of Capua or the theological training of a Giovanni Matteotti, yet for our purposes these shortcomings actually become advantages that allow us a clearer view of how women understood their own religious feelings.[40]

Eustochia's noble mother, we are told, at the age of eighteen had been inspired by the preaching of Friar Matteo de Girgenti to take up the way of the cross. Despite the fact that she had several sons to care for, she put all her efforts into vigorous fasting, long prayer, hard flagellation, and care for the poor and sick. When her husband returned from a five-year absence in the king's service, he was so horrified by his wife's wretched appearance and humiliated by her work among the poor that he beat her. She wanted his permission to vest herself as a Franciscan tertiary but he refused, and so she continued her bread-and-water diet, wearing of a hairshirt, and wailing nightly over the passion of Christ. In answer to her prayers that she might fulfill her husband's desire for a daughter as beautiful as an image of the Madonna, she became pregnant. Because of an outbreak of plague in Messina, they left for their country estate at Annunziata, about three kilometers away, and there in a stable the child was born. She was baptized Smiralda, a precious emerald of God and all men. Three "philosophers" who happened to be present consulted the stars and predicted great things for her.[41]

Miracles and signs appeared early. Although Smiralda's mother had no milk, the infant nourished herself on honey. When the devil made Smiralda fall from the third floor of their villa a beautiful woman caught her and saved her. She joined her mother in repetitive prayer and wore a little hairshirt under her ornate dresses. She hated men, and so when she went out the child would pull her mantle down from her forehead to her mouth and then pretend that passersby were all demons. She very much wanted to learn to read, and although her brothers refused to teach her she mastered the skill on her own. Greater tensions arose when her older brothers, in the absence of their father who was away but in any event shared their views, tried to force her to marry. She was not yet eleven when one of them returned home with a marriage contract he had signed for her against her will. Her prospective husband was a widowed merchant in his thirties. Smiralda went into convulsions (*fece la schiuma a la bocca*) and was broken-hearted over her helpless situation. Fortunately her betrothed was called away on business and so for more than two years she remained free to reflect upon her future. She now wore splendid garments willingly and got along well with her brothers, which suggests that she may have been adjusting to the idea of beginning a married life. However, when she was thirteen something impelled her to return to her birthplace, and there a vision inspired her to alter her course. She firmly resolved to despise worldly things and to treat herself as if it she were made of "excrement and mud." For days she exposed her naked body to the hot sun, thereby blackening and cracking her skin. Upon her return home even her mother was sorely troubled, yet she had little choice but to accede to Smiralda's wish to don a camisole of sackcloth under a dress sewn of cheesecloth and horsehair. The family built her a small cell in the house, where she prayed night and day, never letting herself be seen by them or conversing with them.[42]

Word of Smiralda's conversion spread far and wide, reaching even her betrothed who hastened home laden with beautiful jewels and thoughts of a grand wedding feast. But the sight of this beautiful virgin (and the account, by women, stresses that "he was certain of her virginity") now wasted away by harsh austerity, so traumatized him that in seven days he died. Smiralda's relatives all tried to change her course, even calling in notable holy men to talk some sense into her. Nothing worked, however, and after a brief try at satisfying her spiritual desires by joining in her mother's more socially acceptable charitable activities, Smiralda experienced a fiery vision. In temporary blindness and dead to the world, she withdrew to her cell.[43]

There she fasted on bread and water, often ingesting no more than a crumb of one and a drop of the other. Her body shrank so severely that she was forced to eat a little more. She could not sleep, as devils tormented her brain and thrashed her body; staying at home was like being in hell, and she was determined to enter a nearby monastery. This her parents joined in opposing mightily, her father signing against her will yet another marriage contract. When she secretly spoke with the abbess about her desires, Smiralda's relatives found out and threatened to burn down the monastery if the nuns accepted her. Next the family tried gentler persuasion, her father promising that if she would accompany him on a trip to Sardinia, upon their return he would build her a new monastery. This proposition Smiralda accepted, but within a few days of their arrival in Sardinia her father died. The fourteen-year-old girl suffered great anguish, perhaps blaming herself as the cause of his death, but she persevered despite everything, and by cutting off her hair she renewed her intention to become a nun. The problem of finding a suitable monastery remained, however, since the local abbess was too afraid of retaliation to intercede on Smiralda's behalf; it took another six months, and many battles with demons in the form of hens with giant beaks, before her mother and brothers finally consented and allowed Smiralda to take the name of Eustochia as a novice at the convent of Basicò.[44]

From the outset her penances were extraordinary, far beyond anything allowed for most Franciscan nuns. Eustochia wore a pigskin undergarment that gouged her flesh and another woven of wild branches she had gathered from the mountains. At night she stripped naked, tied herself to a column, and whipped herself from her head to her feet; then she would melt candlewax over her head so that it hardened onto her hair and use ropes to stretch her arms in the form of a cross. To counter her natural beauty she burned her face at the oven and discolored her skin with herbs.[45]

Eustochia's diet reflected both her desire to suffer and the sorry condition of her stomach. Her preference was for bread and water, but at times she would share in whatever the other nuns ate, except that she could not digest soup with oil in it and always added bitter white herbs to all her food. When she was ill and the abbess ordered more delicate fare for her, she "pretended to be unable to eat." Later her sickness came to be less fully under her control, and we are given a detailed clinical description:

[In a later phase of her illness] she could not nourish herself with cereal foods or with meat, because at first she had been able to eat but had chosen not to do so. And when forced to eat, she prayed God that He make her unable to eat. God answered her prayers in such a way that not only was she unable to eat but the mere smell of food upset her stomach and caused her to vomit; for this ["grace"] she was very happy.

Even a perfunctory inquiry from a visiting friar ("Perhaps your constitution has changed?") triggered her to become immobilized "like a tree," and for three-day stretches she neither ate nor slept, often staying in a small cell under the noisy church staircase and imagining that every footstep was a nail being driven into her head.[46]

It is well known that present-day anorexics are obsessed with the act of eating, typically carving a strawberry or two into dozens of precisely equal pieces or subdividing a scoop of mashed potatoes over and over again. Consider, then, the report of Eustochia's companions about lunchtime at the convent.

Often we would lift her up from the table half dead, this because she wanted to refrain from crying. And after an hour or two she vomited anything she had eaten or drunk. Then she began to sob with such passion that it seemed she was at the foot of Christ's cross, and we all fell to crying. This happened nearly every day.

Her only respite was to lose herself in chores, and in particular she constantly wanted to work in the kitchen (again, the modern parallel is evident).[47]

Eustochia's *vita* wanders on from one topic to another and back again, often losing all chronological sense and failing to conform to any of the norms for topical treatment established by male clerics for the proper recounting of a virtuous life. Even the listing of miracles and intercessions is haphazard, and there is precious little effort to name names and document events. The style suggests that the good nuns who wanted a record of Eustochia's life did not have much experience in the art of hagiography. Many were not literate and relied instead on oral traditions passed down within a convent's walls. They were partially immune to the skeptical attitudes of male clerics ever suspicious of the womanly stupidity that Saint Paul had railed against. In their theological innocence they were free to record only what they believed to be important, and it mattered little that their glaring inconsistencies would have been picked up even by a third-rate scholastic.

Not only the causal explanations given but even some of the events themselves seem fanciful. And yet what comes through on every page is Eustochia herself as the protagonist of her holy path. She is not merely God's vessel but an active agent in forging her sanctity. No male confessors appear to guide her, and the unfortunate men who earlier had tried to block her wishes all were visited with a quick death. In sharp contrast to male hagiography, this account describes forthrightly and with anatomical accuracy just how Eustochia stripped down before flagellating and how she macerated her skin with various compounds (women's chemistry). It tells clearly how she had brought upon herself her inability to eat. More sophisticated clerics always described the holy anorexic as doing God's will, but the nuns who admired Eustochia knew clearly that it was the girl's will all along, and they said so.

TABLE 2 provides some numerical indicators of the historical dimensions of holy anorexia that I have tried to trace from individual cases. In Italy, the phenomenon began in the thirteenth century with the rise of the mendicant orders. Evidence of self-assertive piety, it should be noted, exists also at about this time among Cistercian nuns in Germany, at least according to Caroline Bynum. Her work is especially suggestive on two points that are immediately relevant here—that the nuns at Helfta participated in the wider reform efforts launched by men who preceded them, but that they took hold of their own spirituality by forging new modes of piety explicitly for women.[48] Analogously, thirteenth-century mendicancy began with a man, Francis of Assisi; his call for spiritual renewal initiated a drama played out in a man's world— the public squares, highways, and town halls of northern Italy. He and his male followers meant to be seen and to be heard. In humble garments they preached the virtues of Lady Poverty, calling on men to forsake their counting houses and the useless pursuit of material goods. Their message contained a sharp rebuke of the church hierarchy, a problem not put to rest for over a century. Yet even the conflict between Spiritual and Conventual Franciscans in essence was a contest among male holders of power.

For women, beginning with Clare of Assisi, the path had to be different. She, like other women, might be stirred by the mendicant call for worldly renunciation and might feel the urge to for-

TABLE 2 CHARACTERISTICS OF SAINTS OVER TIME (Century of Death of the Saint)

	13th	14th	15th	16th	17th	18th	19th	20th	Overall
					Century				
Number of Cases	*42*	*43*	*50*	*46*	*13*	*19*	*32*	*16*	*261*
Relationship with mother	(%)	(%)	(%)	(%)	(%)	(%)	(%)	(%)	(%)
Hostile	12	18	12	22	31	21	28	6	18
Died early	14	12	8	9	23	26	6	31	13
Neutral	60	65	58	56	23	21	38	19	50
Supportive	14	5	22	13	23	32	28	44	19
Relationship with father									
Hostile	22	21	22	22	38	37	16	6	22
Died early	14	12	12	13	0	10	16	44	14
Neutral	57	58	58	54	38	16	40	19	49
Supportive	7	9	8	11	24	37	28	31	15
Regular nun (not tertiary)	60	35	70	54	92	74	69	63	61
Never left birthplace	26	54	32	50	39	26	31	13	36
Had childhood visions	12	12	14	15	15	26	3	13	13
Never married	83	67	70	83	85	100	81	94	80
Resisted marriage	14	19	24	26	31	5	13	6	18
Central aspects of holy reputation									
Asceticism	43	35	30	35	46	37	9	0	31
Reclusion	31	21	20	28	15	5	28	6	22
Contemplation/mysticism	31	30	16	33	69	42	6	25	28
Compulsive-fasting	41	26	24	24	39	42	9	6	26
Fortitude in illness	33	19	18	26	62	47	47	38	31

Quality of documentation									
Weak	62	67	68	56	0	21	44	25	53
Moderate	31	26	18	20	15	16	25	31	23
Strong	7	7	14	24	85	63	31	44	24
Geographic distribution by place of childhood									
Tuscany	22	37	10	11	23	16	6	19	18
Umbria-Marche	38	30	12	11	0	10	0	13	17
Northeast	19	14	18	26	15	5	9	6	16
Northwest	0	7	4	13	8	16	22	12	9
Lombardy	0	2	24	26	0	11	19	25	14
South and elsewhere	21	10	32	13	54	42	44	25	26
Geographic distribution by place of adulthood									
Tuscany	21	44	8	11	23	16	3	13	18
Umbria-Marche	36	26	26	13	0	21	6	0	20
Northeast	24	7	20	31	15	5	3	6	16
Northwest	0	5	4	13	8	10	13	13	7
Lombardy	0	2	18	28	0	11	19	6	12
South and elsewhere	19	16	24	4	54	37	56	62	27
Family status (excluding 43 cases with missing information)									
Noble (urban or rural)	50	46	54	44	54	26	28	36	43
Urban (non-noble)	32	33	31	35	23	48	58	14	36
Rural (non-noble)	18	21	15	21	23	26	14	50	21
Holy anorexia pattern evident	50	37	38	39	61	47	31	12	39
Saint opposed by male authority figures	38	46	48	39	77	58	41	25	44

sake everything for God. If she did, the theater for her spiritual journey was not the public domain but the private world of her home. There her role was the biologically defined one of procreator. To become a nun, or even to think of doing so, was to demand control of herself. In one sense, of course, this was equally true for women who entered an established Benedictine house. Yet the reformist zeal of the Cistercians elsewhere on the continent had not spread to the Italian scene, and it seems that Benedictine women, even those who were not simply dumped in a convent by relatives, did not share fully in the innovative piety of the thirteenth century.

The adolescent Italian girl who determined to consecrate her virginity to God simultaneously declared a war on two fronts. The external battle was against her parents, especially her father. (Note the consistently high ratios of hostile to supportive fathers shown in table 2 until well after the Reformation.) At the most practical level, she was taking something of cash value—her presumed ability to procreate—from her parents and squandering it in a nunnery of little social standing where she would lead a life of abject poverty. Figures for resistance to marriage refer only to cases where this is discussed in detail, but it is reasonable to assume that in virtually all instances the alternative of marriage was considered. A number of women, ranging from one-sixth in the thirteenth century to double that proportion in the fourteenth, did marry. Certainly in this early period, most never had a meaningful choice about the matter, either because the arrangements were made when they were mere children or because the power relationship with parents overwhelmed them from the outset. Detailed statistical analysis of the subset of married saints shows that the reported qualities of the marriage (whether the husband was understanding, whether the saint loved her husband, and so forth) made no significant difference in the high proportion of married women who fasted compulsively and otherwise displayed an anorexic behavior pattern.[49]

Beyond the practical matter of letting reproductive capacity go to waste, a decision for God usually involved the girl in an intense personal conflict. We can never be certain exactly what caused the thirteenth-century Benvenuta Bojani, for example, to decide to imitate Saint Dominic's penances, nor precisely why the decision impelled her so deeply into an anorexic syndrome. But from her vita, along with all the others, an emotional drama does emerge. Although the composite picture does not amount to an ironclad cause-to-effect model (just as every modern-day girl striving for autonomy who starts dieting does not become an anorexic), it does suggest possibly useful historical generalizations.

The mendicant emphasis on *personal* responsibility for salvation and its characteristic use of familial metaphor, as in the *marriage* to Lady Poverty, appealed to women in an especially direct way. It called upon them, in the name of God and for their own salvation, to take charge of themselves. Nearly half of the forty-two Italian women who lived and died in the thirteenth century and came to be recognized as saints exhibited an anorexic behavior pattern. Thus a new ideal of female piety was forged. The psychological need for autonomy stirred by preachers in the mold of Francis and Dominic inspired women to go beyond the passive, reproductive role of Mary and to seek to become Christ's bride. In this quest their bodies became impediments, painful reminders of the earthly realities they sought to transcend. At first, especially among the younger ones, there may have been a fair amount of toying with bodily urges, testing of willpower as much for the fun of the test as for any well-considered spiritual goal. Diabolic temptation commonly followed and served to remind these women of the enormous dangers inherent in their bodies. They fought their demons by ever-escalating physical tortures and, consciously at first, willfully denied the stimuli of hunger and fatigue. After a time the drives of sex, appetite, and repose were conquered and these holy women became unable to eat or sleep; the sexual drive, or more broadly the emotional need to unite in love, found its expression in mystical union with God. Their hunger was for the host alone, for the body of their husband.

In the fourteenth century and until the Reformation, the percentage of holy anorexics among all female Italian saints dropped somewhat. Yet the intense and compelling qualities of the later *vitae* meant that the impact of the anorexic model actually increased. Geographic distribution widened to include Lombardy and Piedmont (and, I suspect, France and Spain as well). Holy anorexia moved out of the convent and into the home, such that in the fourteenth and fifteenth centuries nearly half of all female Italian saints never became nuns. Hostility to men, a sense of fighting actively against patriarchal structures and the male prelacy, and a need to tell their own stories all increased over time.

Responses by men to the challenge of female piety varied. At one extreme, the Dominican inquisitors Heinrich Kramer and James Sprenger summarized a century of misogyny in the *Mal-*

leus Maleficarum (1486?), as they addressed the question, "Why is it that Women are chiefly addicted to Evil Superstitions?" But our concern is with saints, women of enormous strength and will who succeeded in convincing male authorities of their holiness. Changes in their history necessarily came more slowly and must be extracted from the thickets of male-dominated hagiography. Nevertheless, the year 1500 seems to represent something of a watershed in the history of holy anorexia. Nearly three centuries after it had begun, this behavior pattern reached its zenith. It now embraced even women such as Francesca Romana, who simultaneously carried out her normal wifely duties. It had finally become evident that woman's holiness was the consequence of sacrifice and willpower; no longer could the female saint be viewed simply as a receptacle of divine grace, always in need of male guidance. Woman as object, possessed of no interior spirituality, gave way to woman as subject, creator of her destiny. A living, powerful alternative to the two Marys, the virgin and the converted prostitute, had been recognized and accepted.

6

HISTORICAL DIMENSIONS: DECLINE

EVEN WHILE monks such as Martin Luther posed all sorts of problems for the early sixteenth-century papacy, the Church found time to attend to the challenges raised by holy women in Italy who also forged for themselves new avenues of spiritual expression. These individual seekers of union with God created no revolution, but their piety nonetheless flourished in the confines of their homes or in convents only partially isolated from the religious ferment of the day. Not until the early seventeenth century did Pope Urban VIII establish official procedures for canonization, with formal requirements for proof of doctrinal purity and heroic virtue as well as of miraculous intercession after death.[1] Immediately and for two centuries thereafter (see table 2, p. 146) the number of Italian women whose holiness ultimately would bring them official recognition declined drastically. And yet, among this reduced absolute number, the percentage whose lives displayed the now classic holy anorexia syndrome actually rose sharply. Catholic reform intended to reestablish the Magisterium—leadership of the Church Militant on earth by a hierarchical male prelacy. This meant a counterattack on the lay piety, with its emphasis on individual responsibility, that for three centuries since Bernard of Clairvaux and Francis of Assisi had flourished within mother church's bosom and that now had become its mortal enemy.

Ultimately Catholics would develop a less theologically challenging and nonanorexic model of female holiness, that of the dogooder, but only after much introspection and not until the late eighteenth century. Before this reconciliation, the major impact of the Reformation upon the group of holy women here under study was a much closer scrutiny of their religiosity by clerics growing ever more suspicious but as yet having no alternative model of holiness to offer. The result was to increase the radical, antiestablishment quality of pious expression among the few women who did pass such rigorous screening. As we saw in the case of Veronica Giuliani, often it was their very confessors, fearful of Protestant and then Jansenist tendencies (which these women may have had in their souls long before receiving them from reading books), who spurred them to ever more bizarre, occasionally psychotic, behavior.

The male domination intrinsic to the Reformation, symbolized and actualized by the role of the Jesuits as the first major order to bar women entirely from any share in its work, coexisted with more outright expressions of woman hatred, and such expressions extended even to hagiography and its mode of recounting the lives of holy anorexics. Whereas most pre-1500 accounts convey a heroic quality, certainly to medieval people if not always to us moderns, later *vitae* addressed a more specialized audience. The lives of Clare of Assisi and Catherine of Siena or the writings of Angela of Foligno and the dialogues of Margaret of Cortona were widely retold to lay audiences of women and men. Their purpose was inspirational. After 1500, the *vitae* seem to be aimed more closely at clerics themselves; even as they extol an individual who was in God's grace, they serve to remind confessors of all the false steps and errors that women fall into. Their purpose becomes increasingly didactic. The lesson, however, is not to learn to do likewise but to point out the perils that lurk everywhere if a female tries to strike out on her own. Unless she is inspired purely by the divine, and only male clerics seem able to ascertain this, her piety is not only useless but dangerous, to herself and to all the faithful. Even before the onset of the Reformation, we leave behind stories of heroic chastity to take up accounts of sexual assault and later of child prostitution; the inspired wisdom of female mystics, once recognized even by the misogynous Thomas Aquinas, comes to be replaced by charges of heresy.

We begin with the attempted rape of Colomba da Rieti, as told by one of her confessors, Padre Sebastiano degli Angeli. On Thursday August 21, 1488, the twenty-one-year-old Colomba decided to give a dinner for twelve of her family and friends and so she requested a lamb of her father. He was very pleased, because for the past several years Colomba had been deeply anorexic and mostly had kept to herself in a small cell within her house. The dinner went well and even Colomba ate heartily; only when she asked to wash the feet of each of her guests did everyone realize that the party was not a sign of recovery but some new experiment in piety. Still, she had behaved in far stranger ways before. After the gathering, Colomba went to her room and bolted the door. The next morning her mother was surprised not to see her up and about, but attributing her late sleep to the festivities of the previous night, she waited until noon to summon her daughter. When Colomba did not answer her mother became worried, all the more so because for several weeks strange comets had been seen in the skies. She and her husband broke down the door, only to find the girl's self-created cell empty, except for her Dominican tertiary vestment folded neatly on the floor in the form of a cross. How did she get out and how did she escape through the locked city gates? Where could she have found other clothes? Where had she gone? Years later Padre Sebastiano asked Colomba the same questions, but she could not answer, excusing herself by pleading that she had been in prayer the whole time.[2]

Popular rumor had it that she had gone to the hermitage of a holy man near Foligno and then with him to Spoleto. Others said they had seen a girl followed by a giant black dog or like a shadow in the woods. However she managed it, Colomba was somewhere on the road toward Spoleto, a good forty kilometers or more from home. There, a seemingly kind man invited her to his house for a bite to eat and some rest. After he assured her that his wife and daughters would be there, Colomba willingly accompanied him to a rustic cottage. Seeing no one at home, the man told her to wait and he would go to fetch them. Instead, he returned with two young men carrying provisions for reveling and drinking. Apparently the three men thought that Colomba might be a noble Neapolitan girl named Chiaretta who had been tricked into running away with a false monk and for whose recovery her father had posted a handsome reward.[3]

Once the men realized they had the wrong girl their thoughts turned from money to sex. At first they offered her jewels and pretty clothes; then they pulled out their knives and threatened to kill her if she resisted. Colomba's body became rigid, like marble, and even with great force they could not move her. She warned them of the offense to God they were committing and of the atrocious, eternal punishment that would await them in Hell, but all to no avail. They began to rip off her clothes, stopping only momentarily when they heard what they took to be the jingling of coins in her pocket, but that turned out to be the noise of her crucifix hitting her flagellum as the attackers jostled her about. Still they tore away her vestments, stripping Colomba down to the iron belt three fingers wide with which she punished her naked hips and then to her hairshirt with two studded iron chains strapped around her neck and across her breasts. The sight of her instruments of atrocious self-punishment and of her body scarred with whippings quickly cooled their lust and the two young rapists ran off while the older man fell to his knees and asked her prayers for his dead wife and his daughter, who was actually in a convent.[4]

Colomba felt secure enough to spend the night there, and the next morning the old man accompanied her back to the main roadway and introduced her to a group of women headed in the same direction toward Foligno. Further dangers awaited the young saint from a gang of ribald hunters who eyed the women as easy prey. One of them tried to shove his hand under her dress, but a sudden pang in his heart made him quake and he withdrew, crying and begging forgiveness. Other marauders lay in wait to ambush and ravish her "for love or by force," but Colomba was inspired to stop unnoticed at a roadside statue of the Madonna, so that when the gang asked the other women where she was hiding, they honestly had to answer that they did not know.[5]

The story of Colomba's frightening experiences after she ran away from home reveals much about popular and clerical mentalities. Colomba was a conscious imitator of Catherine of Siena, and in many respects her *vita* is a step-by-step repetition of the earlier Dominican's life. In an almost exact parallel with Catherine, Colomba starved herself to death at the age of thirty-four; both of them faced down male clerics who suspected them of fraud or demonic possession. In many concrete ways then, Colomba's case harks back to an earlier model of female piety, perhaps not surprising since in hagiography there is always a tendency to repeat established conventions over and over again, but also reflecting the profound impact of Catherine's life upon women of great spirituality. Yet the *vita* is hardly a carbon copy, and the differences both reflect early sixteenth-century concerns and foreshadow future changes. First, one notices a vivid new realism, the precise description of exact details of the attempted rape. The language used, especially in Padre Sebastiano's vernacular version but even in the Latin one, is coarse in the extreme, including puns and local "ethnic" jokes. Moreover, God appears nowhere in the account; Colomba must rescue herself by her own effort from a plight of which she is made to seem to be the cause. Not unlike the modern tendency to treat victims of rape as protagonists, the account suggests that it was Colomba's pretty face and lack of proper concern for her safety that contributed to her predicament. In the end, prayers are of no help; it is only the ugliness of Colomba's punished body that dissuades her attackers. The entire episode is recounted is such a way as to make Colomba anything but heroic, and certainly not an inspirational model. There is a voyeuristic concern with how, since she had left her vestments in her cell, she must have been going around naked for quite a while, and in one early account there is a rather irreligious explanation of her "miraculous" exit from home by pointing out that there was a good-sized fissure in the wall.

Later, upon her arrival in Foligno, Colomba forgets to specify which convent named after Catherine she wants and is directed wrongly to the Poor Clares of Catherine of Alexandria instead of to the Dominicans of Catherine of Siena. This causes a good deal of bickering between the two orders, all recorded in embarrassingly petty detail. Finally Colomba heads out for Siena but takes a wrong fork in the road, leaving behind an accompanying priest who has stopped too long to gossip with his fellow clerics, and ends up in Perugia, where she settles down. These are surely not the sorts of mistakes God would make, nor Catherine of Siena for that matter. Ultimately, of course, the hagiographer intends to show the divine will at work, but he does so in such a way that he sheds glory on no one.[6]

Further on in his account, Padre Sebastiano took up the many charges brought against Colomba. This was a bit delicate since one of the accusations was that he and Colomba were guilty of fornication. Initially they were cleared, but suspicion remained and eventually the Padre was replaced as confessor by Friar Michele Genuese, a Master of Sacred Theology. Colomba's troubles went well beyond charges of sexual misconduct. She had caught herself between Cesare and Lucrezia Borgia. Their father, Pope Alexander VI, apparently was favorably disposed toward Colomba, as was Cesare, who as a student at Perugia had witnessed one of her miracles and knew of her extraordinary fasting. But Lucrezia, offended because Colomba once had refused to receive her, convinced her father to issue a decree accusing the putative saint of sorcery. Detractors sprang up everywhere; within her own convent disgruntled nuns claimed that Colomba had been too harsh on novices, even expelling them, and that her arbitrariness and willful-

ness broke the rule of their communal life. Another memorial
attacked both Colomba and Padre Sebastiano.

> She is no saint who does not eat or drink, but rather a glutton
> and something else too . . . And speaking of the devil, she is a
> witch [è una fattuchiera]. In her room we found a collection
> of bones under her bed, and a basket full of hosts she vomited.
> And her confessor is an enchanter himself, and holds the key
> to everything.

Other "dissimulators and hypocrites" sent by "men of high esteem at the Court of Rome" pretended to want to join in her good
works while actually serving as double agents ready to testify on
every aspect of Colomba's personal life. When all their rummag-
ing about the convent could not turn up anything negative, they
used entrapment to induce her into impurity. Another agent posed
as a nun bringing a child to Colomba for cure of a tumor; the ruse
was that the child's tumor previously had been diagnosed by a
Jewish (and therefore reliable seems to be the point) doctor as in-
curable, so that Colomba surely would fail. The saint sensed a
trick, however, and declared that the woman was not a nun, that
the child was illegitimate, and that he soon would die, which indeed happened.[7]

Hardest to deal with was the charge of not eating, and therefore
of being in league with the devil. Here even Colomba's friends did
her more harm than good by their testimony that in fact she did
not eat.

> [We] never saw her taste bread, or fish, or eggs or cheese or
> anything similar, nor any other food except that on some eve-
> nings she would taste a piece of fruit, sort of licking it to draw
> out the juice, and she drank water . . . sometimes she would
> sip a bit of chick-pea soup remaining in the nuns' bowls or
> suck on (but not eat) leftover salad leaves . . . this she did to
> punish her senses because the food had spoiled and was cov-
> ered with flies.[8]

Such eating habits went back to her early years at Rieti. Beginning in 1485, at the age of eighteen, she had fasted for five forty-
day cycles each year. She had a positive nausea toward earthly
food, "springing not from her temperament or from any internal
indisposition, but solely from her total languor that made her
famished for Holy Bread . . . In fact, little by little she began to
deny herself bread entirely, eating only fruit." Colomba's mother,
who had gone to seek the local priest's aid several years earlier

when her daughter had first displayed an anorexic behavior pattern, now became convinced that the child was either possessed or "distracted" mentally by too much concentrated prayer.[9]

As with most holy anorexics, Colomba went through phases of diabolic torment, beginning with a demon who suffocated her and threw her to the ground and painfully extracted a tooth from her mouth, progressing to a handsome youth parading his nude body and inviting her to partake of its pleasures, and arriving finally at the more insidious torture of devils dressed as holy angels, Jesus and his disciples, and the Virgin Mary—all disguises to make her question her piety as well as her sanity. When she became rigid in ecstasy, her mother feared the worst and cried out: "Oh God! She's dead, she's dead! Hurry! Damn that monk . . . who incited her to die of starvation! He has killed her."[10]

But in fact the men of the church consistently had warned Colomba against excessive fasting, had ordered her to eat more, and now were investigating her on charges of sorcery confirmed, it seemed, by her unnatural diet. As a modern study correctly notes, Colomba was inspired by an essentially "medieval" ascetic model; but this was the late fifteenth century, when such behavior was widely taken for the work of Satan. Once when she had been very ill her father had coaxed her to share an egg with him, but as she was about to take a bite a mysterious voice was heard by all who had gathered around: *"Non sit tibi cura de ea: mea est* (It is not yours to be responsible for her; she is mine)." A century earlier everyone would have recognized unquestionably the voice to be God's, but now who could be sure that the Devil had not spoken? Colomba, of course, never admitted to being a witch, but her own testimony reveals her belief that she was possessed; her vomiting, she said, relieved her of evil spirits, just as she had seen in pictorial representations of exorcism.[11]

A visiting Provincial Inquisitor from the Sorbonne observed Colomba and concluded that she might be *areptitia*. The ordinary meaning of the word was "out of her mind" or at least "in error," but especially from an inquisitor, it had a clear juridical sense as well. Colomba was in danger. He had been sent by Rome to investigate her, and his recent success in rooting out a horrible collective invasion by devils in a nunnery in France made him quite certain of what he was looking for. He warned Colomba that her pretenses and foolishness were a disgrace to the Church and that she would end up in hell. The young woman's innocent response; that she knew far less about demons and nunneries in France than he did, disarmed his worst fears. Still, it seems he did not clear her entirely, because other private and public investigations followed. Pope Alexander VI was deeply suspicious when Colomba went into a long, totally rigid ecstasy at his feet. And Cardinal Olivero Caraffa, Protector of the Dominican Order, summoned her to a grand banquet to observe for himself her eating habits. Always the results were the same—not guilty, but not quite innocent either.[12]

Five years before her death Colomba foretold that she would die at the age of thirty-three, in honor of Jesus and of Catherine of Siena. The prediction turned out to be wrong by one year, but the autopsy done to clarify whether Colomba had been a witch or a saint clearly showed that she had starved herself to death. "Not only did she not have the breasts of a woman but truly only little trace of a human body. One could count all her bones as if they were covered only by a clear veil." The skeletal appearance was due not to her terminal illness but to her years of fasting. Her fecal matter was minimal whereas urine seemed normal. Although the medical examiner claimed no special expertise in such matters, he found no clinical reason to doubt the prioress's report that Colomba never menstruated. When alive, her body temperature regularly had been so low that the other nuns tried to warm her with hot bricks, and her pulse was barely measureable even when she was not in ecstasy. But medical inquest did no more to guarantee Colomba's holiness than had the many clerical inquiries undertaken during her brief lifetime. Both priest and physician lacked either the certitude of medieval faith or the confidence of modern science necessary to recognize the holy anorexic for what she was, a woman determined to find her own way to her own destiny.[13]

The themes set forth in Colomba da Rieti's *vita* reappear in various guises throughout the sixteenth century. Again and again, the women strike out on their own, and the men diagnose, command, question, charge, and judge. Even women of considerable standing and influence, such as Osanna Andreasi of Mantua, had to exercise caution. Osanna may have been epileptic, or so her parents feared, and as a teenager she apparently became anorexic in response to her father's efforts to force her to marry. At the age of eighteen she experienced mystical marriage and wore a ring invisible to all but herself; immediately people suspected her of being a fake, even her fellow Dominican tertiaries, who knew well of the same experience told by Catherine of Siena. Not only was Osanna not revered for this grace, but she was threatened with expulsion from the order and denounced before her powerful friend, Duke Frederick of Mantua. The persecution lasted for years, during which time, however, Osanna found ways of fighting back; heavily influenced by the writings of Girolamo Savonarola, she too feared for the future of Renaissance Italy, and even though she revealed only reluctantly the content of her apocalyptic visions, it did come out that she saw Pope Alexander VI going to hell. Other late fifteenth- and sixteenth-century holy anorexics also were driven simultaneously toward both severe private austerity and public authority, but few were as well connected as Osanna and therefore so able to protect themselves from immediate suspicion.[14]

More typical among female saints of this era were tribulations of the kind suffered by Catherine of Racconigi. Catherine was the youngest daughter of a metalworker who had fallen upon hard times. The family was so poor that her mother, who was unable to feed her, sent the infant around in her brother Luigi's arms to beg suckle from healthier village women. Modern experts generally agree that inconsistency in infant feeding, which leads to baffling frustration of the drive for oral gratification, has a deeper psychological impact than either regular deprivation or satisfaction. Catherine's first experiences certainly parallel her adult spiritual life of daily alternation between angelic visions and fierce diabolical torments. And her unhappy childhood can only have exacerbated the emotional difficulties she experienced in infancy: mysterious shoulder pains (from carrying Christ's cross) that kept her bedridden in her seventh year; then attacks of vertigo so severe that her mother prayed that the child would die; constant fighting over money by her parents, relieved only temporarily when Jesus helped her to find coins hidden here and there (was she driven to petty thievery?); such fear of being punished for her clumsiness that she trembled from head to toe as she approached dishwashing and other routine household chores; her mother forced to flee the house to escape her father's wrath when supper was late or meager.[15]

Young Catherine became withdrawn and secretive, comforted only by intense supernatural consolations beginning as early as age five and yet tormented by demons starting in her tenth year. As a teenager she entered upon a severe fasting regimen, her purpose being to make herself so ugly and deformed as to drive away potential suitors. This may have worked as she intended, for Giovanni Francesco Pico della Mirandola, the renowned humanist (and nephew of the even better known Giovanni Pico) whose full-length biography of Catherine is our major source here, notes that she grew shorter and misshapen in the years he knew her. However, what Catherine may not have anticipated is that the devil would enflame every part of her body with such "sexual heat" and fill her head with such "lurid images" that at times, according to her confessor, she could not retain food and vomited what little she had been forced to eat. For ten years, Pico tells us, she vomited anything that entered her stomach except the host. This continued until she was twenty-six.[16]

Shortly thereafter, probably in 1512 or a little later, she was brought before the Sacred Tribunal of the Inquisition of Turin on twin charges of heresy and sorcery. Pico, the author of *Strix* and other works bearing upon magic both white and black, asserts that Catherine was a victim of jealous and envious high prelates who resented her self-assumed role as a spiritual counselor and advisor to political elites. Banned from her homeland by her enemies, she ultimately was cleared and then found refuge at the court of Duke Carlo of Savoy and with Anne, the marquise of Montferrat and a relative of the French king. Finally her detractors repented and asked Pico himself to persuade her to return; however, in a gesture we have seen frequently among holy anorexics, she responded humbly that she gladly would go but that Jesus Christ, her bridegroom, had ordered her not to do so. Later on she refused a similar command from the provincial head of the Dominican Order, which she had joined as a tertiary at the age of twenty-eight—after her trial and perhaps as a requirement of it—

> Father, I am a daughter of obedience, and I am obliged to obey until death in all things governed by the rule to which I am pledged; but those things to which the rule does not obligate me, *for now I do not want to obey.* And since the rule does not require me to do this [return to Racconigi] and especially since it would be against the express will of God, who does not wish me to return home to live, excuse me, but I am not coming back.

The prelate, infuriated by this response, ordered every convent in Lombardy to close its doors to her, thus making her a total outcast for the two years during which he stayed in his post.[17]

For the next twenty years Pico took an active interest in the life of this deformed, subliterate, anorexic, suspected witch. Often he invited her for lengthy stays at his castle at Mirandola, and there

Catherine miraculously cured various members of his family by taking upon herself their assorted aches and fevers. Shortly before 1533, the humanist composed his panegyric on this living heretic/saint, using prologues and epilogues to each of its ten books to attack her enemies with his peculiar mix of neo-Platonic wisdom and awed reverence for such a wonder worker. She would survive Pico by fifteen years, but nothing in the later period changes the picture drawn by her early friends and enemies: a woman in close touch with the supernatural whose strange behavior commanded the attention of scholars, dukes, prelates, as well as of more humble folk. For all of them she was ready with advice and prayer, but to none did she allow any compromise of her spiritual autonomy.[18]

Other lives tell about women of higher social standing whose position only barely allowed them to escape out of the limelight and into a private world of their own. Such a person was Catherine Fieschi of Genoa. Much scholarly controversy surrounds her *vita*, which was not compiled until nearly forty years after her death, and there is also dispute over the authorship of spiritual works attributed to her. We pause here to consider only the incontrovertible evidence of the obstacles that might confront a holy anorexic. Forced to marry Giulio Adorno for reasons of state, Catherine's thwarted spiritual impulses turned inward. The accounts make much of Giulio's philandering ways and general uncouthness, but I have come to suspect that these actually may have had little to do with Catherine's emotional trials. Obvious brutality was easier for male hagiographers to deal with than the more subtle oppression of the fundamental social and physical requirements of marriage. For twenty-three years Catherine was totally unable to eat during Lent and for forty days preceding Christmas. Afraid that she was the victim of some evil delusion, at first she forced herself to take food, but always she vomited. The same thing happened when her confessors ordered her to eat. There is no positive evidence that she induced vomiting in the way, for example, that Catherine of Siena did, so she may not have been bulimic. On the other hand, the sudden beginning and ending of her inability to eat in precise forty-day cycles twice yearly suggests that her condition was not purely somatic.

Pope Benedict XIV, among others, was much troubled about such behavior and in 1737, the very year of Catherine's beatification, he drew up a list of saints who did not eat, carefully distinguishing them from victims of possession. The model for holy fasting, he and others believed, was Simeon the Stylite (died ca.

459), who for twenty-six years observed Lent by total abstinence from food and water. But the parallel is defective and fails to account for holy anorexia. Simeon *chose* to fast, whereas Catherine claimed she did not; Simeon was greatly weakened by his lack of nourishment and after the forty days he would be found barely alive on the ground or else tied by ropes to his pillar; Catherine went cheerily through her forty days, "sleeping well and working around the hospital more than at other times, and she felt stronger than when she ate." Unlike Simeon, Catherine drank—a mixture of water, vinegar, and salt. Beginning with observers during her lifetime and continuing to the present day, even Catholic scholars concede that Catherine's fasts were of neurological origin, probably an expression of suppressed religious desires blocked by her married condition.[19]

From a noble contemporary of Catherine's, Paula Gambara-Costa, we have a letter in her handwriting in which she proposes how she will try to adjust to the marriage she has been forced into.

> At dawn I will get out of bed and go to the palace chapel, where I will say my prayers; I will pray God and the Blessed Virgin to have mercy and remember me, a sinner, and my dear husband, and his family and mine. Then on bent knees I will say the rosary for my [salvation] and for the souls of the departed of both families, and twice a week I will say it for those of my friends and acquaintances; and if I am bedridden I will say it in bed. After finishing the rosary I will attend to a few household chores and to my husband's needs. Then I will attend mass at the Brothers of St. Francis . . . and then another one after that. When I return home I will attend to house duties; after lunch I will say the Office of the Madonna and read a bit of the book sent to me by Rev. Padre Angelo, *The Glories of Wives*, or something similar. There will follow household chores, and I will devote myself as best as I can to charity for the poor, as I noted elsewhere. And in the evening before supper I will do another spiritual exercise and after supper before going to bed I will repeat the rosary and my other prayers . . . I will always obey my husband and I will put up with his defects and I will make sure that these faults are not revealed to others. In sum, I will do all I can to save my soul.[20]

His "faults" came to include installing his mistress in the palace to spy on his wife and then accusing Paula of poisoning this rival. The regimented life Paula had intended for herself simply was not sufficient to fortify her against such tribulations, and she drifted into a pattern of compulsive praying and fasting that often in the winter left her unconscious and nearly frozen to death on the floor. As in the case of Catherine of Genoa, however, the relevant psychological matrix for holy anorexia seems not to be the obvious presence of male cruelty but the more subtle pressures involved from the outset. It was Padre Angelo, holy man that he was, who had convinced Paula to wed in the first place, had given her books to read on the joys of the married condition, and had encouraged her to accept a life of subjugation. When his prescription failed her, she had only herself to turn upon, and at the age of forty-two she died of her austerities.[21]

Even women who refused immediate domination by a husband and opted for monastic life increasingly came under male scrutiny. Domenica dal Paradiso had been troubled since her early years. So taken was she with anguish over her purity that she would not let her older sister bathe her. "Hatred of myself," she vowed, "will be my way of fleeing from sin." And she prayed: "Oh God, teach me to hate my body and to despise myself. Give me your love, and my hatred." In her childish desire to get literally closer to heaven, she was wont to sneak out of her house at night and climb on the roof to pray. At the age of eight she fashioned herself a hairshirt of goatskin, slipped out of her mother's featherbed to sleep on a wooden board, and flagellated herself nightly with a knotted rope. Once in the garden she saw the devil approaching in the shape of a bear with long arms and hands, yellow feet, his tongue sticking out, eyes on fire, and a hideous human head; Domenica jumped into a spring, where she would have drowned had not the Virgin Mary rescued her. A more subtle devil tried to test her innocent wisdom by telling her that in fasting and sharing her meals on the sly with the poor she was being disobedient to her mother, who wanted her to eat, and was abetting thieves dressed as beggars who actually were out to steal from her mother. At the age of ten she tied together a bunch of candles, lit them, and set fire to her shoulder. She believed that "if a man were to even touch her hand she would instantly lose her virginity," and so she spent nine years jumping out of windows and climbing over high walls to avoid a young relative who lived under their roof.[22]

Then suddenly the narrative bursts forth with its didactic purposes. "The Devil's heart burned with envy that such a vile little peasant girl—crude, ignorant, incapable of all noble virtue by reason of her birth, education, age, and experience—should soar so high in her saintliness that she leaves behind the nobles, patricians, and wise men of the city." What we have here, quite simply, is a fairytale meant to be used by rural priests in instructing their presumably simple-minded charges. Whether it has any factual base is beside the point. It goes on to tell how Domenica, whose father had died when she was six, dusted and scrubbed the whole house, cooked the food, set the table, washed the clothes, weeded the garden, plowed and planted, hoed and reaped, fed the animals, stored the vegetables, cleaned the stalls, carried manure to the fields, and every evening stabled the pigs, oxen, asses, and mules; in the morning she got up before dawn to bring produce to her brother at the town market and in the late evening she sewed miraculously well. No wonder her mother was sorry to see her leave to become a nun when she was twenty.[23]

At the Augustinian monastery in nearby Candeli the novice Domenica was immediately put to work in the vegetable garden. There she was kept so busy that she had no time to pray or to meditate; moreover, the novice mistress refused to let her use any of her tools for self-mortification or even to do extended prayer vigils. Her superior stayed by her side all the time, so that she had to work all day and sleep all night with no time out for God. Then Domenica became ill with pestilential fever; after several months she was no better, even though ultimately she broke her earlier vow never to let anyone touch her and did allow medicines to be applied to her body "with maximum possible decency." Her physicians ordered her to return home, apparently a wise decision since there she quickly regained her health. Then Domenica returned to the monastery, where once again she found herself trapped in a work/sleep routine; now she was not even allowed to fast because the nuns believed that her not eating might have been the cause of her earlier illness. She reflected upon how she would be better off letting her bridegroom Jesus set the rules for her life than to follow the regimen of a convent, and so she delayed her profession as a nun. It happened one day that Domenica heedlessly tripped and banged her eyebrow on a doorknob; although she passed it off as nothing at the time, the bruise got steadily worse until her whole face became swollen and she bled profusely from her nostrils. She seemed about to die and once more the other nuns, anxious that her spiritual merits should glorify their order urged her to be vested. Domenica promised to do only as Jesus commanded, and thus after due consultation she had to tell her would-be sisters that he had said no. The *vita*, of course, was written by Dominicans, the order she ultimately joined, and not by the Augustinians she was now about to leave for the second time once successful surgical intervention relieved the abcess that had formed around the original bruise. Later, when her mother and others tried to bring her back to the monastery at Candeli, her head wound immediately opened up and started bleeding again.[24]

As she recovered from the operation Domenica found herself becoming disgusted by the smell and the taste of meat, eggs, and milk. These items made her vomit with such violence it seemed she would burst open. On top of this "natural" change in her appetite, she voluntarily decided to give up bread, wine, and everything but herbs, tubers, some fruits, and plain water. She always fasted totally for three days when she received communion and on other occasions for stretches of eight, fifteen, and forty days. Domenica ate on her knees and as she chewed, ever so slowly, she meditated on Christ's passion. She fixed her mind especially on the nails driven into his hands and feet, so that often the food in her mouth became as hard as iron and tormented her throat as she swallowed. Domenica now lived at home in a special cell where she prayed and flagellated all the time, never going out to work in the fields or help around the house. Her mother and brother became very irritated and cursed at her constantly, the more so because she took from the family supplies to give to the poor. There came a day Domenica could not stand the scolding any longer and ran to her room, but her mother chased after her, and shoving open the door, caught Domenica behind it with such force that a vein in her chest burst and she nearly bled to death. Even after a miraculous cure of this wound, her mother and brother never let up their hostilities, saying they wanted to slit her throat and cut her up into little pieces. In 1499, at the age of twenty-seven, Domenica ran away from home in Paradiso and came to Florence.[25]

There she entered the strict Dominican orbit and placed herself under the guidance of the monks at San Marco. She was especially taken with the apocalyptic spirit of the recently executed Girolamo Savonarola, whom she venerated as a saint. She contributed further to the persecution about to beset her by agreeing to stand as godmother for a friend's baby and then predicting that in a few days the infant would be in heaven. When the baby indeed died, Domenica came under immediate suspicion of practicing the black arts. To make sure the charge would stick, her enemies hired a young and errant priest to come and pray at her door at night so as to lead the local gossips to think she was hardly a virgin. When a bleeding kidney caused Domenica to evacuate blood one of her nasty neighbors, Filippa, accused the good woman of having self-induced an abortion. Another girl, Angela, secretly put some bread crumbs in Domenica's vegetables to see if she would vomit as she claimed. Finally her enemies injected a bunch of grapes with a powerful poison and gave them to her as a peace offering. At the first bite Domenica became blind and deaf, falling to the ground in a swollen mass. She was saved only because she vomited with such force that even her poisoned teeth came out! A few years later Filippa died of tongue cancer and Angela of atrocious stomach pains, but this was God's punishment, we are told, not Domenica's since she always forgave her enemies.[26]

It is hardly surprising that a young woman who came to Florence from the countryside and quickly found herself accused of casting "the evil eye" to kill innocent babies, who had very strange eating habits, and who meddled in people's marital relations would fall into official hands. She was cited by the Curial Nuncio before the Vicarial Tribunal on charges of witchcraft and suspected heresy; although the verdict is not recorded, Domenica was placed under the direction of the Vicar to "correct her and restore her mental health." After a year of "cure" she was brought before the Archbishop of Florence and a group of Canons on three explicit charges of heresy; although the judges found her innocent, the Vicar ordered her to enter a monastery. She refused, saying she would submit to no rule unless Jesus told her otherwise, an impasse that was resolved only when the Vicar canvassed every monastery in the diocese and found none willing to receive her.[27]

In a vision, Domenica received a habit directly from Saints Dominic and Catherine of Siena, the standard Dominican dress of a white tunic and black hood. Regularly she wore the outfit on her missions around the city, much to the consternation of more orthodox Dominicans, but apparently with the support of at least some of the brothers at San Marco. When the Master General of the Order spotted her walking about, he was furious; once again Domenica found herself up on charges before the Archbishop and furthermore, the Master General warned the *piagnoni* at San Marco "not to be facile propagandists of her visions, prophecies and private revelations." He forbade them to have anything to do with her and also ordered that no house of the order was to receive her. The Archbishop, who had tangled with this woman before, allowed her to keep her supernatural habit if she would agree to add something to it to distinguish it from standard Dominican dress. This she did, sewing on a red cross exactly like the one used as an insignia by the confraternities instituted by her martyred hero Savonarola. Ultimately she founded her own monastery and although she tried to flee to "the desert," a threat of excommunication convinced her to serve effectively as its head until her death four decades later in 1553.[28]

Sister Domenica's case for formal beatification is still pending in Rome, even though it was first introduced in 1611. The reason for the long delay seems to be her close association with remnants of the group at San Marco that supported Savonarola even after he was excommunicated and condemned for heresy and schism. Church politics aside, our interest in this *vita*, written fifty years after her death but based on extensive, contemporary manuscript materials still preserved at Santa Croce, is in what it tells us about holy anorexia.

Contrasts with earlier *vitae* abound, and overall we see clear indications of a decline in the coherence and religious vitality of the holy anorexic behavior model. Instead of a detailed, individualized, compassionate accounting of the tribulations of childhood and adolescence, there are only trite stories, perhaps aimed to instill fear of their own bodies in children. The chapters of Domenica's *vita* are more like a caricature of the ill-considered morality lessons that some readers may recall from their early years in "Catholic school" than like the self-assured texts of the fourteenth century which we have examined. Gone completely is the hagiographer's attempt to understand the contradictions and mysteries that inevitably appear in anyone's growth cycle. Concern is for the lesson, not the person and, indeed, the author betrays a lack of confidence in the instructional clarity of the life itself by his constant and simplistic exhortation. He is ever ready to sling mud on other religious orders or to treat every bad turn done to Domenica by church authorities as a further test from God. What he cannot allow is that male authority may simply be wrong, may not understand God's will, may be too quick to condemn the ways of women. In earlier centuries more self-confident biographers— one thinks immediately of Raymond of Capua, but Tommaso da Celano and many others might be added—admitted their awe of female piety and even confessed to errors themselves. By the late sixteenth century, however, male prelates were under attack on many fronts, and while they might extol a woman's harsh asceticism they showed little concern for its deeper emotional fabric. We are left only with the self-punishment and abasement, not the person whose iron will drove her to command her own destiny. Appropriation of holy women's lives by male prelates for didactic purposes that overrode concern with the inner dynamics of the persons involved became complete with Cardinal Federigo Borromeo's *vita* of Catherine Vannini. This eminent scholar and champion of the Catholic Reformation is remembered primarily for his role in the infamous punishment for sexual transgression and ultimate pardon of the nun of Monza (Suor Virginia in real life but better known as the Suor Gertrude of Alessandro Manzoni's *Fermo e Lucia*, and actually guilty of murder in addition to her sins of the flesh). But it is his treatment of Catherine, who he says had been a child-prostitute, that interests us here. Although her noble family had fallen on hard times, Catherine and her widowed mother had lost none of their taste for fine clothes, jewels, and rare perfumes. By the time she was eleven years old, the precocious child had earned such a reputation for licentious behavior in her native Siena that she and her mother were persuaded to ply her talents at Rome. There she triumphed as a young courtesan, establishing herself in a richly adorned house where she gave suppers for her numerous lovers and admirers, leaving behind a train of broken hearts. And yet she suffered episodes of severe depression, lost her appetite, attempted suicide, and was troubled by strange illuminations. Unable to find a way out of her predicament, and admired all the more as her melancholy gave her a haunting beauty none could resist, she threw herself totally into passion, provoking scandal and ruin among the nobles and high prelates who initiated a "contest" over who could lavish the most money on her.[29]

For this, in 1574 Pope Gregory XIII ordered her arrest, and at the age of twelve she was imprisoned in his fortress of Castel Sant' Angelo. When she became ill with bronchitis the Pope conditionally offered to release her, but she refused, saying that she "had no desire either to marry or to convert by force." Fearful that her death in his prison might cause the Church even further embarrassment, Gregory released her anyway but banished her from Rome. Upon her return to Siena, as she hovered near death, she called for a confessor and accepted his order that she give away all her possessions. Once she recovered, however, she returned to a life of total abandon. When she was fourteen a sermon on Mary Magdalen converted her again, this time permanently, and all the passion she had devoted to wickedness she now dedicated to penance. She stripped herself of everything, keeping only temporarily a gold chain or two with which to flagellate herself. After almost a decade of harsh punishment at home, in 1584 at the age of twenty-two, she was accepted by the *convertite*, where for four years she buried herself in a cell so small that she became crippled and only on crutches could she accept the Archbishop of Siena's order that she move to slightly larger quarters, where she stayed for the remaining sixteen years of her life.[30]

Borromeo's *vita* goes on to describe in glowing detail Catherine's "incredible" fasting, her bloody flagellations, her lurid demons, her ecstasies—all in a pattern we have seen repeatedly among holy women. While he obviously was fascinated with this living saint and went out of his way to visit her and speak with her through the small grating between her cell and the altar, our concern is with how he understood such behavior. His attitude, according to the canonization proceedings begun in 1606, the year of her death, was similar to that of the many powerful men who admired her and very unlike that of the other *convertite* who lived with Catherine and who despised her and even accused her of having had sexual relations with her visitors and of being pregnant. Certainly he was familiar with many of the *vitae* considered in this and the preceding chapter, and he drew explicit comparisons between "his" saint and Catherine of Siena. For several years he wrote regularly to Catherine Vannini, and although she apparently followed his wishes and destroyed all his letters to her, her correspondence to him is at least partially preserved. In contrast with Manzoni's portrait of the Cardinal as a serene, dedicated servant of God, the letters reveal a troubled man, inclined toward melancholy and in deep need of affection and nurture.[31]

Catherine, too, pours out in her letters her desire, repressed but not eradicated by years of solitary confinement, for human love, not in a directly physical sense to be sure, and yet with all the possessiveness we saw earlier in Angela of Foligno. She warns Borromeo against cultivating friendships with any other nuns, prays for his recovery from various illnesses, protests that his confidential messenger is reading their secret correspondence, and coyly suggests that if he vacillates again in trusting the veracity of her visions she will reveal nothing more to him. Describing himself as her devoted son, the Cardinal begs her to let him have a portrait of her, to be painted by their mutual friend Francesco Vanni, but the ex-prostitute humbly resists. Borromeo nonetheless includes in his *vita* a detailed physical description of Catherine's facial features, most unusual in hagiographic literature. It is he, not she, who seems to want her to be not a "daughter" but a "sister," who relies on her as a spiritual director, who gives her a tunic and insists that she console him by wearing it next to her body, and who sends her small boxes of roses and violets. It is she, not he, who puts limits to their relationship by rejecting his gift of a silver ball, by refusing his repeated pleas that she write at least a line or two every day, and by sending him practical, almost maternal, advice on his diet and dress.[32]

The discovery half a century ago of Catherine Vannini's letters to Federigo Borromeo sparked a lively scholarly and popular controversy. Her salutation as his *piccinina* (little one) and his "only one," the flowers and gifts, the chitchat and banter easily led to a sharp revision of Manzoni's version of the high prelate as a calm rationalist immune to female wiles. Defenders of the cleric's reputation explained away as much as possible, but failed to offer any alternative portrait that might account for his choice of penpals. Only within the larger context of the history of holy anorexia since the thirteenth century do the letters and Borromeo's *vita* of Catherine become explicable.

Beginning at the dawn of the Reformation in the early sixteenth century, male understanding of female piety changed dramatically. The earlier models—Clare's retiring, innocent holiness and Catherine of Siena's troubled, aggressive, individualistic spirituality—although usually recorded and even partially shaped by male clerics, were forged by women for other women. The men might be amazed, baffled, respectful or fearful, but they did not control female religiosity. Holy anorexia was an accepted behavior pattern indicating God's special favor bestowed upon a woman of enormous interior strength. With the Reformation, however, autonomous female piety came to be seen variously as insane, demoniacal, and heretical. While women's needs and expressions remained relatively constant, male responses became increasingly suspicious and negative. Woman's innate weakness, her insatiable lust, her disobedient nature inherited from Eve and confirmed in the classical myth of Pandora, came to dominate religious literature. Interest in the cult of Mary Magdalen reached new heights. It is hardly surprising then that Federigo Borromeo, like his cousin Saint Carlo and his close friend Saint Filippo Neri (all three superbly controlled fasters) a quintessential hero of the Catholic Reformation, would take a special interest in reformed prostitutes and promiscuous nuns. The details of their confessions and the explicit retelling of their sexually charged dreams, apart from their self-evident vicarious fascination, confirmed for male clerics exactly what they wished to believe about all women. Armed with the certainty that even the holiest of women might purify their minds and bodies only after years of complete solitude and hard punishment, leaders of the Church Militant confidently expanded their control over female religiosity, placing themselves squarely between the penitent and her God, jealously guarding the prerogatives of a male-only priesthood.[33]

Cardinal Borromeo seems to have yearned throughout his life for the security of the maternal nurture he once had known; yet, like other Reformation men, he projected the lust he feared in himself onto woman. Psychologically unable to deal with the sexuality of his mother, as a man he could be neither son nor father. Explicitly rejecting spiritual "daughters," he called instead for "sisters," "little ones" whose deepest sinfulness was fully known to him alone. Some scholars argue that much of his *vita* of Catherine is fictional, created for purposes of edification either by him or by a troubled woman who embellished her wickedness to please him and perhaps to satisfy her own need for self-abasement. The letters from Catherine reasonably may be read in this way. Such invention, of course, justifies yet further a psychohistorical approach, one that may help to make sense not only of two individuals but also of larger questions about the consequences of Catholic Reformation. The legacy of this controlled reformation was an erosion of woman's established avenues for the self-expression of outstanding holiness and personal unity with God.

Mary Magdalen, the converted prostitute, appears to be a most inappropriate name for Catherine de' Pazzi, only daughter of that illustrious family, to have chosen on entering the Carmelite convent of Santa Maria degli Angeli in Florence at the age of sixteen. She was much concerned with names and had been greatly upset (*grandissimo scontento*) because her parents habitually called her Lucrezia instead of her proper name, which she took to be in honor of Saint Catherine of Siena. Actually, Catherine was her maternal grandmother's name and Lucrezia that of her father's mother, so the parents simply may have been trying to be equitable. Even as a child, however, Catherine attributed deep motives to everything, and for her the denial of her baptismal name seems to have had an effect not unlike Dante's lines in the Inferno which punished equivocators with namelessness. Anything she did, she did with all her heart. Magdalen Mary was her noble mother's name, and by taking its inversion as her own name in religion, I believe Catherine was expressing both her psychological identification with the archetypal sexual sinner and her final triumph over her mother.[34]

Mary Magdalen de' Pazzi's life is very thoroughly documented, with full-length biographies by two of her confessors, a significant contemporary *vita* by Sister Maria Pacifica del Tovaglia, abundant testimony at the remissorial hearings held within two years of her death, and her own extensive writings. She has been the subject of much investigation by modern scholars as well, and heated debate continues over Eric Dingwall's assertion that she was a "masochistic exhibitionist" with "a slight sadistic streak." In her whipping of other nuns and in her self-mortifications, he argues, she was turning into reality her sexual fantasies and gaining intense pleasure as her ego suffered aggression by her superego. In carefully drawn rebuttals appearing in *Carmelus*, experts in psychiatry have conceded much to the necessity of understanding Mary Magdalen de' Pazzi's emotional turmoil, even though they do not accept Dingwall's extreme conclusions.[35]

My own view is that the entire controversy suffers from a lack of historical dimension. Looking back over the *vitae* of holy anorexics we have explored, it becomes evident that Mary Magdalen de' Pazzi, who definitely had read the works of Catherine of Siena, followed, albeit not always consciously, a well-established path of religious expression for women. The response of the Catholic hierarchy to such behavior was changing rapidly, however, and so during her lifetime and continuing to the present day, she became the subject of medical inquiry. Illness now emerges as the main theme of holy anorexics' lives—how they are visited by God with strange, painful maladies; how they suffer and thereby grow spiritually; how death ultimately allows them to fully embrace their bridegroom in heaven. Illness becomes the alternative to heresy, sorcery, or insanity as the male clerical explanation of holy anorexic behavior.[36]

Mary Magdalen had been an exceedingly strong-willed child, praised for her obedience and serious piety while behaving in distinctly disobedient fashion. Always she wanted to have her own way and to get it she was willing to cry, to suffer illness, and to fight back. As with Catherine of Siena, the authority figure in her household appears to have been her mother, and it was against this woman that the girl waged her most severe emotional battles. When her mother and aunt ordered her to leave them alone to continue their discussions (of God), little Catherine/Lucrezia pretended to obey but then sneaked back to listen to them. She pestered her mother with constant questions about how there could be a Trinity and yet only one God, driving the frustrated woman to tell her to keep quiet and wait until she grew up before thinking about such mysteries. Upon returning from a summer in the countryside she cried so insistently over the loss of a working-class playmate she had been instructing in religion that her mother had to have the girl brought to their palace for more lessons from the enthusiastic Catherine. Sister Maria Pacifica's *vita*, which certainly was based on conversations at the convent with the would-be saint, is especially revealing about the parental relationship. Catherine

> had much more compassion for her father when she saw him commit some imperfection than for her mother, believing that he was kinder, and that in his heart there was a certain natural goodness . . . but her mother, because she was more enlightened and led a spiritual life, was obliged to render more to God.[37]

The child engaged in a contest against her mother for her father's affection and lost, at least temporarily. At the age of fourteen, when he accepted the post of governor of Cortona, it was she, not her mother, who was placed (abandoned) in a convent. There she outperformed all the nuns in her devotions and first displayed the classic anorexic eating pattern. Fifteen months later her mother, either because they were returning to Florence or perhaps because she finally became alarmed at reports of her daughter's emaciated condition, removed her and followed medical advice that the girl go to the countryside and take a restorative tonic. When her father then began making marriage arrangements for his only daughter, Catherine went to him and said: "I tell you, father of mine, that I have decided to let my head be cut off rather than not be a Religious."[38]

Faced with such resolution, Ser Pazzi did what I suspect he had done many times before; with tears of affection filling his eyes he said nothing and left it to his wife and her relatives to change the girl's mind. Nothing, however, could prevent Catherine from becoming more holy than her devout mother, and thereby from triumphing over her in the eternal battle for *the* Father's love. She became despondent, refusing to speak, never smiling, not eating. The more her mother tried to display affection toward her, the more Catherine turned away. She did this calculatingly, writes one of her biographers, so that her mother would lose all tender love for her and let her go her own way. In August of 1582 she entered Santa Maria degli Angeli for a fifteen-day trial period, and three months later, against the will of her mother but with apparent paternal approval, since he paid the extra dowry required because the convent already was at its legal limit of nuns, began her novitiate.[39]

Immediately her radical holiness caused problems in this environment where obedience and nondifferentiation were the rule and where she faced another stern mother. Before she had completed the year of her novitiate, a time came when seven other novices were ready to make their profession. Mary Magdalen begged the Mother Prioress to bend the rules and let her also profess; the Mother refused, but promised to let her do so at the proper time. She took this to mean at year's end, but again the Mother denied her, saying it was their custom to wait until several novices were ready to profess together. And to this Mary Magdalen shot back: "I will not make my Profession with the others, but you will be forced to let me make mine alone, and to your sorrow." Within a short time she suddenly was struck in the dining hall with coughing fits, chest pains, and a high fever. For two months her condition deteriorated and confounded the wisest medical advice her distraught father could pay for. Modern experts speculate that something may have lodged in her bronchial tract or that she had tuberculosis. In any event, Mary Magdalen seemed about to die, and so on May 27, 1584, her Mother Superior agreed to let her profess, alone and bedridden. Immediately Mary Magdalen entered into the first of fifty lengthy ecstasies she would experience over the next forty days, recorded for posterity by two nuns who attended her and transcribed her words into what became the important and difficult mystical work, *The Forty Days*. During these ecstasies all signs of illness disappeared. Further confirmation of the psychological dimensions of her coughing fits, fever, and pain comes in their overnight disappearance when in July she decided to reject all further medical treatment and prayed instead for the intercession of Mary Bartolomea Bagnesi, another holy anorexic, whose corpse was buried at the monastery.[40]

Ever the rebellious teenager, the new nun out of humility refused to join her full sisters and instead remained in novice quarters and under obedience to the Novice Mistress for another two years. During this time, beginning in 1585 when she was not yet twenty, God commanded her to restrict her diet to bread and water except on Sunday, and these in minuscule amounts; her superiors ordered her to eat more and to obey the regulations governing all nuns in the convent, but they were helpless against "God's" will and ultimately had to yield to Mary Magdalen's special compact and her forced vomiting. So also she slept only for the few moments God allowed, and her feet swelled so that she could not wear sandals as the Prioress directed but God forbade. Throughout these five years she experienced constant diabolic attacks. Craving for food tormented her. As she walked by the dispensary, locked cabinets flew open and displayed before her their culinary treasures. At times other nuns reported seeing Mary Magdalen (or a devil who took her appearance) gobbling down food in secret. To combat temptations against her purity she whipped herself, lay naked upon thorns, poured icy water on her breasts to cool them, and gouged her flesh with sharp metal. Upon attaining the post of Novice Submistress she had the right to inflict similar punishments on others and also to make them beat and defile her. All this she did to drive away the devil. Beginning in 1595 she prayed for *il nudo patire*, the atrocious death from painful illness that began for her only nine years later, when the combined impact of her physical torments and unhealthy diet culminated in a three-year terminal illness marked by excruciating toothaches, head and chest pains, fever, and coughing. She wanted to suffer, and everyone else also came to want this for her, for only in this way could she be certain that she was the holiest of all.[41]

The importance of painful illness and heroic response to such involuntary testing by God as a principal theme in holy women's lives increased notably beginning in the late sixteenth century. The statistical outlines of this increase may be seen in table 3. Figures for "Century of Death," when read vertically to reveal the percentages of all Italian female saints (261 cases) whose *vitae* concentrated heavily, moderately, or only slightly on illness as a component of their sanctity, seem to show little change over time—the bedridden female saint is a constant in hagiography. However, upon reading horizontally the figures in parentheses, which adjust for variation in the absolute numbers of saints over time, the historical change we are dealing with becomes clear. Fully 61 percent of the female Italian saints who died in the seventeenth century were bedridden for much of their holy lives, and their spiritual strength in the face of illness is a primary factor in their *vitae*. This percentage is two to three times greater than fig-

TABLE 3   CHARACTERISTICS OF SAINTS AND "ILLNESS" PATTERNS

	High	Moderate	Low	Over-all
Number of Cases	81	57	123	261
Relationship with mother	(%)	(%)	(%)	(%)
Hostile	32	14	11	18
Died early	20	14	8	13
Neutral	30	44	66	50
Supportive	18	28	15	19
Relationship with father				
Hostile	41	21	10	22
Died early	16	19	10	14
Neutral	26	42	67	49
Supportive	17	18	13	15
Regular nun (not tertiary)	62	60	61	61
Never left birthplace	37	35	37	36
Had childhood visions	24	19	3	13
Never married	86	75	77	80
Resisted marriage	26	25	11	18
Central aspects of holy reputation				
Asceticism	61	26	13	31
Reclusion	37	12	17	22
Contemplation/mysticism	58	25	9	28
Compulsive fasting	59	18	8	26
Quality of documentation				
Weak	27	47	72	53
Moderate	28	37	13	23
Strong	45	16	15	24
Geographic distribution by place of childhood				
Tuscany	15	19	19	18
Umbria-Marche	11	21	19	17
Northeast	16	20	15	16
Northwest	8	7	11	9
Lombardy	12	12	16	14
South and elsewhere	38	21	20	26
Geographic distribution by place of adulthood				
Tuscany	16	18	18	18
Umbria-Marche	15	23	21	20
Northeast	15	21	15	16
Northwest	7	5	8	7
Lombardy	10	10	15	12
South and elsewhere	37	23	23	27

TABLE 3 CONTINUED

	High	Moderate	Low	Over-all
Number of Cases	81	57	123	261
Family status (excluding 43 cases with missing information)	(%)	(%)	(%)	(%)
Noble (urban or rural)	42	42	46	43
Urban (non-noble)	30	36	40	36
Rural (non-noble)	28	22	14	21
Holy anorexia pattern evident	76	39	15	39
Saint opposed by male authority figures	69	44	28	44
Century the saint died				
Thirteenth	17 (33)	14 (19)	16 (48)	16
Fourteenth	10 (18)	12 (16)	23 (66)	17
Fifteenth	11 (18)	30 (34)	19 (48)	19
Sixteenth	15 (26)	14 (17)	21 (57)	18
Seventeenth	10 (61)	7 (31)	1 (8)	5
Eighteenth	11 (47)	5 (16)	6 (37)	7
Nineteenth	19 (47)	12 (22)	8 (31)	12
Twentieth	7 (37)	6 (19)	6 (44)	6

ures for previous centuries (18–33 percent) and indicates, I believe, the solution by male prelates of the Catholic Reformation to the puzzlement in their heads over what to make of female piety generally and holy anorexia in particular. Whereas men might achieve sainthood as champions of the faith who spread the true word around the globe, woman's path to official recognition confined them to a sickbed. Even mystical wisdom such as that attributed to Mary Magdalen de' Pazzi's *Forty Days* declines, leaving only the suffering.

These post-Reformation *vitae* may evoke compassion or pity, but they are not the inspiring models of earlier holy anorexics. Little in them is new. The high percentages for hostile parents suggest that illness may have involved a retreat from battles against authority, a failure to achieve autonomy not unlike that found among nineteenth-century American "hysterical" spinsters and "chlorotic" female adolescents.[42] Consistent strong scores for extreme asceticism, fasting, and mystical contemplation indicate replication of the holy anorexic behavior pattern, and yet what the numbers cannot reveal is that the vitality of the earlier accounts generally is absent. Beginning in the seventeenth century, and more fully by the nineteenth, women inspired to outstanding holiness turned away from self-mortification and toward tireless charity, teaching, and care as their mode of self-expression. The sanctity of Mother Francesca Cabrini, Maria De Mattias, Maddalena Canossa, Rosa Venerini, or Lucia Filippini—all missionaries, teachers, founders of new orders for women—has little or nothing to do with holy anorexia.

While the *vitae* of Giacinta Marescotti, Maria Margherita Allegri, Maria Geltrude Salandri, Maria Diomira del Verbo Incarnato, Teresa Verzeri, Caterina Volpicelli, and especially Gemma Galgani prove that penance, self-mortification, and painful illness continue to be revered by some among the faithful, to tax the reader with detailed accounts of these modern saints would not advance the present effort to understand holy anorexia when it was both holy and anorexic. Only in the rare post-Reformation cases where holy women were allowed to speak for themselves do the *vitae* have much psychohistorical interest, as we saw with Veronica Giuliani's five autobiographies. Even the Congregation of Rites, as shown by the canonization proceedings for Gemma Galgani, has been too much influenced by Freud to treat such behavior as an unqualified proof of God's mystery at work. Although "Poor Gemma" is officially a saint, the papacy explicitly declined to comment upon or approve in any way her more exotic spiritual experiences, all of which her defenders argued had been found as well in the lives of Catherine of Siena, Francesca Romana, Veronica Giuliani and others we have come to know. Both sides are correct.

Behavior once deemed to have been supernaturally inspired may well be seen in a different light as the product of human emotional development. Nor is the spiritual achievement rendered any less meaningful because it is human. The holy anorexia of Clare of Assisi or Catherine of Siena was, in its time, both holy and anorexic, a positive expression of self by a woman in response to the world that attempted to dominate her. With the Reformation, however, female religious autonomy came to be seen as heretical or as the work of the devil. Since the Church was passing judgment upon proposed saints, something less negative was bound to emerge, and it did in the model of the suffering holy female, immobilized and racked by pain. However, while male prelates found this acceptable as proof of saintliness, holy women came to do so less frequently, turning instead to good works. Ultimately even male authority conceded that illness was not saintly, and so holy anorexia disappeared as an inspired mode of religious self-assertion.

EPILOGUE

WILLIAM N. DAVIS

Holy Anorexia is a stimulating and thought-provoking book. Its content is entirely unique in that it identifies specifically anorectic behavior patterns four hundred years before they first were described in medical reports. Moreover, Rudolph Bell has been able to present the holy women that he studied in both a historical and a social psychological context. This is quite unlike most theoretical or clinical discussions of anorexia that focus primarily upon narrowly defined psychodynamic issues.

The purpose of this commentary is to bridge the centuries that stand between medieval Italy and today in order to explore the relationship between holy anorexia and anorexia nervosa. Several important questions are raised by Bell's discovery of saintly starvation. To begin with, was Catherine of Siena, or Veronica Giuliani, or Mary Magdalen de' Pazzi actually anorectic? In other words, did these women suffer from the syndrome of anorexia nervosa as it is known in the present day? More important, perhaps, what can be said about the analysis that is presented in *Holy Anorexia*, and what are its implications? Does the hypothesis that holy anorexia is in part a response to the patriarchal social structure of medieval Catholicism have any relevance for current understanding and treatment of anorexia nervosa? In what follows, the perspective will be that of a clinical psychologist who specializes in the psychotherapy of anorexia and bulimia. As such, there will be no comment about the validity of the historical scholarship that is illustrated by *Holy Anorexia*. I will simply take it to be accurate and concentrate instead on how this book relates to, and has affected my thinking about, anorexia nervosa.

In one very important way it appears that the holy women described by Bell did not suffer from the eating disorder known today as anorexia nervosa. No doubt the saints starved themselves, lost in excess of 25 percent of their normal body weight, and experienced all the physical symptoms that accompany extreme malnourishment. Just as certainly, they purged themselves, denied their nutritional needs, and strongly resisted external efforts to get them to eat. But missing from Bell's accounts of holy anorectic behavior is a dread of fatness, and a self-conscious, unremitting pursuit of thinness. This is the hallmark of anorexia nervosa, its single most telling diagnostic sign.

However, a more thoughtful look at the data suggests that this apparent discrepancy is more illusory than real, and that holy anorexia and anorexia nervosa represent remarkably similar conditions. Bell makes an important comment in Chapter 1 when he remarks that the distinction between holy anorexia and anorexia nervosa may be more a matter of the modifiers than anything else. That is, both states are characterized by an unwillingness to eat, but one is driven by the desire to be holy and the other by the desire to be thin. The point is that anorectics in the fourteenth century and those in the twentieth century do not want to eat because they abhor the consequences. And, whether in the service of holiness or thinness, they determinedly relish the effects of starvation.

A review of Feighner's diagnostic criteria that refer to attitudinal states exposes a marked similarity between holy anorexia and anorexia nervosa when holiness is juxtaposed with thinness.[1] For example, instead of "a distorted, implacable attitude towards eating, food or weight that overrides hunger, admonitions, reassurance, and threats," read a distorted, implacable attitude toward holiness that overrides hunger, admonitions, reassurance, and threats; or instead of "apparent enjoyment in losing weight with overt manifestation that food refusal is a pleasurable indulgence," read apparent enjoyment in gaining holiness with overt manifestation that food refusal is a pleasurable indulgence; or instead of "a desired body image of extreme thinness," read a desired body image of extreme holiness. The superficial discrepancy mentioned above is transformed into a fundamental parallel when holiness for a holy anorectic is understood to be similar to thinness for a present-day anorectic.

Furthermore, there is good reason to equate medieval holiness with contemporary thinness. Both represent ideal states of being

in the cultural milieus under consideration. In medieval Italy holiness was held in the highest regard, and was a much sought after
way of life. According to Bell, female holiness in particular received a great impetus with the appearance of Clare of Assisi and
Catherine of Siena. Women were presented with specific models
of holiness toward which they could aspire. Struggling to live up
to them could provide new and enhanced experiences of self-
esteem. Similarly, in contemporary western culture thinness is
constantly extolled as the feminine ideal. Adolescent females are
literally deluged with cultural messages that place enormous
value upon the ability to get slim and to stay slim. This has been
especially true during the last several decades. As with the advent
of new kinds of female holiness in medieval Italy, the hyper-
emphasis on female thinness in recent years has been attended by
a rapid increase in the recognition of anorectic behavior patterns.

Quite apart from the overt symptomatology there are other star-
tling and profound parallels between holy anorexia and anorexia
nervosa. Both in medieval Italy and in the twentieth century anorectics are hyperactive, perfectionistic, and never satisfied or comfortable with the results of their efforts to be holy or thin. They
constantly experience themselves to be in grave danger of losing
control over their fanatically pursued aims, and so are forever
watchful and self-critical. Their thoughts are obsessively focused
upon holiness or thinness, so much so that there is little time or
energy for anything else. Holy anorectics and their modern-day
counterparts profess to be uninterested in ordinary human relationships. They see themselves as extremely self-sufficient and
independent, always ready to care for others but entirely unwill-
ing to receive care from others.

The relationship between holy anorexia and anorexia nervosa
with regard to internal needs and desires deserves special emphasis. Holy anorectics detested their bodily desires and were ter-
rified at the possibility of their unbidden appearance. In order to
be holy it was necessary to have no needs, be they sexual, narcissistic, or nutritional. The sine qua non for holiness was purity,
and so attractive men, or opportunities to be selfish, or food had to
be obsessively avoided. It is here that there is an explicit connection between holiness and starvation. The avoidance of food is
part of the path to saintliness. Modern-day anorectics are just as
suspicious of their bodies, and just as frightened that they will
suddenly be betrayed by their bodily needs. Food and the desire to
eat are paramount, but all primary anorectics are also repulsed by

sexuality and disgusted by selfishness. The notion of bodily purity and cleanliness is just as significant for them as it was for
holy anorectics. Thinness means the absence of desire just as
surely as it means emaciation.

The medieval women who became holy anorectics were not
only in search of spiritual perfection. Through their individualized quest for purity of mind and body, they might attain a direct
connection with God. There are repeated references throughout
Holy Anorexia to the saintly women's seeking union with God.
Purity was necessary for this life-sustaining and totally fulfilling
union. Again, there may be a parallel with anorexia nervosa.
Modern-day anorectics are peculiarly unable to make connections
with other people. As mentioned, they avoid the care and nurturing that are offered by others, preferring instead to maintain an
apparently independent and self-sufficient stance. Yet anorectics
are involved in a deeply connected relationship, not with people
but with their diet. The relationship is intensely personal and private. There are no intermediaries. Nutritional purity in particular
and bodily purity in general enable the anorectic to maintain her
connection with the diet. While recovering, and as the importance
of the diet recedes, the anorectic often expresses a deep yearning
for connection, as if she is missing some part of herself that she
needs to feel complete. Indeed, successful and lasting recovery frequently turns on the anorectic's capacity to accept less of a union
with others than she had experienced with her diet. The point is,
both holy anorectics and those today express a powerful urge to
feel deeply, intensely, and consistently connected in a way that is
beyond the abilities of most human relationships. The psychodynamic term "symbiotic merger" springs to mind, but this sounds
only pathological and therefore too pejorative. Perhaps there is
more here than illness, suggesting the need for further thought
rather than quick diagnosis.

Holy Anorexia is, of course, more than a gripping historical account of those medieval women who starved themselves in their
search for saintliness. It is also a significant attempt to document
a relationship between gender conflict and anorectic behavior patterns. Rudolph Bell emphasizes that saintly anorectics had to do
battle with the Catholic male clergy in order to attain their desired state of holiness. Again and again there is mention made of
the saints' need to resist tradition and to conquer or overcome patriarchal authority. Implied are male-female power struggles and
the ultimate triumph of feminine will. Several points are worth

noting here. In the first place, the gender struggles that no doubt occurred do not appear to have been of primary importance for the holy anorectics. Bell comments that "even among these holy anorexics there is no reason to suggest that they intended in a careful and planned way to appropriate male prerogatives." Instead, the battles are a by-product of the quest for holiness. They happened because the definition of holiness could not tolerate worldly intervention of any kind, not because there was a self-conscious rebellion against male domination of religion. Certainly gender conflict took place, but perhaps it occurred in order to find union or connection, not power and mastery. From this perspective holy anorexia might be described as a particularly profound example of feminine striving for direct, personal connection in a predominantly patriarchal world.

The feminist scholar Carol Gilligan has recently completed an extremely important book, *In a Different Voice*.[2] In it she proposes the intriguing hypothesis that all extant psychological theory misunderstands women because it is based primarily upon male development and male phenomenology. Gilligan suggests that women have a basic need for affiliative relationships, and that much of their apparently confusing and unintelligible behavior is more easily understood when thought about in the context of a person searching for and needing to maintain interpersonal connection. Therefore, holy anorectics might be best understood as women with especially strong feminine needs, who were courageously autonomous not simply in order to express their will, but in order to feel deeply and ultimately affiliated. Moreover, for a holy anorectic to be truly in control of herself might mean more, or other, than conquering her bodily needs and desires. It might mean that she wanted above all to be deeply connected to just herself, independent of the needs that would inevitably bring her into a hierarchic, submissive, and "possessed" relationship with men. Bell's analysis of Angela of Foligno in Chapter 4 certainly suggests such a conclusion.

In fact, a variation on this theme may be central to the current dramatic increase in the incidence of anorexia nervosa. In contemporary culture, women are inundated with the image of the "liberated female," someone who is defined as aggressive, assertive, and ambitious. Traditionally these characteristics have been a part of the male role, and it is only recently that women have been exhorted to conquer, overcome, and master. As a result, adolescent females may be faced with a cultural mandate for which they are ill prepared, and which also runs counter to their basic psychological dispositions. If women have strong natural needs to secure and maintain interpersonal connections, then requiring them to ignore affiliation and focus instead upon acquiring power might easily produce deep confusion, uncertainty, and fear. Anorexia nervosa is one way to "resolve" a psychological dilemma wherein going on with life leads to an unbearable sense of inadequacy. Indeed, anorexia could be seen as a tragic caricature of the disconnected, self-sufficient female, unable to affiliate and driven by an obsessive desire for power and mastery.

There is an ironic aspect to the gender conflict portrayed in *Holy Anorexia*. On the one hand the saintly women struggled desperately to free themselves of the shackles of male authority. Yet, in doing so, they may have unwittingly colluded with the very forces they were attempting to bypass. The holy anorectic's resolve to be absolutely free of bodily desires so as to unite with God seems to underscore the idea that femininity, in its natural or perhaps instinctive state, is dangerous and potentially sinful. Furthermore, to the extent that God, or Christ, is a psychological equivalent of earthbound fathers or men in general, the implication may be similar. In order for a woman to be worthy of uniting or connecting with a man, she must rid herself of all her "baseness." Such an attitude is completely congruous with the deeply embedded belief that women are somehow a threat to men and to society as a whole, and so must be kept in check, controlled, and forced into a subservient position. From this perspective the church fathers would have done well to remain awestruck by the religiosity of the holy anorectics in their charge. They did not have to enforce their domination via suspicions of demonic possession or complicated formulas for beatification. The saints themselves were unknowingly supporting their cultural values by equating bodily purity with essential holiness. Or, to put it another way, the women who struggled to express their sense of self by becoming holy did so in a way that reinforced a male interpretation of female psychology.

To return to anorexia nervosa, Bell's social psychological analysis has real significance for current understanding of eating disorders. Indeed, the ideas expressed in *Holy Anorexia* complement contemporary feminist theory. As such, they may represent an independently derived source of support for feminist hypotheses regarding the nature of anorexia. Susie Orbach is perhaps the best known writer in this area. Most recently she has argued that anorexia nervosa is the quintessential symbol of female oppression in a male-dominated culture.[3] According to Orbach, women are raised to care for others rather than for themselves, and because of this to expect less than they might want by way of personal satisfaction and fulfillment. As a result, every generation of daughters reaches adulthood steeped in the necessity for self-deprivation. These cultural prerogatives are passed on from mothers to daughters in a never ending cycle. Adding to the deprivation that any daughter is taught to expect is the hidden resentment her mother feels about giving to her child when she has not received herself. Consequently, mothers form ambivalent attachments to their daughters, never able to nurture comfortably, and by the same token never able to easily encourage secure and self-confident separation. Orbach does not intend to accuse mothers of poor mothering. Instead, she is arguing that on a cultural level women are trapped in these psychological circumstances. The trap is promoted unconsciously but profoundly by a patriarchal culture that requires female submissiveness and servitude, and is deeply threatened by the prospect of secure, self-confident, and genuinely self-assertive women.

In anorexia nervosa Orbach finds the expression of every woman's plight. The disorder poignantly and graphically depicts the self-starved female who is unable to feed or nurture herself, who must reject her own needs and desires, and who is too frightened and uncertain to find a means for authentic self-assertion. Of course, this picture implies a very different meaning for anorectic behavior patterns than is suggested by *Holy Anorexia*. Here, anorexia represents the helplessness, and inevitably the impotent rage, of women trapped, whereas holy anorectics are illustrative of some women's capacity to overcome the pervasive influence of cultural forces. Nevertheless, the theme of gender conflict is a common denominator, suggesting its crucial importance in the genesis of anorectic behavior. In fact, one wonders about the difference mentioned above. Where self-starvation is regarded as an illness, as it is today, it seems reasonable to assume that the "ill" will feel helpless and impotent; where it is regarded with reverence and awe, as it was in medieval Italy, it seems likely that those who are "awesome" will feel triumphant and self-expressed.

At present the treatment of anorexia nervosa is a difficult undertaking. It is frequently time consuming, often frustrating, seldom inexpensive, and rarely guaranteed of success. The treatment modalities currently in use range over the entire spectrum of

available psychiatric and psychological services. There are anorectic patients being treated with rather orthodox psychoanalysis,
with dynamically oriented psychotherapy, with behavior therapy,
with group psychotherapy, and as part of family therapy. In addition, there are many hospital based treatment programs, some
using milieu techniques, others relying on behavior modification
principles, and still others that focus upon a variety of forced feeding regimens. There is even an occasional recommendation for
electro-shock treatment. All of the above methods may or may not
employ a number of different psychiatric medications as a treatment adjunct. Moreover, across the country and throughout western Europe there are countless self-help organizations, each with
its own system, all devoted to assisting anorectics and their
families. This plethora of treatment approaches implies what is
true: not enough is known about how to most effectively treat
those who suffer with anorexia nervosa. Certainly there are many
anorectics who do recover and are able to lead fulfilling, produc-
tive lives; but there are still too many who do not receive sufficient help. Either these anorectics lapse into a chronic condition where life has a marginal and desperate quality, or they die.
Anorexia nervosa has the highest mortality rate of any psychiatric
disorder.

Holy Anorexia does not and cannot provide the answer to the
treatment questions that confront contemporary therapists. Still,
its contents are instructive, and offer important implications for
modern day efforts to deal with anorexia nervosa. For example, it
is interesting to note that the response of the Catholic hierarchy
to holy anorexia bears some resemblance to current treatment
techniques. In general, the priest-confessors who were close to
many if not all of the saints are reminiscent of twentieth-century
individual psychotherapists. Like the confessor, the modern therapist struggles to listen, to understand, and to offer appropriate interventions. Moreover, both usually represent the "system," and
attempt to influence anorectic behavior patterns in the direction
of established convention.

Numerous examples of behavior modification principles appear as part of the priestly and conventual response to holy
anorexia. Then as now, the idea was to establish a system of rewards or punishments in order to manipulate and control behavior. Also, the various dietary rules and routines that were frequently suggested for saints in an effort to moderate their
abstinence sound similar to the modern physician or nutritionist

who offers meal plans and caloric counseling to the anorectic.

What is most striking, and perhaps more relevant, about the official Catholic response to holy anorexia is that it had little apparent impact. In other words, the "treatment" techniques employed to confront directly and to alter specifically the pursuit of holiness were generally unsuccessful. Most often, the church hierarchy could finally do little more than stand aside in puzzled awe and bewildered reverence. Perhaps this happened because no one in official authority really understood the holy anorectics. In fact, it is just possible that these medieval anorectics were declared holy precisely because no one understood. As Bell comments, medieval people were prone to attribute to heaven what could not be comprehended on earth. In other words, regardless of whether holy anorectics were driven primarily by a need for autonomy or primarily by a deep desire to experience a profound personal connection, the men of their era were not able to grasp the genuine meaning of their behavior.

It is conceivable that contemporary men in general, and therapists in particular, are in a similar situation. Interestingly, while there are many female therapists treating anorexia nervosa, the commonly acclaimed experts in the field—those who publish the most and therefore are most influential regarding treatment techniques—are almost all male. If anorexia nervosa, like holy anorexia, represents an expression of women in search of a new self-definition or a new self-experience, then the contemporary male-initiated and male-controlled treatment approaches may actually be missing the point. All current treatment, whether individual psychotherapy or hospital based behavior modification, may be inadvertently focused on a misunderstanding of the anorectic experience. For example, the psychological issue of separation is often assigned a crucial role in the psychodynamics of anorexia. Following Gilligan, suppose this is, unconsciously, a male category of interpretation that does not have the same meaning for women as it does for men? Suppose successful psychological separation and individuation is not particularly relevant for women because that is not really what they want or need? The general issue here is the necessity to take seriously how *little* may actually be known about female psychology, and it implies the crucial importance of educating therapists in the field to what is currently known. Furthermore, it suggests that modern treatments of anorexia nervosa may not be genuine treatments at all. Instead they may be deeply experienced by the anorectic patients as further entrapments rather than as sources of psychological liberation.

At the level of actual, ongoing clinical practice these comments present a therapeutic dilemma. Anorexia nervosa is a life threatening illness. Still today anorectics have the capacity to instill a sense of awed wonder. Treating anorexia, however, requires an ability not to be awestruck and consequently paralyzed. It necessitates taking action, sometimes drastically, in order to save a life. At the least it means making an effort to dramatically and significantly engage the patient so that her powerful need to choose thinness instead of a future and a diet instead of people can be reversed. From this perspective there is not the time to regard anorexia nervosa with the respect and curiosity it may deserve theoretically. Of course, ideally there is room for the therapist to try to understand the anorectic experience, with all that it may imply about female psychology and unconscious, culture based gender conflicts. Indeed, there is a real struggle here for the therapist that may in a sense be like that for the anorectic. Known treatment methods are not working consistently. There is more to know and more to do. A new way to connect with anorectic patients must be found in order to promote reliable and genuinely fulfilling recovery. The danger, of course, is that therapists will feel overwhelmed by their inadequacy and so revert to practices that are more comfortable psychologically but that actually represent a retreat from furthering the treatment experience.

On the other hand, at the present time, none of the above is relevant when a life is in danger. Given the modern definition of anorexia nervosa as an emotional disorder, self-starvation is evidence only of a pressing need for hospitalization. Unfortunately, therefore, the pressures of therapeutic responsibility may have the unnoticed side effect of diminishing a genuine willingness to listen or understand in new and different ways. The treatment of the eating disorder bulimia with antidepressant medication is perhaps a good example. Bulimia is closely related to anorexia nervosa in that many bulimics have experienced a period of self-starvation prior to becoming trapped in the "binge-purge" cycle—periods of gorging food followed by vomiting, or the use of laxatives, or complete fasting. The incidence of bulimia is rising extremely rapidly, and its medical complications are serious and upon occasion life threatening. Recently, several studies have shown an apparent relationship between treating bulimia with medication and a marked diminution of binging and purging.[4] As a result, there is growing support for a more biological explanation of bulimia within the eating disorders community and a corresponding deemphasis on psychological issues. Worth recalling, however, are Bell's comments about the changes that took place in the Catholic hierarchy as holy anorexia gained a more and more prominent position among medieval females. Reverence and awe were replaced by a growing suspicion of demonic possession, and then by efforts to more carefully legislate saintliness, as well as the growing "realization" that holy anorectics were actually ill. What in effect happened was that little, if any, new understanding of women was achieved, while the patriarchal clergy moved steadily toward a reassertion of its power and authority. In the absence of more compelling evidence, treating bulimia solely with antidepressant medications (as well as the periodic efforts to establish a biological or biochemical etiology for anorexia nervosa) has a somewhat similar ring to it. In this case, the male dominated medical and psychiatric establishment may be moving toward a redemonstration of its unique authority to correctly understand and treat bulimia.

There is another and very different implication to Bell's description of the changing response to holy anorexia within the Catholic hierarchy. That is, as the definition of holiness was altered, so eventually was the incidence of holy anorexia. When, finally, female saints came to be recognized in terms of their capacity to do good works, the phenomenon of holy anorexia largely disappeared. Self-starvation lost its appeal for Catholic women when it became irrelevant as a means to gain the highly valued state of holiness. Similarly, it follows that the incidence of anorexia nervosa will be reduced when the cultural ideals for feminine beauty and the "liberated" woman are no longer connected with thinness. In these circumstances, dieting should lose its special status and self-starvation much of its allure. It seems possible, in other words, to influence anorexia nervosa without a more authentic understanding of female psychology. However, this is not to say that the distinctive importance of feminine needs and desires should be ignored. Above all else, *Holy Anorexia* makes it clear that the experience of being female deserves respectful and profound attention. This message is as relevant and as significant today as it should have been in medieval Italy. Indeed, it is not just anorectic behavior patterns that are involved, for undoubtedly it is poorly understood or quite unconscious gender conflicts that underlie much of the contemporary struggle to achieve truly collaborative and fulfilling human relationships.

NOTES

I. RECOGNITION AND TREATMENT

1. Association for Research in Nervous and Mental Disease, *The Hypothalamus and Central Levels of Autonomic Function* (Baltimore, 1940), especially the contributions of Fulton, Ranson, Bard, Sheehan, Harrison, Alpers, and Zimmerman. For recent findings, see S. L. Jeffcoate, ed., *The Endocrine Hypothalamus* (New York, 1978).

2. On mortality rates see Katherine A. Halmi, "Anorexia Nervosa: Recent Investigations," *Annual Review of Medicine* 29 (1978): 137–48. The most readable general account of anorexia nervosa is Hilde Bruch's *The Golden Cage: The Enigma of Anorexia Nervosa* (Cambridge, Mass., 1978) but also see her earlier work, *Eating Disorders: Obesity, Anorexia Nervosa, and the Person Within* (New York, 1973). Other basic and indispensable works are Peter Dally, *Anorexia Nervosa* (New York, 1969); Moses Kaufman and Marcel Heiman, eds., *Evolution of Psychosomatic Concepts: Anorexia Nervosa, A Paradigm* (New York, 1964); Salvador Minuchin, *Psychosomatic Families* (Cambridge, Mass., 1978); Mara Selvini-Palazzoli, *Self-Starvation: From Individual to Family Therapy in the Treatment of Anorexia Nervosa* (New York, 1978; for translation by Arnold Pomerans of *L'anoressia mentale* [Milan, 1974]); Robert Vigersky, ed., *Anorexia Nervosa* (New York, 1977); and Richard J. Wartman and Judith J. Wurtman, eds., *Disorders of Eating: Nutrients in Treatment of Brain Diseases* (New York, 1979), esp. 1–70, 101–16. For a bibliography of over 1300 entries, see Aldo Borghi et al., *L'anoressia nervosa* (Rome, 1975).

3. John P. Feighner et al., "Diagnostic Criteria for Use in Psychiatric Research," *Archives of General Psychiatry* 26 (1972): 57–63.

4. Richard Morton, *Phthisiologia or, A Treatise of Consumptions*, 2d ed. (London, 1720), pp. 8–9. Morton immediately thereafter reports a case of anorexia in a young male in which he effected a full recovery. Petr Skrabanek, "Notes Towards the History of Anorexia Nervosa," *Janus: Revue internationale de l'histoire des sciences, de la médecine de la pharmacie et de la technique* 70 (1983): 109–28, provides ample evidence of earlier anorexic behavior.

5. Ilza Veith, *Hysteria: The History of a Disease* (Chicago, 1965), pp. 146–51; Giorgio Baglivi, *The Practice of Physick*, 2d ed. (London, 1723), pp. 160–72. For a fascinating look into the extraordinary range of Baglivi's interests see Dorothy M.

Schullian, *The Baglivi Correspondence from the Library of Sir William Osler* (Ithaca, N.Y., 1974).

6. Veith, *Hysteria*, pp. 153-74; George Cheyne, *The Natural Method of Cureing the Diseases of the Body and the Disorders of the Mind Depending on the Body*, 2d ed. (London, 1742), esp. pp. 90-96 on the links between lunacy and diet; *The Works of Thomas Sydenham, M.D.*, trans. with a "Life of the Author" by R. G. Latham (London, 1850), 2:85-96, 231-35; William Cullen, *First Lines of the Practice of Physic* (Edinburgh, 1791), 3:231-64 on dyspepsia or want of appetite discusses anorexia separately from hypochondriasis (pp. 265-86) and hysteria (4:94-111), but the distinctions are never clearly drawn; Bernard de Mandeville, *A Treatise of the Hypochondriack and Hysteric Passions*; Robert Whytt, *Observations on the Nature, Causes, and Cure of those Disorders which have been commonly called Nervous, Hypochondriac, or Hysteric* (Edinburgh, 1767); Benjamin Rush, *Medical Inquiries and Observations upon the Diseases of the Mind*, 4th ed. (1815; reprint ed., New York, 1972), 1:85.

7. Philippe Pinel, *A Treatise on Insanity* (New York, 1962 for reprint of translation by David D. Davis of *Traité médico-philosophique sur l'alienation mentale, ou la manie* [Paris, 1801]), pp. 78-81 for the particular difficulties of treating "insanity from religious enthusiasm" and pp. 237-39 on demoniacal possession; Veith, *Hysteria*, pp. 175-84.

8. William W. Gull, "The Address in Medicine Delivered before the Annual Meeting of the B.M.A. at Oxford," *Lancet* 2 (1868): 171-76; "Apepsia hysterica. Anorexia Nervosa," *Transactions of the Clinical Society* 7 (1874): 22-28; "Anorexia Nervosa," *Lancet* 1 (1888): 516-17; Jacques Decourt, "L'Anorexie mentale au temps de Lasègue et de Gull," *La Presse Médicale* 62 (1954): 355-58.

9. Charles Lasègue, "De l'anorexie hystérique," *Archives générales de médecine* 21 (1873): 385-403.

10. Jean-Martin Charcot, *Clinical Lectures on Diseases of the Nervous System*, trans. Thomas Savill (London, 1889), 3:211-14.

11. Josef Breuer and Sigmund Freud, *Studies on [in] Hysteria* (1893; London, 1955 ed. trans. James Strachey as vol. 2 of *The Standard Edition of the Complete Psychological Works of Sigmund Freud*), pp. 21-47.

12. Ibid., pp. 48-105.

13. Ibid., p. 89.

14. Pierre Janet, *The Major Symptoms of Hysteria*, 2d ed. (New York, 1920), pp. 227-44.

15. Jack L. Ross, "Anorexia Nervosa: An Overview," *Bulletin of the Menninger Clinic* 41 (1977): 418-36.

16. A judicious appraisal of symptoms primarily related to starvation itself rather than to anorexia nervosa may be found in Dally, *Anorexia Nervosa*, pp. 8-9, 35-41.

17. Raymond L. Vande Wiele, "Anorexia Nervosa and the Hypothalamus," *Hospital Practice* (December 1977), pp. 45-51.

18. Kelly M. Bemis, "Current Approaches to the Etiology and Treatment of Anorexia Nervosa," *Psychological Bulletin* 85 (1978): 593-617 places the voluminous recent literature on anorexia nervosa into a context similar to the one I have set forth here.

19. Helmut Thoma, "On the Psychotherapy of Patients with Anorexia Nervosa," *Bulletin of the Menninger Clinic* 41 (1977): 437-52.

20. Donald Weinstein and Rudolph M. Bell, *Saints and Society: The Two Worlds of Western Christendom, 1000–1700* (Chicago, 1982), pp. 220–38.

21. David Stannard, *Shrinking History: On Freud and the Failure of Psychohistory* (New York, 1980), clearly has earned the description "obsessive-compulsive."

22. Bruch, *Eating Disorders*, pp. 250–51.

23. The psychological import is discussed in Fawn M. Brodie, *Thomas Jefferson: An Intimate History* (New York, 1974), p. 45.

24. In addition to Bruch, who remained enough of a Freudian that she placed more emphasis on maternal nurturing practices than I do, see esp. Minuchin, *Psychosomatic Families*, pp. 22–73; and R. S. Kalucy, A. H. Crisp, and Britta Harding, "A Study of 56 Families with Anorexia Nervosa" (presented at the Second Congress of the International Colloquium on Psychosomatic Medicine, Rome, 1975).

2. I, CATHERINE

1. Caterina (Santa) da Siena (Caterina Benincasa), *Epistolario di Santa Caterina a cura di Eugenio Dupré Theseider*, vol. 1 (Rome, 1940), letter number 92 (using Tommaseo's numbering). This edition remains incomplete but is most valuable for the critical notes on letters it does contain. For other letters, nearly four hundred in all, see Caterina (Santa) da Siena (Caterina Benincasa), *Le lettere di S. Caterina da Siena ridotte a nuova lezione e in ordine nuovo disposte con note di Niccolò Tommaseo a cura di Piero Misciattelli*, 6 vols. (Siena, 1913–21; reprint ed., Florence, 1939–40). Useful notes also will be found in Girolamo Gigli, *L'opere di Santa Caterina da Siena*, 4 vols. (Siena and Lucca, 1707–21). A more readily available complete edition, unfortunately with introductory essays that are not always historically accurate, is Santa Caterina da Siena, *Epistolario* (Rome, 1979). Only sixty-four of the letters currently are available in English translations in Vida D. Scudder, ed., *Saint Catherine of Siena as Seen in Her Letters* (London, 1905). On translation problems and forthcoming complete English editions see Suzanne M. Noffke, "Translating the Works of Catherine of Siena into English: Some Basic Considerations," in Congresso Internazionale di Studi Cateriniani (CISC), *Atti* (Rome, 1981), pp. 470–82. For his unstinting assistance on this and other translations I am indebted to Professor Joseph Chierici of Rutgers University.

2. Raimundus Capuani, "Legenda maior" in *Acta Sanctorum*, April vol. 3, para. 167. Hereafter cited as Raymond of Capua, *Legenda*, followed by the paragraph numbering used in the *Acta* and in the more worthy translations and commentaries on this work. A good scholarly yet officially approved full-length modern biography of Catherine is Innocenzo M. Taurisano, *Santa Caterina da Siena: Patrona d'Italia* (Rome, 1948); see esp. pp. xviii–xlviii, 35–50, and 208–15, for various points discussed in this chapter; also see Giorgio Papasogli, *Sangue e fuoco sul ponte di Dio* (Rome, 1971). The excessive nature of Catherine's fasting encouraged lively controversy even centuries ago. In his multivolume *Histoire ecclésiastique* the Abbot of Fleuri concluded that Catherine's many visions were a direct consequence of her inability or refusal to eat. This position was sharply contested in Ambrogio Tantucci, *Dissertazione teologico-critica del P. Maestro F. Ambrogio Ansano Tantucci dell' Ordine de' Predicatori, In cui risponde colla Dottrina specialmente de S. Tommaso D'Aquino a cio, che si legge nella storia ecclesiastica dell' Abate di Fleuri spettante alla serafica Santa Caterina di Siena, Ed ai Direttori della medesima* (Milan, 1749), esp. pp. 20–36.

3. The fundamental study of the sources for Catherine of Siena's life remains Robert Fawtier, *Sainte Catherine de Sienne: Essai de critique des sources*, vol. 1, *Sources hagiographiques* (Paris, 1921), and vol. 2, *Les oeuvres de Sainte Catherine de Sienne* (Paris, 1930). For five centuries before the appearance of Fawtier's work, no one had brought a deeply critical, secular, historical spirit to an examination of the problems raised by Raymond of Capua's *Legenda* and related materials. By the very ferocity of his relentless questioning of everything, Fawtier spurred scholars to return to the basic documents and examine them more closely. The result has been an outpouring of meticulous and sometimes exhaustingly detailed works that continues to the present day. Lina Zanini, *Bibliografia analitica di S. Caterina da Siena, 1901–1950* (Rome, 1971), which by no means is complete, gives over 1000 entries. As with most historical documents, the *Legenda* can be used but must be subjected to appropriate methods of verification. A case in point relevant to the analysis that follows is the matter of Catherine's date of birth. Raymond of Capua gave her age at death in 1380 as thirty-three, the same age as Jesus Christ. For Raymond this was another sign of her sanctity, one that later faithful admirers, especially "Caffarini," embellished. Fawtier suspected a trick and built an elaborate argument that Catherine was born sometime between 1333 and 1338, a decade or more earlier than her traditionally assumed birth year. To support his contention, Fawtier turned Raymond into a mastermind at selectively manipulating and destroying telltale documents, brushed aside the internally inconsistent dates of an anonymous panegyric whose historical value he greatly overestimated, misread a list of names by claiming it referred to a single year when close examination shows this to be highly improbable, and asserted that Catherine's efforts to foil her family's plans to marry her off came when she was twenty-five or thirty years old and had been a Dominican tertiary for more than a decade. Perhaps nothing is impossible, but such a chronology makes little sense for fourteenth-century Siena. All these and other points are explored at length in E. Jordan, "La date de naissance de Sainte Catherine de Sienne," *Analecta Bollandiana* 40 (1922): 365–411. Also see Robert Fawtier and Louis Canet, *La double expérience de Catherine Benincasa* (Paris, 1948), and Eugenio Dupré Theseider, "La duplice esperienza di S. Caterina da Siena," *Rivista Storica Italiana* 62, fasc. 4 (1950): 533–74; and Francesco Valli, *Saggi sulla letteratura religiosa italiana del trecento* (Urbino, 1943), pp. 91 and 136–55. The result is to reestablish on a firmer basis (given the absence of an actual birth register) 1347 as the most likely year of Catherine's birth but to be skeptical about assigning much significance to her age at death since neither she nor the disciples gathered around her did so in 1380. Generally, Raymond of Capua interpreted and moralized a bit excessively, but he was writing about a life so extraordinary and about which so many popular tales already flourished that he hardly needed to add his own fictions.

On Catherine's appearance before a Dominican inquisitorial commission in Florence, see Innocenzo Taurisano, *L'ambiente storico cateriniano* (Siena, 1934); Fawtier, *Sainte Catherine*, 1:92; Anonimo Fiorentino, *I miracoli di S. Caterina da Siena*, ed. Francesco Valli (1374; Florence, 1936), introduction; and for a reevaluation that convinces at least this reader that Fawtier was correct in concluding that Catherine was in real danger of being found guilty of heresy at this point, see Timoteo M. Centi, "Un processo inventato di sana pianta," *S. Caterina fra i dottori della chiesa*, ed. T. Centi (Florence, 1970), pp. 39–56.

On Raymond of Capua, see Fawtier, *Sainte Catherine*, 1:118–30; and Giacinto M. Cormier, *Il Beato Raimondo da Capua* (Rome, 1900). On translation and publication of his biography see the recent edition of Giuseppe Tinagli (Siena, 1978), introduction by Giacinto D'Urso; and, more generally, Francesco Valli, "La mentalità agiografica del B. Raimondo da Capua," *La Diana* 8 (1933): 191–209. On hagiography and history, see Donald Weinstein and Rudolph M. Bell, *Saints and Society: The Two Worlds of Western Christendom, 1000–1700* (Chicago, 1982), pp. 1–15. And for an anthropological perspective see Alessandro Falassi, *La santa dell'oca: Vita, morte e miracoli di Caterina da Siena* (Milan, 1980), esp. pp. 13–16.

4. Raymond of Capua, *Legenda*, 162, 163, 399, and 413.

5. Ibid., 167. An independent contemporary account of the stages of Catherine Benincasa's anorexia, one that Raymond of Capua probably was not familiar with, is Anonimo Fiorentino, *I miracoli*. Pages 5–9 and 23–25 differ slightly in detail but confirm the progressive character of Catherine's loss of appetite. Page 9 especially reads like a textbook case of anorexia nervosa and includes a reference to hypothermia.

6. Raymond of Capua, *Legenda*, 171. On Catherine's enemies, see also Anonimo Fiorentino, *I miracoli*, pp. 13–16. On devotion to the sacrament see also Thomas Antonii de Senis (Caffarini), *Libellus de Supplemento: Legende Prolixe Virginis Beate Caterine de Senis*, ed. Iuliana Cavallini and Imelda Foralosso (Rome, 1974), pp. 70, 75–120. This edition, with its erudite notes, takes precedence over the versions previously translated or published, although still of literary interest despite its incompleteness and inaccuracy is *Supplimento alla vulgata leggenda di S. Caterina da Siena che forma il tomo secondo della sua vita. Scritto gia in lingua latina dal B. Tommaso Nacci Caffarini ed ora ridotto nella Italiana dal P. Amb. Ansano Tantucci Sanese* (Lucca, 1754). On philological questions, see Ezio Franceschini, *Leggenda Minore di S. Caterina da Siena* (Milan, 1942). On the eucharist more generally see the deeply insightful work of Caroline Bynum, "Women Mystics and Eucharistic Devotion in the Thirteenth Century," *Women's Studies* 11, nos. 1 and 2 (1984): 179–214.

7. Telesforo Bini, *Laudi spirituali del Bianco da Siena* (Lucca, 1851), pp. 167–68, for *Laude* LXXII. On the context of the *laude* see Franca Ageno, *Il Bianco da Siena: Notizie e testi inediti* (Città di Castello, 1939), pp. x and xvi–xvii; Fawtier, *Sainte Catherine* 2:286–88; Hyacinthe Laurent, ed., *Fontes Vitae S. Catharinae Senensis Historici: Il Processo Castellano* (Florence, 1942), pp. 338–39.

8. Raymond of Capua, *Legenda*, 176–77. On her confessor's skepticism, see ibid., 87–90. On sainthood and witchcraft more generally, see Marcello Craveri, *Sante e streghe: Biografie e documenti dal XIV al XVII secolo* (Milan, 1980). On the emergence of concern with witchcraft (distinct from demonic possession), especially within Dominican circles, see Franco Cardini, *Magia, stregoneria, superstizioni nell' Occidente medievale* (Florence, 1979), pp. 58–92.

9. Catherine of Siena, *The Dialogue*, trans. Suzanne Noffke (New York, 1980), pts. 9, 11, and 104. See letter 213 to Suor Daniella da Orvieto on discretion and 340 to Monna Agnesa da Toscanella on the dangers of love of penance for its own sake.

10. Accounts written by Catherine's contemporaries based either directly on Raymond of Capua's *Legenda* or with full knowledge of his work cannot be considered "independent" in the same way as the anonymous Florentine's *I miracoli*. Thus, as Fawtier argues at length, a seemingly large number of testimonies all must be treated cautiously since the "witnesses" were aware of and may have felt obliged to confirm what Raymond had written. What is significant about these briefer or less reliable accounts is that they include extensive references to

Catherine's anorexia, generally laboring with some difficulty to explain such strange, potentially demonic, seemingly scandalous behavior. Collectively, they do not necessarily prove that Catherine was anorexic, but they do document a portrait, however fictionalized, of a young woman whose loss of appetite was not simply religious asceticism. These "facts," their authors must have believed, deserved prominent mention and captured the attention of Catherine's followers. Explicit reference to Catherine Benincasa's extraordinary fasting appears in the Bull authorizing her canonization issued by Pope Pius II on June 29, 1461. For references by contemporaries to her loss of appetite, see Felix Battaglia and Hyacinthe Laurent, eds., *Fontes Vitae S. Catharinae Senensis Historici: Leggenda Abbreviata di S. Caterina da Siena di F. Antonio della Rocca* (Siena, 1939), pp. 6–7; Laurent, ed., *Il Processo Castellano*, esp. the testimonies of Stefano Maconi and Bartolomeo Dominici, pp. 257–73, 281–323; Girolamo Gigli, ed., *L'opere della serafica Santa Caterina da Siena* (Siena, 1707), 1:460–89 and esp. 473 on self-induced vomiting; Francesco Grottanelli, ed., *Leggenda minore di S. Caterina da Siena e lettere dei suoi discepoli* (Bologna, 1868), pp. 63–70, and Ezio Franceschini, *Leggenda minore di S. Caterina da Siena* (Milan, 1942), pp. ix–xii and 121–22 on its relationship to the *Legenda Maior*; and Thomas Antonii de Senis, *Libellus de Supplemento*, pp. 20, 34–35, 60, 101–2. Even scholars who attempt to refute the evidence on Catherine's eating habits recognize her as an early "feminist"; see Umberto Mattiolo, "S. Caterina da Siena nella storia della donna," in *Caterina da Siena: Una donna per tutte le stagioni: Atti del seminario cateriniano del Circolo Carlo Tincari, Bologna 1979–80*, ed. G. F. Moria (L'Aquila, 1981), pp. 101–24.

11. Raymond of Capua, *Legenda*, 25–28; Francesco Valli, *L'infanzia e la puerizia di Santa Caterina da Siena: Esame critico delle fonti* (Siena, 1931), discusses in depth the historical context of all the relevant contemporary sources.

12. Erik Erikson, *Childhood and Society*, 2d ed. (New York, 1963), esp. pp. 247–73 for the theory, and *Young Man Luther: A Study in Psychoanalysis and History* (New York, 1958) for a provocative application of his ideas in a historical setting. Raymond of Capua, *Legenda*, 191 for the quotation and 416 for the "exchange." And see Thomas Antonii de Senis, *Libellus di Supplemento*, p. 100: *Pater, quemadmodum puer habens in ore suo ubera matris sue, ex habundantia lactis per os eius versatur sive diffunditur, ita Dominus michi facit.*

13. Caterina da Siena, *Epistolario*, letter 18 to her brother Benincasa. Consider also her "miraculous" restoration of milk to the mothers of her godchild and her niece, as told in Thomas Antonii di Senis, *Libellus de Supplemento*, pp. 62–63.

14. Giovanni Boccaccio, *The Decameron*, trans. Mark Musa and Peter Bondanella (New York, 1982), p. 9.

15. On the Benincasa's business fortunes, see Hyacinthe Laurent and Francesco Valli, eds., *Fontes Vitae S. Catharinae Senensis Historici: Documenti* (Florence, 1936), pp. 13–21, and Giovanni Battista Regoli, ed., *Documenti relativi a S. Caterina da Siena* (Siena, 1859), pp. 23–37.

16. Raymond of Capua, *Legenda*, 26 is very explicit on the details of Catherine's weaning and Lapa's inexperience, which suggests that Lapa's shortcomings remained significant to her many years later or else one presumes she would not have bothered to tell them to Raymond after four decades. Especially insightful on the maternal relationship is Ruth Lechner Von Behren, "Woman in Late Medieval Society: Catherine of Siena—a Psychological Study" (Ph.D. diss., University of California, Davis, 1972), pp. 37–58.

17. Caterina da Siena, *Epistolario*, letter 239 to Pope Gregory XI; Emile Gebhart,

Moines et papes: Essais de psychologie historique, 7th ed. (Paris, n.d.), pp. 63–133, and esp. 111–12 on the importance of this letter; also see Edmund G. Gardner, *Saint Catherine of Siena: A Study in the Religion, Literature and History of the Fourteenth Century in Italy* (London, 1907), pp. 193–94.

18. Giovanni Getto, *Letteratura religiosa dal due al novecento* (Florence, 1967), 2:109–267, is the fundamental work on Catherine's literary style. Also see Tommaso Gallarati-Scotti, ed., *Le più belle pagine di Caterina da Siena* (Milan, 1927), introduction; Franco Mancini, *Ispirazione e linguaggio di Caterina da Siena* (Trieste, 1951), pp. 49–65; Giacinto D'Urso, "Il valore autobiografico del linguaggio cateriniano," *S. Caterina da Siena,* n.s., 3 (April–September 1951): 56–77, aptly concludes that "Catherine did not invent symbols because life offered them to her."

19. For other important adult references by Catherine to breastfeeding and weaning, see Caterina da Siena, *Epistolario,* letter 26 to her niece Eugenia, letter 84 to Filippo di Vannuccio and Niccoló di Pietro di Firenze, and letter 333 to Raymond of Capua. That Catherine was aware of the more usual positive religious metaphors involving breastfeeding and weaning is evident from Tommaso "Caffarini"'s letter to her printed in Grotanelli, ed., *Leggenda minore,* pp. 253–58. On Catherine's recurring call to "virility" as the path of holiness, see Umberto Mattioli, "La tipologia 'virile' nella biografia e nella letteratura cateriniana," in CISC, *Atti,* pp. 198–222.

20. Raymond of Capua, *Legenda,* 27, and Valli, *L'infanzia,* pp. 51–64. Alvaro Grion, *Santa Caterina da Siena: Dottrina e fonti* (Cremona, 1953), pp. 260–74, attributes to Catherine a very early ability to read and suggests that this is how she learned about Euphrosyne, but such a contention is unlikely.

21. Anonimo Fiorentino, *I miracoli,* pp. 2–3, gives the version of this first vision reported here and accepted also by Arrigo Levasti, *My Servant, Catherine,* trans. Dorothy M. White (London, 1954), p. 8. The account in Raymond of Capua, *Legenda,* 29–31, differs in details such as how Jesus was dressed but concurs that Catherine kept the experience to herself. The Levasti biography estimably combines thorough scholarship with profound insight but inexplicably has no footnotes. With the invaluable aid of Padre Innocenzo Colosio, director of the Biblioteca della Spiritualità Levasti, I have tried to reconstruct as fully as possible what made Levasti write what he did. The influence of his work extends throughout the present chapter.

22. Levasti, *My Servant, Catherine,* pp. 12–13; Raymond of Capua, *Legenda,* 35–38; Valli, *L'infanzia,* pp. 48–49, 73–76.

23. Anonimo Fiorentino, *I miracoli,* pp. 3–4; Raymond of Capua, *Legenda,* 35–38; Valli, *L'infanzia,* pp. 48–49, 73–76.

24. Raymond of Capua, *Legenda,* 41–44; Mariano Sardi, "Bonaventura Benincasa," *S. Caterina da Siena* 4 (1925): 123–27; Francesco Valli, *L'adolescenza di Santa Caterina da Siena: Esame critico delle fonti* (Siena, 1934) offers the same thorough treatment of sources for Catherine's adolescence as his earlier work did for her childhood.

25. Raymond of Capua, *Legenda,* 45; Martino St. Gillet, *La missione di S. Caterina da Siena,* trans. Giacomo Dati (Florence, 1946), pp. 47–50, is especially good on this point despite its sexism; Valli, *L'adolescenza,* pp. 57–65.

26. Raymond of Capua, *Legenda,* 46; Anonimo Fiorentino, *I miracoli,* p. 6. The identification of Bonaventura's husband as Niccolò Tegliacci is from ibid., p. 2.

27. Raymond of Capua, *Legenda,* 25, tells of Bonaventura's visible weight loss

and wasting away in the context of praising Giacomo Benincasa's good character, and it is only a passing remark so that perhaps one should not build too much on it. But there is at least a possibility that Bonaventura had experienced anorexia at some point, that Catherine had seen this behavior pattern at first hand, and that in this aspect of her asceticism she began by consciously imitating her dead sister.

28. Fawtier, *Sainte Catherine*, 1:135.

29. Thomas Antonii de Senis, *Libellus de Supplemento*, p. 64. Raymond of Capua, *Legenda*, 241–44, cites three witnesses to Catherine's prayer and gives a version even more businesslike and demanding in tone, with phrases such as "established terms," "defrauded," and "promises made." For a similar prayer on behalf of her brother, see Thomas Antonii de Senis, *Libellus de Supplemento*, p. 61: *Ego non recedam hinc donec tu michi facias gratiam pro eo . . . Da michi peccata sua et ego satisfaciam pro eo.*

30. Anonimo Fiorentino, *I miracoli*, pp. 5–7; Raymond of Capua, *Legenda*, 47–48; Eugenio Lazzareschi, "Il colore dei capelli di Santa Caterina da Siena," *Memorie Domenicane* 38 (1921): 183–90.

31. Raymond of Capua, *Legenda*, 48.

32. Raymond of Capua, *Legenda*, 49–50; Valli, *L'adolescenza*, pp. 67–72.

33. Raymond of Capua, *Legenda*, 54–56. For Catherine's understanding of obedience, which she casts heavily in familial metaphors, see Caterina da Siena, *Il dialogo della divina provvidenza*, 3d ed., ed. Tito S. Centi (Siena, 1980), pp. 346–78. On her father see Mariano Sardi, "Giacomo Benincasa," *S. Caterina da Siena* 5 (1926): 39–43.

34. Raymond of Capua, *Legenda*, 57–63; Anonimo Fiorentino, *I miracoli*, p. 7, states that the length of Catherine's "moratorium" of hard penance in a private cell at home lasted seven years, which would be approximately from Bonaventura's death in August 1362 until early 1370, about eighteen months after her father's death. This time sequence does not in fact conflict with Raymond of Capua's version, the latter being more detailed.

35. Raymond of Capua, *Legenda*, 66–68.

36. Raymond of Capua, *Legenda*, 69; Valli, *L'adolescenza*, pp. 73–86.

37. For the rules governing the Sisters of Penance see Hyacinthe Laurent and Francesco Valli, eds., *Fontes Vitae S. Catharinae Senensis Historici: Tractatus de ordine FF. de Paenitentia S. Dominici di F. Tommaso da Siena* (Florence, 1938), pp. 169–78.

38. Raymond of Capua, *Legenda*, 70–72; Valli, *L'adolescenza*, pp. 87–98.

39. Raymond of Capua, *Legenda*, 73–76. Anonimo Fiorentino, *I miracoli*, p. 8, implies that Catherine and Lapa joined the Mantellata together, which would explain why Lapa plays such a large role in Raymond of Capua's version and also the statement in *I miracoli* that Giacomo died before Catherine took vows. However, there most likely is here an erroneous collapsing of events; Giacomo definitely died in 1368 and Catherine probably joined the Sisters of Penance in late 1364 or early 1365. The date of Lapa's vestition is unknown, but it probably occurred sometime after her illness in October 1370 and before Catherine's appearance in Florence in May 1374.

40. Raymond of Capua, *Legenda*, 73–79, simply asserts God's plan; Diana P. Cristadoro, *Dialogo e contestazione in Santa Caterina da Siena* (Poggibonsi, 1980), pp. 21–22, and Levasti, *My Servant, Catherine*, pp. 25–29, emphasize Catherine's reforming spirit; Augusta Drane, *Storia di S. Caterina da Siena e dei suoi compagni* (1887; reprint ed., Siena, 1911), p. 36, and Emilia De Sanctis

Rosmini, *Santa Caterina da Siena* (Turin, 1930) stress humility; François Vanden-broucke, *La spiritualité du Moyen âge* (Paris, 1961), pp. 489–98, suggests that Catherine had an active hostility to monasticism, a contention sharply denied in Francesco Scalvini, "La vera Caterina da Siena e la Caterina del benedettino Fr. Vandenbroucke," in *Saggi sulla spiritualitá domenicana*, ed. Innocenzo Colosio (Florence, 1961), pp. 151–84. Ample precedent for the choice of tertiary status by urban young women existed in the Low Countries, but for the Italian scene Catherine's decision was innovative.

41. Indeed, nothing in the regulations governing the various Dominican con-gregations of women required Lapa's consent. Catherine certainly was strong-willed enough to join on her own had she wished to do so and had she chosen the expected path toward second orders. See Laurent and Valli, eds., *Tractatus de or-dine FF. de Paenitentia S. Dominic*, p. 171, for admission rules requiring consent of living spouses but not of parents.

42. Raymond of Capua, *Legenda*, 220–23, 416. Giovanni Francesco Pico, *Com-pendio delle cose mirabili della beata Caterina da Racconigi* (Chieri and Turin, 1858), p. 100, discusses the earlier Catherine as an inspirational model for the later Catherine he is defending.

43. Caterina da Siena, *Epistolario*, esp. letters 196, 206, 218, 229, 233, 252, and 255 to Pope Gregory XI. See Grotanelli, ed., *Leggenda minore*, pp. 259–383, for letters among Catherine's disciples consistently referring to her as "dolcissima Mamma" (not Madre) and Innocenzo Taurisano, ed., *Santa Caterina da Siena nei ricordi dei discepoli* (Rome, 1957).

44. On her saving her brothers during the 1368 revolt in Siena, see Anonimo Fiorentino, *I miracoli*, pp. 12–13; Fawtier, *Sainte Catherine*, 1:158–59; and Levasti, *My Servant, Catherine*, p. 73. On her brothers' business misfortunes, see Grotanelli, ed., *Leggenda minore*, pp. 209–14; and for the correction to 1373 (not 1397 as misread by Fawtier and others) of the document proving their indebted-ness, see Laurent and Valli, eds., *Documenti*, pp. 26–30. Caterina da Siena, *Epis-tolario*, letters 10, 18, and 20 to Benincasa and letter 14 to her three brothers; The-seider's notes suggest that in addition to all his other troubles Catherine's brother Benincasa had a nagging, unhappy wife. For Catherine's stomach disorders and a vision of her brother frequenting a brothel, see Thomas Antonii de Senis, *Libellus de Supplemento*, p. 38. Also see Christopher N. L. Brooke, "Aspetti del matri-monio e della famiglia nel mondo di Santa Caterina e di San Bernardino," in *Atti del simposio internazionale cateriniano-bernardiniano*, ed. Domenico Maffei and Paolo Nardi (Siena, 1982), pp. 877–89, on Catherine's prayer that her brothers be impoverished.

45. Caterina da Siena, *Epistolario*, letters 1, 6, 117, and 240 to Lapa. The quota-tion is from letter 240. On Catherine's close relationship with Alessia, see Ray-mond of Capua, *Legenda*, 299 and 338; and Thomas Antonii de Senis, *Libellus de Supplemento*, p. 46.

46. Levasti, *My Servant, Catherine*, pp. 380–95. For Catherine's prayer, see Ca-terina da Siena, *Le orazioni*, ed. Giuliana Cavallini (Rome, 1978), p. 175; in her last recorded prayer on January 30, 1380, the day after her collapse, she repeated the offer of martyrdom (*denuo offero vitam meam pro dulci sponsa tua*); see ibid., p. 283. Also see Thomas Antonii de Senis, *Libellus de Supplemento*, pp. 268 ff., and esp. p. 268, which makes clear that Catherine *could* not swallow food or water but *would* not even wet her lips with a drop of water; Gigli, ed., *L'opere*, 1:481–89 for Barduccio di Piero Canigiani's account of her death; and Misciattelli, ed., *Epis-*

tolario, 6:148-53 for a different version of the same account.

47. Raymond of Capua, *Legenda*, 365.

3. THE CLOISTER

1. Ida Magli, "Il problema antropologico-culturale del monachesimo femminile," in *Enciclopedia delle religioni* (Florence, 1972), 3:627-41, and more recently her highly controversial *Gesù di Nazaret: Tabù e trasgressione* (Milan, 1982).

2. For the most complete available bibliography concerning Veronica Giuliani, see Felix a Mareto, "Bibliographia vitae et operum sanctae Veronicae Giuliani monialis capuccinae (1727-1961)," in *Sancta Veronica Giuliani: Vitae spiritualis magistra et exemplar tertio ab eius nativitate exeunte saeculo*, ed. Instituti Historici Ordinis Fr. Min. Capuccinorum (Rome, 1961), pp. 215-307; and in the same volume Marianus ab Alatri, "Conspectus bibliographicus decennalis (1951-1961) de S. Veronica Giuliani," pp. 344-60; and for approved works published since 1961 the *Bollettino del santuario di S. Veronica* (Città di Castello, 1965-).

3. For the official version of her infancy and early years, see Sacra Rituum Congregatione, *Beatificationis, & Canonizationis Ven. Servai Dei Sor. Veronicae de Julianis Monialis Professae in Ven. Monasterio S. Clarae Capuccinarum Tiferni seu Summarium Super Dubio An constet de Virtutibus Theologalibus Fide, & Spe, & Charitate erga Deum, & Proximum; ac de Cardinalibus Prudentia, Justitia, Fortitudine, & Temperantia, earumque adnexis in gradu heroico, in casu, & ad effectum &c.* (Rome, 1762), pp. 4-31; and Sacra Rituum Congregatione, *Beatificationis, & Canonizationis Ven. Servae Dei Sor. Veronicae de Julianis Monialis Professae in Ven. Monasterio S. Clarae Capuccinarum Tiferni. Responsio Ad Animadversiones·R.P. Fidei Promotoris Super Dubio An constet de Virtutibus Theologalibus Fide, Spe, & Caritate erga Deum, & Proximos, ac de Cardinalibus Prudentia, Justitia, Fortitudine, & Temperantia, earumque adnexis in gradu heroico, in case &c.* (Rome, 1763), pp. 2-7. Hereinafter cited respectively as *Summarium* and *Responsio* followed by the section number and page numbers. Oreste Fiorucci, see below note 4, asserts (5:5, n. 3) that the fourth sister also became a nun, but the contemporary accounts do not confirm this. For a typical example of hagiographical treatment of divinely inspired infancy see [G. Longino], *Vita della Madre Suor Veronica Giuliani Abbadessa Cappuccina nel Monastero di S. Chiara di Città di Castello* (Venice, 1734), pp. 5-7.

4. The most readily available edition of her writings is Oreste Fiorucci, ed., *"Un Tesoro Nascosto" ossia diario di S. Veronica Giuliani*, 5 vols. (Città di Castello, 1969-74). For variations in the explanatory notes see Petrus Pizzicaria, *Un tesoro nascosto ossia diario di S. Veronica Giuliani religiosa Cappuccina in Città di Castello scritto da lei medesima pubblicato e corredato di note dal P. Pietro Pizzicaria D.C.D.G.*, 8 vols. (Prato, 1895-1905) plus the ninth and tenth volumes edited by the Comitato per il II Centenario (Città di Castello, 1928). On the circumstances of the various autobiographies see Fiorucci's introduction to Veronica Giuliani, *Il mio Calvario: Autobiografia* (Città di Castello, 1976), pp. 9-16; and Antonio Minciotti, ed., *Il purgatorio d'amore (inedito) con indice veronichiano* (Città di Castello, 1980), pp. 27-46. The Fiorucci edition places the second autobiography in volume 1 and the others, confusingly numbered 1-4 (thus creating two second autobiographies) in volume 5. Hereinafter the autobiographical works will be cited as 1st *rel.*, 2d *rel.*, etc. (as Pizzicaria numbered them) followed by the volume and page number in the Fiorucci edition. Diary entries will be *Diario* fol-

lowed by the date and then the volume and page number in the Fiorucci edition. 1st *rel.*, 5:2–3; 2d *rel.*, 1:5; 3d *rel.*, 5:35; 5th *rel.*, 5:101. On Veronica Giuliani and Marian devotion, see Stefano De Fiores, "La mariologia al tempo di Santa Veronica Giuliani," in *La Madonna in Santa Veronica Giuliani*, ed. Curia Provinciale dei Frati Cappuccini-Ancona (Ascoli Piceno, 1982), pp. 19–35.

5. For an orthodox yet insightful treatment of this and other childhood incidents see Contessa de Villermont, *Vita di S. Veronica Giuliani*, 2d ed. (Città di Castello, 1977), pp. 3–82. For a serene reflection on her own childhood see 4th *rel.*, 5:85–94, written when she was fifty-four years old.

6. 1st *rel.*, 5:3; 2d *rel.*, 1:14; 3d *rel.*, 5:36–37.

7. 2d *rel.*, 1:2–4; 3d *rel.*, 5:39.

8. 2d *rel.*, 1:7, 14; for a sympathetic and generally accurate account see Raffaello Cioni, *S. Veronica Giuliani* (Città di Castello, 1965), esp. pp. 29–82.

9. 5th *rel.*, 5:100; Francesco Maria da San Marino, "La famiglia di Santa Veronica Giuliani," in Atti del Convegno di Studi (1978), *Santa Veronica Giuliani dottore della chiesa? . . .* (Città di Castello, 1979), pp. 117–28, is notably astute on this point.

10. The negative self-appraisal appears especially in the first three autobiographies and is much richer than the conventional humility of a saint would require. For the quote see 2d *rel.*, 1:14.

11. 1st *rel.*, 5:4–5; 3d *rel.*, 5:40; 5th *rel.*, 5:105. Historian Richard Kieckhefer, in a communication to the author, suggests that Orsola's desire to hold the host (*che con la mia mano la volevo pigliare*) may have involved sacerdotal aspirations or fantasies, which would suggest that the child may have intended to save her mother's soul rather than to replace her as death's victim.

12. 1st *rel.*, 5:6 also relates that Orsola stole wooden pieces to decorate her altars.

13. 3d *rel.*, 5:41; *Summarium* 6:17–24; see *Responsio* 6:3 for the official version that drops most such testimony, whether by Veronica herself or by witnesses, in favor of a flatly wrong assertion that she was quiet and cooperative. Yet even "official" biographers could not help but convey Orsolina's capriciousness; see, for example, Filippo Maria Salvadori, *Compendio della vita di Santa Veronica Giuliana Abbadessa delle Cappuccine nel Monastero di S. Chiara di Città di Castello tratto da' processi apostolici e dal libro scritto da Filippo Maria Salvadori* (Florence, 1839), pp. 11–12, on the potmaker.

14. See especially Appendix 1 in the Fiorucci ed. 5:137–42, for Veronica's account, probably written around 1700, of her arduous prayers to liberate her father from purgatory.

15. 1st *rel.*, 5:7; 3d *rel.*, 5:42–43.

16. 1st *rel.*, 5:7–8.

17. 1st *rel.*, 5:8–9; 2d *rel.*, 1:14–15; 3d *rel.*, 5:46.

18. 1st *rel.*, 5:9–11; 2d *rel.*, 1:16; 3d *rel.*, 5:47–49.

19. 1st *rel.*, 5:12; 3d *rel.*, 5:45.

20. In the fragment cited in n. 14 above Veronica laments that she did not do more to rescue her father from his sinful ways when he was still alive. Lazaro Iriarte, *S. Veronica Giuliani: esperienza e dottrina mistica* (Rome, 1981), p. 76, sets Veronica's return to Mercatello when she was not yet twelve but this seems too early and conflicts with Fiorucci, 5:17, n. 3, and with 3d *rel.*, 5:54.

21. 1st *rel.*, 5:13–15; 3d *rel.*, 5:53–54.

22. 1st *rel.*, 5:17.

23. 1st *rel.*, 5:18.

24. 1st *rel.*, 5:18–19; 2d *rel.*, 1:19.

25. 3d *rel.*, 5:55–56.

26. 1st *rel.*, 5:19; 3d *rel.*, 5:57–60.

27. 1st *rel.*, 5:22–23; 3d *rel.*, 5:61–65, 69.

28. 1st *rel.*, 5:24–26.

29. 2d *rel.*, 1:21–24; *Diario*, 23 Dec., 1693, 1:181–82 for a continued sense of desolation even years later.

30. 2d *rel.*, 1:25; 3d *rel.*, 5:77. For an understanding modern analysis of Veronica's difficulties as a novice see Desire des Planches, *La passione rinnovata: S. Veronica Giuliana*, 3d ed. (Siena, 1981), esp. pp. 102–12.

31. 2d *rel.*, 1:28–34, also tells of more positive experiences but all these are personal, not communal, and seem to occur despite the abbess and her ways; 3d *rel.*, 5:78–80.

32. See esp. Appendix 2 in the Fiorucci ed., 5:143–50, for Veronica's account, probably written in 1686 when she was twenty-six. On the length of her novitiate, see 2d *rel.*, 1:35.

33. Ibid., 150–52; 2d *rel.*, 1:36, 73–75.

34. On popular and official criteria for canonization, see Donald Weinstein and Rudolph M. Bell, *Saints and Society* (Chicago, 1982), pp. 141–63.

35. Her own description is found in 2d *rel.*, 1:86–91, and 96 on vomiting. For the testimony of others see *Summarium* 16:372–74.

36. 2d *rel.*, 1:56, 61, 119 on sleeplessness, hyperactivity, and hypothermy; *Summarium* 17:378–79, 383.

37. *Summarium* 16:374; 17:379.

38. *Summarium* 17:379–81, 384, 389.

39. *Responsio* 160–72:75–81.

40. 2d *rel.*, 1:124–25 on contaminated food; *Summarium* 16:367; 17:379, 383, 386.

41. *Summarium* 18:404.

42. *Summarium* 17:375, 386.

43. *Summarium* 17:378; 18:392, 397–98, 402, 405.

44. 2d *rel.*, 1:47–48, 86, on denial of communion; *Summarium* 16:365–66; 18:391, 393, 400.

45. 2d *rel.*, 1:44–45. For her letters to her sisters see Oreste Fiorucci, ed., *Lettere di Santa Veronica Giuliani* (Città di Castello, 1965), pp. 1–25; for other letters also see Davide M. Montagna, "Cinque autografi di S. Veronica Giuliani," *Moniales Ordinis Servorum* 3 (1965): 126–36. On diet see *Summarium* 17:385. Her instruments of flagellation, an unusually varied collection, along with other devices for self-mortification are carefully preserved and may be viewed at the Capuchin monastery in Città di Castello. I thank Dott. Alberto Ferroni for his kindness in allowing me to view and study these artifacts as well as the photocopies of the original *Diario. Responsio* 173–78:81–84; 182–87:113–17. On her "relapse," or severe fast, in the 1690s see *Diario* 20 March, 1695, 1:459 ff.

46. On Veronica's asceticism and mysticism see Metodio da Membro, *Misticismo e missione di S. Veronica Giuliani, Cappuccina (1660–1727)* (Milan, 1962), esp. pp. 49–88; on the content of the convent library see Iriarte, *Esperienza e dottrina mistica*, pp. 27–38; *Diario* 26 May, 1722, 4:610–12, is typical of the later entries and their serene trust in God.

47. *Summarium* 14:316–29.

4. WIVES AND MOTHERS

1. Maria Consiglia DeMatteis, ed., *Idee sulla donna nel Medioevo: Fonti e aspetti giuridici, antropologici, religiosi, sociali, e letterari della condizione femminile* (Bologna, 1981), esp. pp. 8–24; K. E. Borrensen, *Natura e ruolo della donna in Agostino e Tommaso* (La Cittadella, 1979), pp. 25–58. For an excellent introductory bibliography, see Ida Magli, *La donna: Un problema aperto: Guida alla ricerca antropologica* (Florence, 1974), pp. 243–97.

2. On the Cistercians see Caroline Walker Bynum, *Jesus as Mother: Studies in the Spirituality of the High Middle Ages* (Berkeley, 1982), esp. pp. 170–262 on sacerdotal functions. On women and heresy the classic work remains Gottfried Koch, *Die Frauenfrage und Ketzertum in Mittelalter* (Berlin, 1962); also see the materials cited in Bynum, *Jesus as Mother*, p. 249.

3. On Aquinas see Borrensen, *Natura e ruolo della donna*, pp. 144–90. On the Franciscans see Mariano D'Alatri, ed., *I frati penitenti di san Francesco nella società del Due e Trecento* (Rome, 1977); O. Schmucki, ed., *L'ordine della penitenza di san Francesco d'Assisi nel sec. XIII* (Rome, 1973); Mariano D'Alatri, ed., *Il movimento francescano della penitenza nella società medievale* (Rome, 1980); Anna Benvenuti Papi, "Le forme comunitarie della penitenza femminile francescana. Schede per un censimento toscano," in *Prime manifestazioni di vita comunitaria maschile e femminile nel movimento francescano della penitenza*, ed. R. Pazzelli and L. Temperini (Rome, 1982), pp. 389–449.

4. For Umiliana de' Cerchi the basic text is "Vita beatae Humilianae de Cerchis," *Acta Sanctorum*, May vol. 4 (Antwerp, 1685), pp. 385–418, hereinafter cited as *Vita* followed by the section number in the *Acta*. For Margaret of Cortona the text in the *Acta Sanctorum* is incomplete, and instead one should use the critical edition by [Lodovico da Pelago], *Antica leggenda della vita e de' miracoli di S. Margherita di Cortona scritta dal di lei confessore Fr. Giunta Bevegnati* (Lucca, 1793), hereinafter cited as *Antica leggenda* followed by the chapter and section numbers, or page numbers for Pelago's "dissertations" in part 2. This allows cross-reference to the more available *Acta Sanctorum* edition for the parts it contains. For Angela of Foligno, in the absence of a single critical text, I used the best three scholarly editions: M. Faloci Pulignani, ed., *L'autobiografia e gli scritti della beata Angela da Foligno pubblicati e annotati da un codice sublacense* (Città di Castello, 1932), hereinafter cited as FP followed by the section number; Paul Doncoeur, ed., *Le Livre de la bienheureuse Angèle de Foligno: Texte Latin* (Paris, 1925), hereinafter cited as Doncoeur followed by the page number; M. J. Ferré, *Sainte Angèle de Foligno. Le livre de l'expérience des vrais fidèles: Texte latin publié d'après le manuscrit d'Assise* (Paris, 1927), hereinafter cited as Ferré followed by the section number only where this differs from Faloci Pulignani.

5. *Vita* 1. For an excellent analysis of the political and economic struggles in which Umiliana's *vita* and cult must be understood, see Anna Benvenuti Papi, "Umiliana dei Cerchi. Nascita di un culto nella Firenze del Duecento," *Studi Francescani* 77 (1980): 87–117.

6. On family background, see Francesco Cionacci, *Vita della beata Umiliana de' Cerchi vedova fiorentina del Terz' Ordine di San Francesco* (Florence, 1682), pp. 16–17; and Anna Benvenuti Papi, "Il modello familiare nell' agiografia fiorentina tra duecento e quattrocento. Sviluppo di una negazione (da Umiliana dei Cerchi a Villana delle Botti)," *Nuova DWF* 16 (Spring 1981): 80–107.

7. *Vita* 2, 5; also see Guido Battelli, ed., *La leggenda della beata Umiliana de'*

Cerchi (Florence, 1932), p. 15, for a similar opening in an anonymous thirteenth-century vernacular account.

8. *Vita* 3–4.

9. *Vita* 6, 14, 16, 43; Cionacci, *Vita*, p. 25. On the plight of the widowed mother in a somewhat later period, see Christiane Klapisch-Zuber, "La 'mère cruelle.' Maternité, veuvage et dot dans la Florence des XIVᵉ–XVᵉ siècles," *Annales ESC* 38 (September-October 1983):1097–1109.

10. *Vita* 6, 7, 13, 25, 37, 51; Cionacci, *Vita*, p. 26.

11. I Tim. 5:9–15; *Vita* 7, 29.

12. *Vita* 8.

13. *Vita* 10, 11, 13, 35, 37.

14. *Vita* 16–21, 28, 30, 34.

15. *Vita* 34, 52–55.

16. *Antica leggenda* 5:23; 8:4; 12:49; dissertation, pp. 31–34. Francesco Marchese, *Vita di Santa Margarita di Cortona* (Venice, 1752), is monumental but adds nothing reliable to the basic *vita* by Friar Giunta.

17. *Antica leggenda* 1:2; 2:14.

18. *Antica leggenda* 1:2.

19. Ibid.

20. Ibid.

21. *Antica leggenda* 1:3; 2:1. The "I will be called a saint" phrase from the *Antica leggenda* is repeated in the remissorial proceedings of the Sacred Congregation of Rites held at Cortona from 1629 to 1640; see Ottorino Montenovesi, "I fioretti di Santa Margherita da Cortona," *Miscellanea Francescana* 46 (1946): 253–93, esp. 257. Other saints also had a "sense" of their holiness, but Margaret's explicit statement about her future place in heaven and the cultic veneration that would be accorded her is completely lacking in humility and due respect for Church authority.

22. *Antica leggenda* 2:2, 7; 5:40; 8:17; 9:27; dissertation, pp. 34–42, 112–15.

23. *Antica leggenda* 4:1; 9:13; on the story of Dante's visit, see Mariano Nuti, *Margherita da Cortona: La sua leggenda e la storia* (Rome, 1951), pp. 122–53.

24. *Antica leggenda* 2:14; 4:2; 8:4.

25. Nuti, *Margherita da Cortona*, pp. 74–81; *Antica leggenda* 5:3, 6, 10.

26. *Antica leggenda* 10:7.

27. Eliodoro Mariani, ed., *Leggenda della vita e dei miracoli di santa Margherita da Cortona* (Vicenza, 1978), p. xiii, in the preface of his fine modern translation of the *Antica leggenda* emphasizes the centrality of Margaret's links to social realities.

28. *Antica leggenda* 2:1, 3.

29. *Antica leggenda* 2:4–5, 8; 5:2.

30. *Antica leggenda* 2:15.

31. *Antica leggenda* 3:1.

32. *Antica leggenda* 3:2.

33. *Antica leggenda* 3:5; 4:5; 7:17; 10:5.

34. *Antica leggenda* 3:7; 5:8.

35. *Antica leggenda* 5:43; 6:18; 9:9, 42; 10:9.

36. *Antica leggenda* 11:14; dissertation, pp. 52–61, on Margaret's confessors. For the wider context see Anna Benvenuti Papi, "Margherita Filia Jerusalem. Santa Margherita da Cortona ed il superamento mistico della crociata," in *Toscana e Terrasanta nel medioevo* (Florence, 1982), pp. 117–37.

37. For a good early bibliography see Michele Faloci Pulignani, *Saggio biblio-grafico sulla vita e sugli opuscoli della beata Angela da Foligno*, 2d ed. (Foligno, 1889). For a typically embellished account by the author of one of the excellent critical editions which in reality show how little is known of Angela's life see M. J. Ferré, *La spiritualité de Sainte Angèle de Foligno* (Paris, 1927), esp. pp. 10–17. By contrast, see his "Les principales dates de la vie d'Angèle de Foligno," *Revue d'histoire franciscaine* 2 (1925): 21–34. Even Arrigo Levasti seems to fall back on these hagiographic speculations; see his *Mistici del Duecento e del Trecento* (Milan, 1935), p. 990.

38. Ferré, FP 34; Doncoeur, p. 21.

39. Ferré, FP 34, 35; Doncoeur, pp. 22–23.

40. Ibid.

41. Faloci Pulignani, ed., *L'autobiografia*, pp. x–xxx; Doncoeur, ed., *Le livre*, pp. ix–xli; M. J. Ferré, ed., *Le livre*, pp. xli–xlvii; Pasquale Valugani, *L'esperienza mistica della beata Angela da Foligno nel racconto di Frate Arnaldo* (Milan, 1964), pp. 14–41.

42. Ferré, FP 3–12; Doncoeur, pp. 7–11.

43. Ferré, FP 36; Doncoeur, p. 27.

44. Ferré, FP 21; Doncoeur, p. 15.

45. Ferré, FP 64, 71, 98–99, 101; Doncoeur, pp. 56, 64, 80, 81.

46. Ferré, FP 36, 42, 44, 64; Doncoeur, pp. 27, 32–33, 34–35, 58.

47. Ferré 48, 49, 53, 61, 175–77, 183; FP 48, 49, 53, 61, 134–36, 182–83; Doncoeur, pp. 39–40, 40–41, 46–47, 53, 152–54, 161–65.

48. Ferré 52, 74, 135; FP 52, 74, 169; Doncoeur, pp. 46, 65, 117–18.

49. Sergio Andreoli, "La beata Angela da Foligno contempla Gesù Cristo," *L'Italia Francescana* 55 (1980): 35–55; Antonio Blasucci, "Il Cristocentrismo spirituale e la vocazione alla mistica in una grande Beata francescana," *Vita Cristiana* 13 (1941): 44–71; Innocenzo Colosio, "La Beata Angela da Foligno," *Rivista di Ascetica e Mistica* 9, no. 6 (1964): 3–28.

50. Ferré, FP 44, 45, 88; Doncoeur, pp. 34–35, 36–37, 72–73.

51. Ferré 130; FP 156; Doncoeur, pp. 107–8.

52. Ferré 172–74, 190–207; FP 130–33, 214–31; Doncoeur, pp. 150–52, 173–82.

53. Ferré 58, 186, 159, pp. 516–17; FP 58, 232–33, 236, 256; Doncoeur, pp. 50, 165–66, 136–37, 199.

54. Ferré 121, pp. 494–99; FP 121, 243–44; Doncoeur, pp. 96, 188–90.

5. HISTORICAL DIMENSIONS: ASCENT

1. These and other numerical findings are drawn from a new data base compiled by the author in a format similar to that described at length in Donald Weinstein and Rudolph M. Bell, *Saints and Society: The Two Worlds of Western Christendom 1000–1700* (Chicago, 1982), pp. 281–84. The 261 cases are drawn from the *Bibliotheca Sanctorum*, 12 vols. (Rome, 1961), and include all females listed therein who were born in Italy (defined by its modern boundaries) and who died after 1199. A machine-readable copy of the data set and a complete coding guide may be obtained with the author's permission from the Rutgers University Center for Computational Information Services Library. Because the total number of cases is small, and the number for whom abundant information exists is even smaller, the numerical findings here and in the tables that follow should be taken only to indicate general trends. Since a "sample" is not involved, the usual tests of

statistical significance are not appropriate. Whether the data have historical significance depends on the question being raised, as well as on the degree of concern with "representativeness." In the present instance, for example, I take the high proportion of youngest children among all saints, as well as the high proportion of them who were known for compulsive fasting, to be worthy of some effort at explanation. But the numbers themselves reveal only what is to be explained, not the solution ipso facto to a useful historical problem. Any explanation can come only by intensive analysis of individual *vitae*, and these are too few to allow more extensive, multivariate statistical treatment.

2. For the biblical references see Matt. 4:1-4 and Luke 4:1-4. Mark 1:12-13 does not mention fasting or any other specific temptation.

3. Relevant passages are Matt. 9:14-15, 11:19, 12:1-8, and 15:16-20; Mark 2:18-20, 23-28, and 7:18-19; and Luke 5:33-35, 6:1-5, 7:33-34, 10:7, and 22:30.

4. Relevant passages are: Acts 9:9; Rom. 14:2-3, 20-21; Col. 2:16-23; 2 Tim. 3:6-9; and Titus 2:3-5.

5. Here I am relying heavily on secondary materials. Ernesto Buonaiuti, *Le origini dell' ascetismo cristiano* (Pinerolo, 1928), is the fundamental work. Herbert Musurillo, "The Problem of Ascetical Fasting in the Greek Patristic Writers," *Traditio* 12 (1956): 1-64, explores fully the varieties of religious motivation revealed in the patristic sources. Among other useful works are Alfonso M. di Nola, "Ascesi," *Enciclopedia delle religioni* (Florence, 1970): 1:626-38; Maurilio Adriani, "Quadro storico-religioso del monachesimo," *Enciclopedia delle religioni* 4:575-630; Ernesto Buonaiuti, *I rapporti sessuali nell' esperienza religiosa del mondo mediterraneo*, 2d ed. (Rome, 1949), esp. pp. 71-90; and A. J. Festugière, *Les moines d'orient: Culture ou sainteté*, vol. 1 (Paris, 1961), pp. 59-74. Also see W. K. C. Guthrie, *A History of Greek Philosophy*, vol. 1 (London, 1962), pp. 146-340 on the Pythagoreans.

6. Gottardo Gottardi, ed., *Storia Lausiaca* (Siena, 1961), esp. pts. 34, 41, 57, 61, and 69; also see Ernesto Buonaiuti, *Storia del Cristianesimo*, vol. 1 (Milan, 1942), esp. pp. 464-95, on monasticism.

7. Gregorie de Nysse, *Traité de la virginité*, trans. Michel Aubineau (Paris, 1966); Saint Gregory of Nyssa, *Ascetical Works*, trans. Virginia Callahan (Washington, D.C., 1967), p. 71, for the quote, and pp. 163-91, for an important early example of detailed hagiography that does *not* emphasize fasting for women.

8. Lorenzo Dattrino, *Il primo monachismo* (Rome, 1984), pp. 83-120, for book 5 of Cassian's *Cenobitic Institutions* and more generally for an excellent discussion of this writer's role in shaping western cenobitic practices. This is not to say that there were no practitioners of harsh asceticism; see Carl A. Mounteer, "Guilt, Martyrdom, and Monasticism," *Journal of Psychohistory* 9, no. 2 (Fall 1981): 145-71.

9. *Rules of St. Benedict*, chap. 39.

10. *Acta Sanctorum*, May vol. 7 (Antwerp, 1688), pp. 144-64; Giuseppe Sainati, *Vite dei santi, beati e servi di Dio nati nella diocesi pisana* (Pisa, 1884), pp. 132-49; some of the text problems are pointed out in Fusio Bartorelli, *Santa Bona di Pisa* (Bari, 1960).

11. The *Acta* life is not the earliest available and instead I used Olinto Pogni, ed., *Vita di S. Verdiana d'incognito autore, estratta dal codice latino trecentesco esistente nella Biblioteca Mediceo-Laurenziana di Firenze* (Empoli, 1936).

12. For Gerardesca see *Acta Sanctorum*, May vol. 7, pp. 164-80, and Sainati,

Vite dei santi, pp. 158−69; for Sperandea see *Acta Sanctorum*, September vol. 3 (Antwerp, 1750), pp. 890−913, and a modern devotional life by Guglielmo Malazampa, *Vita di S. Sperandia Vergine Protettrice di Cingoli* (Cingoli, 1901).

13. Nello Vian, ed., *Il processo di Santa Chiara d'Assisi* (Milan, 1962), pp. 7−8, 15−16; Zeffirino Lazzeri, "Il processo di canonizzazione di S. Chiara d'Assisi," *Archivum Franciscanum Historicum* 13, fasc. iii−iv (July-October 1920): 403−507.

14. On Francis and Clare see *Fonti Francescane* (Padua, 1980). Substantial additional evidence on gender distinctions with regard to fasting is being brought to light by Caroline Bynum, who shared with me her forthcoming essay, "Fast, Feast and Flesh: The Religious Significance of Food to Medieval Women." It is my belief that the range and different emphases of Bynum's work will enhance whatever I have been able to contribute to our understanding of medieval female piety in the present study; it did not seem to us to be useful or necessary at this point, when we are doing related but totally independent work still in progress, to divide up the turf too narrowly or to direct our notes to each other's interpretations rather than to the sources.

15. *Fonti Francescane*, p. 2252 for the rules and p. 2292 for the quotation. See Richard Kieckhefer, *Unquiet Souls: Fourteenth-Century Saints and Their Religious Milieu* (Chicago, 1984), p. 13, for a similar admonition in the *vita* of Mary of Oignies.

16. Tommaso da Celano(?), *Vita di S. Chiara Vergine d'Assisi*, trans. Fausta Casolini, 3d ed. (Assisi, 1976), pp. 35−37.

17. *Fonti Francescane*, pp. 2415−17; *Analecta Franciscana* (Quaracchi, 1897), 3:173−82.

18. Ibid., pp. 2402−4.

19. Carla Casagrande, ed., *Prediche alle donne del secolo XIII* (Milan, 1978), pp. 61−112, for a selection of the Franciscan Gilberto da Tournai's sermons inviting pious women to follow Clare's example.

20. See n. 1 above for the basis of these numerical findings.

21. Bernardi Mariae de Rubeis, *Vita Beatae Benvenutae Bojanae de Civitate Austria in Provincia Forijulii, Quae nunc primum latine, ex Originali Codice Ms. in lucem prodit cum Praefatione, et Annotationibus* (Venice, 1757); also see M. C. de Ganay, *Les bienheureuses dominicaines*, 3d ed. (Paris, 1924), pp. 91−108; Anonymous, *Vita della beata Benvenuta Bojani del terz' ordine di San Domenico coll' aggiunta di alcune note tratte dal Padre de Rubeis* (Udine, 1848), pp. xi−xxv on various editions of the *vita*; and *Acta Sanctorum*, October vol. 13 (Antwerp, 1883), pp. 145−85.

22. *Acta*, chap. 1; de Rubeis, *Vita*, chaps. 2 and 3; anon., *Vita*, pp. 11−12, 20−21.

23. *Acta*, chap. 1; de Rubeis, *Vita*, chap. 4; and anon., *Vita*, pp. 24−27.

24. *Acta*, chap. 2; de Rubeis, *Vita*, chap. 4; and anon., *Vita*, pp. 27, 35−36, and 39.

25. *Acta*, chaps. 3 and 5; de Rubeis, *Vita*, chaps. 6 and 10; and anon., *Vita*, pp. 41−44.

26. *Acta*, chap. 3; de Rubeis, *Vita*, chap. 7; and anon., *Vita*, pp. 50−51, 54.

27. *Acta*, chaps. 4, 8, and 11; de Rubeis, *Vita*, chaps. 8−25; and anon., *Vita*, pp. 56−68, 82−83, 137, and 143−48.

28. Luigi Passarini, ed., *Leggenda della beata Giovanna (detta Vanna) d'Orvieto* (Rome, 1879), provides an early fifteenth-century version (the earliest

known) of the *vita* by Joan's contemporary, Friar Giacomo Scalza. It is attributed to "Caffarini" and may have been copied in 1400.

29. *Acta Sanctorum*, April vol. 2 (Antwerp, 1675), chap. 1; also see *Compendium vitae, virtutem, et miraculorum, necnon actorum in causa canonizationis B. Agnetis Montis Politiani monialis professae Ordinis Praedicatorum* (Rome, 1726) for ongoing concern with explaining her eating habits.

30. *Acta*, chaps. 7 and 8.

31. *Acta*, chap. 13 and Part 2: chaps. 6, 12, and 13.

32. Placido Tommaso Lugano, ed., *I processi inediti per Francesca Bussa dei Ponziani (Santa Francesca Romana) 1440–1453* (Vatican City, 1945); Placido Tommaso Lugano, "I processi del 1440 e del 1451," *Rivista Storica Benedettina* 3 (1908): 42–110; Mariano Armellini, ed., *Vita di S. Francesca Romana scritta nell' idioma volgare di Roma del secolo XV (1469)* (Rome, 1882); a useful modern study is Berthem-Bontoux [pseud. for Bontoux, Berthe M.], *Sainte Françoise Romaine et son temps (1384–1440)* (Paris, 1931); Giulio Orsino, *Vita di S. Francesca Romana* (Padua, 1616) adds little and Virgilio Cepari, *Vita di S. Francesca, fondatrice dell' Oblate di Torre de' Specchi* (Rome, 1641) embellishes too much for historical use. The Matteotti biography is most easily found in *Acta Sanctorum*, March vol. 2 (Antwerp, 1668), pp. 92–103, and is followed by his summaries of her visions (pp. 103–52) and diabolic conflicts (pp. 152–75).

33. Arnold Esch, "Tre sante ed il loro ambiente sociale a Roma: S. Francesca Romana, S. Brigida di Svezia e S. Caterina da Siena," in *Atti del simposio internazionale cateriniano-bernardiniano: Siena, 17–20 aprile 1980*, ed. Domenico Maffei and Paolo Nardi (Siena, 1982), pp. 89–120. See also his "Die Zeugenaussagen im Heiligsprechungverfahren für S. Francesca Romana als Quelle zur Sozialgeschicte Roms im frühen Quattrocento," *Quellen und Forschungen aus italienischen Archiven und Bibliotheken* 53 (1973): 93–151.

34. *Processi*, pp. 8–11.

35. *Processi*, pp. 12–18, 39–40, and 243.

36. *Processi*, pp. 50–58 and 246–48.

37. Quoted, for example, in Herbert Thurston and Donald Attwater, eds., *Butler's Lives of the Saints* (New York, 1956), 1:530.

38. *Acta*, pp. 152–75; *Processi*, pp. 50–58.

39. Jacob Burckhardt, *The Civilization of the Renaissance in Italy*, Modern Library ed. (New York, 1954), p. 292.

40. The *Acta* contains only a brief mention of Eustochia among the *praetermissi*, but the erudite work of Michele Catalano now makes this *vita* accessible. See Geronima Vaccari and Cecilia de Ansalono, *La leggenda della beata Eustochia da Messina. Testo volgare del sec. XV restituito all' originaria lezione*, 2d ed. Michele Catalano (Messina, 1950), pp. 6–52 on authorship questions. For a recently discovered mystical work on the Passion attributed to Eustochia see Francesco Terrizzi, ed., *Il "libro della Passione" scritto dalla b. Eustochia Calafato, clarissa messinese (1434–1485)* (Messina, 1975). The best starting point on the subject of female religious language in the late Middle Ages is Caroline Bynum Walker, "Women's Stories, Women's Symbols: A Critique of Victor Turner's Theory of Liminality," in *Anthropology and the Study of Religion*, eds. Robert L. Moore and Frank E. Reynolds (Chicago, 1984), pp. 105–24.

41. Catalano, ed., *La leggenda*, pp. 53–57; Terrizzi, ed., *Il Libro*, pp. 5–6.

42. Ibid., pp. 56–61.

43. Ibid., p. 65.

44. Ibid., pp. 58−69.

45. Ibid., pp. 74−76.

46. Ibid., pp. 85−87, 135−36, and 175.

47. Ibid., pp. 274−75.

48. Caroline Walker Bynum, *Jesus as Mother: Studies in the Spirituality of the High Middle Ages* (Berkeley, 1982), pp. 170−262, as well as her published and forthcoming works cited in chap. 2, n. 6 and chap. 5, n. 14.

49. Unpublished paper by Jane Teepe. The respective percentages for compulsive fasting are 26 percent of those who never married, 21 percent of married saints who had no children, and 28 percent of those who had married and are known to have borne children.

6. HISTORICAL DIMENSIONS: DECLINE

1. Pierre Delooz, *Sociologie et canonisations* (Liège, 1969), pp. 105−7.

2. *Acta Sanctorum*, May vol. 5 (Antwerp, 1685), pp. 319*-98* contains the life by Sebastiano degli Angeli written between 1501 and 1506, within five years of Colomba's death. Useful for its literary flourishes but essentially drawn from this account is Leandro degli Alberti, *Vita della Beata Colomba da Rieto dil Terzo ordine di S. Domenego: Sepolta a Perugia* (Bologna, 1521). [Domenico Viretti], *Vita della Beata Colomba da Rieti* (Perugia, 1777) is important for evidence on changing emphasis in hagiography and for its efforts to untangle the confused chronology of earlier accounts. Among the modern accounts two are noteworthy for their scholarly contributions: Ettore Ricci, *Storia della B. Colomba da Rieti* (Perugia, 1901); and Baleoneus Astur, *Colomba da Rieti: "La seconda Caterina da Siena" 1467−1501* (Rome, 1967). The latter is especially valuable for its extensive use of a vernacular version of Sebastiano degli Angeli's *vita*, written by himself, that was unknown to the Bollandists. It clarifies and amplifies numerous points that are obscure or simply incorrect in the faulty transcription contained in the *Acta*. On the wider context of Colomba as a "living saint" see the insightful analysis of Gabriella Zarri, "Le sante vive. Per una tipologia della santità femminile nel primo Cinquecento," *Annali dell' Istituto Storico Italo-germanico in Trento* 6 (1980): 371−445. She dates the decline of the female saint who modeled herself on Catherine of Siena at 1530, rather than around 1500 as I propose. Since Zarri concentrates on public influence, cult activity, and promotion by the orders, her date makes sense. My concern, however, is with the inner dynamic of these *vitae* and with the immediate response of male clerics to female innovation; from this perspective, as Zarri concedes in her analysis of heresy and sorcery charges, holy women were increasingly viewed with skepticism and suspicion even before the Reformation.

3. *Acta*, chap. 23; Leandro, chaps. 21−22; [Viretti], pp. 40−41; Astur, pp. 100−104.

4. *Acta*, chap. 24; Leandro, chap. 22; Astur, pp. 103−6.

5. Leandro, chap. 23; [Viretti], p. 42 falls back on the divine help *topos* and skips the grim details; Astur, pp. 107−8.

6. Leandro, chap. 21; [Viretti], pp. 43−46; on "popular mentality" see Giuseppe Balestra da Loreto, *Vita della B. Colomba da Rieti, Fondatrice del nobilissimo Monastero delle Colombe di Perugia. Raccolta da più Vite stampate, e manuscritte, e de Processi fabricati per la sua Canonizzazione in Perugia* (Perugia,

1652), p. 204, which lists 167 witnesses to her sanctity divided as follows: sixteen medical doctors, eleven priests, forty-seven gentlemen, four canons, nineteen monks, twenty nuns, twenty-six citizens, and twenty-four plebians. For a comparison with earlier hagiographical treatment of attempted rape, see the wondrous supernatural interventions that protected Catherine of Sweden, while she was in Rome, from the designs of Latino Orsini and told in *Acta Sanctorum*, March vol. 3 (Antwerp, 1668), pp. 503–31, esp. chap. 3.

7. *Acta*, chap. 40; Leandro, chaps. 33 and 38; [Viretti], p. 66; Astur, p. 190.

8. Leandro, chaps. 25, 28, 30, and 33 for the quote; Astur, p. 192.

9. Leandro, chap 9; [Viretti], pp. 21–22; other details are added in Alberto Fabri, *La Colomba Angelica overo la vita, et historia della serva di Dio Suor Colomba detta communemente La Beata Colomba da Rieti del Terzo Ordine di Penitenza di S. Domenico* (Rome, 1650), pp. 11, 21–22.

10. Ricci, pp. 9–10, 22–39 is especially astute in analyzing the familial dimensions of Colomba's spiritual quest; Astur, p. 66.

11. *Acta*, chap. 18; Astur, pp. 69, 76, 91, and 128. Zarri, "Le sante vive," pp. 410–12 concludes that abstinence from food was considered a sign of sanctity even in the sixteenth century, but the very *vitae* she cites show that prelates increasingly were questioning this "popular" belief.

12. *Acta*, chap. 32; [Viretti], pp. 70–71; Astur, pp. 141–43, 163, 173–76, 178–80.

13. Leandro, chaps. 29, 43, 44; [Viretti], pp. 94, 107; Astur, pp. 227–28 citing the vernacular version, chaps. 37 and 40, and its differences from the *Acta* text.

14. *Acta Sanctorum*, June vol. 3 (Antwerp, 1701), pp. 667–800; Giuseppe Bagolini and Lodovico Ferretti, *La beata Osanna Andreasi, Vita* (Florence, 1905), pp. 42–79, esp. p. 71 on her eating habits; also see Francesco da Ferrara, *La vita della beata Osanna da Mantova, partita in sei libri* (Mantua, 1590), pp. 12–14 and 20–22 for a lively vernacular account of Osanna's fasting and the persecution by other tertiaries.

15. On inconsistent infant feeding and anorexia, see esp. Hilde Bruch, *Eating Disorders: Obesity, Anorexia Nervosa, and the Person Within* (New York, 1973), pp. 55–58. On Catherine's childhood see Giovanni Francesco Pico [updated by Pietro Martire Morelli], *Compendio delle cose mirabili della beata Caterina da Racconigi* (Chieri and Turin, 1858 reprint of 1681 original), book 1, chaps. 1 and 4; book 2, chaps. 2 and 9; book 5, chaps. 3–5; Giovanni Giovenale Ancina, *Vita della beata Caterina Matei da Raconisio* (reprint ed. of MS, Mondovi, 1899), pp. 2–22; Giovanni Bonetti, *Vita della Beata Caterina Mattei* (Turin, 1878), pp. 33–52, based on a manuscript *vita* by her confessor, Gabriele Dolce da Savigliano in the parochial archives at Garessio. Also see Zarri, "Le sante vive," pp. 389–91.

16. On Catherine's fasting see Pico, book 1, chap. 2; book 2, chap. 1; book 2, chap. 4 for explicit comparison with Colomba da Rieti; book 6, chaps. 10 and 11; Ancina, p. 115; on sexual temptation see Pico, book 6, chap. 12 and books 7 and 8; Bonetti, pp. 71–73; and Ancina, pp. 87–90.

17. On *Strix* see Peter Burke, "Witchcraft and Magic in Renaissance Italy: Gianfrancesco Pico and His Strix," in *The Damned Art: Essays in the Literature of Witchcraft*, ed. Sidney Angelo (London, 1977), pp. 32–52; Giovanni Bosco, *Vie de la bienheurese Catherine de Racconigi de l'ordre de la penitence de Saint-Dominique* (Paris, 1865), pp. 69–73; Bonetti, pp. 112–17; Pico, book 5, chap. 12 for the quotation, italics added; book 9, chap. 3 on counseling nobles.

18. Pico, book 1, chaps. 3 and 16; book 2 Proemio and chap. 14; and book 5 on defense of Catherine against her enemies; on cures of his family see Pico, book 3, chap. 14 and book 5, chap. 16.

19. Umile Bonzi da Genova, *S. Caterina Fieschi Adorni*, vol. 1, "Teologia mistica di S. Caterina da Genova" (Turin, 1961), vol. 2, "Edizione critica dei manoscritti cateriniani" (Turin, 1962), supersedes all other works on this saint and, even if it cannot put to rest all the controversy about her, sets the disputes on a more fruitful path. The text editions of vol. 2 render the *Acta* account obsolete. In Weinstein and Bell, *Saints and Society*, pp. 95–96, we concentrated on Giuliano's brutal treatment, but further reflection leads me to conclude that such emphasis was misplaced. For Simeon's *vita* see *Acta Sanctorum*, January vol. 1 (Antwerp, 1643), pp. 261–64. Benedictus XIV, *De servorum Dei beatificatione et beatorum canonizatione* (Bologna, 1737), pp. 375–77, gives a list of saintly fasters and how to distinguish them from cases of possession. Also see Hippolyte Delehaye, *Les saints stylites* (Paris, 1923). Friedrich von Hügel, *The Mystical Element of Religion as Studied in Saint Catherine of Geona and her Friends*, 2 vols. (London, 1908), remains of great importance. For writings attributed to her see S. Caterina da Genova, *Opere*, ed. Giuseppe de Libero (Milan, 1963).

20. Paula Gambara-Costa to Blessed Angelo of Chiavasso, quoted in Roberto Bollano da Cervasca, *Vita, e venerazione della B. Paola Gambara-Costa del terz' ordine del serafico Padre S. Francesco* (Turin, 1765), pp. 25–26.

21. Ibid., pp. 43–51.

22. Ignazio del Nente, *Vita e costumi ed intelligenze spirituali della venerabil madre Suor Domenica dal Paradiso, fondatrice del Monastero della Croce di Firenze dell' ordine di S. Domenico*, 2d ed. (Florence, 1743), pp. 28–55.

23. Ibid., pp. 84–85.

24. Ibid., pp. 114–31.

25. Ibid., pp. 134–54, 190–92 on later loss of sense of taste and smell. Also see Benedetto Maria Borghigiani, *Intera narrazione della vita, costumi, e intelligenze spirituali della venerabile sposa di Gesù Suor Domenica dal Paradiso, fondatrice del Monastero della Croce di Firenze* (Florence, 1719), pp. 266–67, 374, 400–401, and 470–72.

26. Ibid., pp. 157–59.

27. Ibid., pp. 162–63.

28. Ibid., pp. 254–57; *Bibliotheca Sanctorum* (Rome, 1961), 4:678–80. Continued interest in her case is revealed in anonymous, *Fatti ammirabili ed istruttivi nella vita della Serva di Dio Suor Maria Domenica del Cuor di Gesù, fondatrice primaria delle Religiose Osservanti del Terzo Ordine di S. Domenico in Conegliano. Opera donata alle suore, ed indiritta alle educande del detto monistero* (Venice, 1742), and Aladino Moriconi, *La Venerabile Suor Domenica dal Paradiso: La popolare mistica taumaturga del secolo d'oro fiorentino 1473–1553 ancora tra noi viventi coi luminosi esempi di sua vita colle sue profezie e colle sue intercessioni* (Florence, 1943).

29. On the punishment of the nun of Monza, see Piero Misciatelli, *Caterina Vannini: Una cortigiana convertita senese e il cardinale Federigo Borromeo alla luce di un epistolario inedito* (Milan, 1932), pp. 11–12; Agostino Saba, *Federico Borromeo e i mistici del suo tempo con la vita e la corrispondenza inedita di Caterina Vannini da Siena* (Florence, 1933), pp. 127–30 for chaps. 1–3 of the *vita* originally published in 1618.

30. Saba, *Federico Borromeo*, pp. 131–35, for chaps. 4–6.

31. Ibid., pp. 138–91, for the remainder of the *vita*; the reevaluation of Borromeo and the examination of canonization proceedings is from Misciatelli, *Caterina Vannini*, pp. 45–47, 61–89. For Manzoni's portrait of Borromeo see *I promessi sposi*, chap. 22.

32. Caterina Vannini to Cardinal Federigo Borromeo, undated letters using Misciatelli's numbering; see especially letters 3, 5, 17, 25, 29, and 30 for the points raised here.

33. For the controversy engendered by Misciatelli's work, in addition to Saba, *Federico Borromeo*, see Giovanni Cecchini, "Precisazioni intorno al carteggio di Caterina Vannini col cardinale F. Borromeo," *Osservatore Romano* (Nov. 5–6, 1934); "L'epistolario di una mistica senese," *La Nazione* (March 16, 1933); *Bibliotheca Sanctorum* 12:948–50; Giovanni Cecchini, "Federigo Borromeo e Caterina Vannini in due recenti pubblicazioni," *Bullettino senese di storia patria*, n.s. 4 (1933): 314–46. On the Mary Magdalen theme see Richard Kieckhefer, *Unquiet Souls: Fourteenth-Century Saints and Their Religious Milieu* (Chicago, 1984), pp. 33–35.

34. Maria Pacifica del Tovaglia, "Breve Ragguaglio della Vita della Santa Madre fatto dalla Madre Suor Maria Pacifica del Tovaglia per ordine del Benvenuti secondo confessore della Santa," in *Tutte le opere di Santa Maria Maddalena de' Pazzi: I Quaranta Giorni*, ed. Fulvio Nardoni (Florence, 1960), pp. 69–70.

35. The confessors' biographies are Vincenzo Puccini, *La vita di Santa Maria Maddalena de' Pazzi nobile Fiorentina*, first published in 1609 with variations in the title of the (Bologna, 1707) edition which I used, and Virgilio Cepari, *Vita della serafica vergine S. Maria Maddalena de' Pazzi fiorentina dell' ordine carmelitano*, first published in 1669 and reprinted in the (Prato, 1884) edition I used. Also essential are the seven volumes of her works edited by Nardoni and Ludovico Saggi, *Summarium actionum, virtutum et miraculorum servae dei Mariae Magdalenae de Pazzis ordinis carmelitarum ex processu remissoriali desumptorum* (Rome, 1965). For the modern controversy about her psyche see Eric Dingwall, *Very Peculiar People: Portrait Studies in the Queer, the Abnormal and the Uncanny* (New Hyde Park, N.Y., 1962), pp. 119–44; Leonardo Ancona, "S. Maria Maddalena de' Pazzi alla luce della psicologia," *Carmelus* 13, fasc. 1 (1966): 3–20; and Claudio Catena, "Le malattie di S. Maria Maddalena de' Pazzi," *Carmelus* 16, fasc. 1 (1969): 70–141. For the quotation see Dingwall, *Very Peculiar People*, p. 127. Also important for its psychological insight is Benedetta Papasogli and Bruno Secondin, *La parabola delle due spose: Vita di Santa Maria Maddalena de' Pazzi* (Turin, 1976).

36. For the connection with Catherine of Siena see S. Thor-Salviat, *La dottrina spirituale di Santa Maria Maddalena de' Pazzi* (Florence, 1939), esp. p. 243, and more generally Ermano Arcilli, *Santa Maria Maddalena de' Pazzi: Estasi, dottrina, influsso* (Rome, 1967) with its annotated bibliography of 473 items.

37. For the quotation see Maria Pacifica del Tovaglia, "Breve ragguaglio," p. 76. On other childhood incidents see Saggi, ed., *Summarium*, pp. 42–48; Cepari, *Vita*, chaps. 2 and 5; and Puccini, *La vita*, chaps. 1–7.

38. For the quotation see Maria Pacifica del Tovaglia, "Breve ragguaglio," p. 84. On the convent at Cortona see Saggi, ed., *Summarium*, pp. 49–57; Cepari, *Vita*, chaps. 9–12; and Puccini, *La vita*, chap. 8.

39. Saggi, ed., *Summarium*, pp. 58–65; Cepari, *Vita*, chaps. 12 for the maternal contest and 15–17; Puccini, *La vita*, chaps. 9–13.

40. For the quotation see Maria Pacifica del Tovaglia, "Breve ragguaglio," p. 90. On the illness see ibid., pp. 91–92; Saggi, ed., *Summarium*, pp. 58–65; Cepari, *Vita*, chaps. 18–21 and 25; Puccini, *La vita*, chaps. 15–21; and the analyses of Dingwall, Ancona, and Catena cited in n. 35 above. In addition to *The Forty Days* itself, see Ernest E. Larkin, "The Ecstasies of the Forty Days," *Carmelus* 1, fasc. 1 (1954): 29–71. On Maria Bartolomea Bagnesi see [Agostino Campi], *Vita della beata Maria Bartolomea Bagnesi, nobile fiorentina del Terz' Ordine di S. Domenico scritta da un sacerdote della Compania di Gesù* (Parma, 1804, printing of the biography by her confessor) or *Acta Sanctorum*, May vol. 6 appendix (Venice, 1739), pp. 321–48. In her infancy this holy woman nearly starved to death at the breast of a wetnurse who had too little milk but kept the child anyway and let her crawl around licking bread crumbs or begging an egg. This is a strong case for connecting holy anorexia to infant feeding practices, especially considering that the adult saint felt grateful for her deprivation in infancy, which she believed had set her on the path of asceticism and illness that kept her bedridden for forty years and allowed her to grow spiritually.

41. Saggi, ed., *Summarium*, pp. 131–41; Cepari, *Vita*, chaps. 26, 37–42, and 61–63; Puccini, *La vita*, chaps. 22, 32, 33, 38–48, 53, 107–12, 120, 138, and 139.

42. Joan Jacobs Brumberg, "Chlorotic Girls, 1870–1920: A Historical Perspective on Female Adolescence," *Child Development* 53 (1982): 1468–77; see also her forthcoming work on the development of the concept of anorexia in the nineteenth century. Here and elsewhere I am also influenced by the provocative work of Jane Van Buren, esp. her 1983 American Historical Association paper, "The Holy Family in Harriet Beecher Stowe and Mary Cassatt: The Mythic and Semiological Structures in Two American Women Artists."

EPILOGUE

1. J. P. Feighner, E. Robins, and S. B. Guze, "Diagnostic Criteria for Use in Psychiatric Research," *Archives of General Psychiatry* 26 (1972): 57–63.

2. C. Gilligan, *In a Different Voice* (Cambridge, Mass., 1982).

3. S. Orbach, "The Construction of Femininity: Some Critical Issues in the Psychology of Women" (paper presented at the third annual conference of the Center for the Study of Anorexia and Bulimia; New York, 1984).

4. For example, H. G. Pope and J. I. Hudson, *New Hope for Binge Eaters* (New York, 1984).

BIBLIOGRAPHY

The list below cites for each of the 261 women included in this study the principal sources I consulted. The volume and page refer to the *Bibliotheca Sanctorum* and the names are in the form used therein rather than as in the original sources, or rendered into English as I did often in the text for ease of reading. The list is in date-of-death order (with approximations where necessary).

The entry BSS indicates that I did not or could not go beyond the information contained in the *Bibliotheca Sanctorum*.

Alphabetic designations following a date of death indicate: a = after this date; c = approximate; d = disputed; e = early in this century; l = late in this century; m = around mid-century.

Vol	Page	Death	Name	Source
12	731	1206	Ubaldesca	*Acta Sanctorum*, May vol. 6 (Antwerp, 1688), pp. 854–59 for a late *vita* by Silvano Razzi; Lorenzo Donati di Campiglia, *I reflessi della gratia overo vita di Sta. Ubaldesca vergine pisana* (Lucca, 1694) and Giuseppe Sainati, *Vite dei santi, beati, e servi di Dio nati nella diocesi pisana* (Pisa, 1884), pp. 122–29, provide all of what little exists on this saint.
3	234	1207	Bona di Pisa	See chapter 5, note 10.
9	785	1213d	Nazzarei, Mattia	*Acta Sanctorum*, June vol. 5 (Antwerp, 1709), p. 533, contains a brief notice.
5	1002	1218	Franca di Piacenza	*Acta Sanctorum*, April vol. 3 (Antwerp, 1675), pp. 379–404, for a 1326 *vita*.
2	995	1226	Beatrice I d'Este	*Acta Sanctorum*, May vol. 2 (Antwerp, 1680), pp. 598–603.

Vol	Page	Death	Name	Source
1	1190	1230c	Angela da Sciacca	This saint is historically confused with Angela of Bohemia (see *Acta Sanctorum,* July vol. 2 [Antwerp, 1721], pp. 350–59), but for Angela da Sciacca there is no reliable biographical information.
4	1247	1231d	Enselmini, Elena	*Acta Sanctorum,* November vol. 2 pt. 1 (Brussels, 1894), pp. 512–17, for a fifteenth-century *vita;* Clara Daneluzzi Messi, *B. Elena Enselmini: Un angelo sulle orme del Santo di Padova* (Padua, 1954), includes a good critical bibliography.
4	593	1236	Diana d'Andalò	*Acta Sanctorum,* June vol. 2 (Antwerp, 1698), pp. 363–68; Hyacinthe-Marie Cormier, *La bienheureuse Diane D'Andelò et les bienheureuses Cécile et Aimée* (Rome, 1892), is thorough and includes an anonymous contemporary *vita* of considerable interest.
8	754	1236	Mareri, Filippa	Aniceto Chiappini, "S. Filippa Mareri e il suo monastero di Borgo S. Pietro de Molito nel Cicolano," *Miscellanea Francescana* 22 (1921): 65–119, includes a full text of the earliest *legenda* (fourteenth century).
2	994	1239	Beatrice d'Este	BSS.
6	344	1239	Giacomina de' Settesoli	L. Oliger, "S. Francesco a Roma e nella Provincia Romana," in *L'Italia francescana nel VII centenario della morte di S. Francesco* (Assisi, 1927), pp. 79–84.
2	712	1240	Balbina di Assisi	Ludovico Iacobilli, *Vite de' santi e beati dell' Umbria* (Foligno, 1647), 1:186–87.
12	1023	1242	Verdiana	See Chapter 5, note 11.
3	1132	1246	Cerchi, Umiliana dei, da Firenze	See Chapter 4, notes 4–7.
5	1007	1200m	Francesca da Coldimezzo	Zeffirino Lazzeri, "Il processo di canonizzazione di S. Chiara d'Assisi," *Archivum Franciscarum Historicum* 13, fasc. iii–iv (July-October 1920): 470–74, gives what little is known.
8	1027	1250d	Maria di Pisa	Giuseppe Sainati, *Vite dei santi, beati e servi di Dio nati nella diocesi pisana* (Pisa, 1884), pp. 276–81.

Vol	Page	Death	Name	Source
11	413	1252	Rosa da Viterbo	Giuseppe Abate, "S. Rosa da Viterbo, Terziaria Francescana (1233–1251): Fonti storiche della vita e loro revisione critica," *Miscellanea Francescana* 52, fasc. i–ii (January-June 1952): 112–278, supersedes all earlier works.
1	369	1253	Agnese di Assisi	See Chapter 5, note 17.
3	1201	1253	Chiara da Assisi	See Chapter 5, notes 13–16.
4	323	1253a	Cristiana di Assisi	Zeffirino Lazzeri, "Il processo di canonizzazione di S. Chiara d'Assisi," *Archivum Franciscarum Historicum* 13, fasc. iii–iv (July-October 1920): 470–74, includes a mention.
5	810	1253	Fina di San Gimignano	*Acta Sanctorum*, March vol. 2 (Antwerp, 1668), pp. 235–42, should be supplemented with the contemporary vernacular account of Giovanni del Coppo in Guido Batelli, ed., *Leggenda di S. Fina di Sangimignano* (Florence, 1919).
3	1087	1254	Cecilia da Spello	Ludovico Iacobilli, *Vite de' santi e beati dell' Umbria* (Foligno, 1661), 3:391–92, provides a brief notice.
2	712	1254	Balbina di Assisi, la Giovane	Ludovico Iacobilli, *Vite de' santi e beati dell' Umbria* (Foligno, 1647), 1:310.
1	936	1254c	Amata (de Corano) da Assisi	Ibid., p. 272.
2	1251	1257c	Benvenuta da Perugia	Ibid., p. 144.
2	1089	1260	Benedetta di Assisi	Ludovico Iacobilli, *Vite de' santi e beati dell' Umbria* (Foligno, 1647), 1:324.
2	996	1262	Beatrice II d'Este	Girolamo Baruffaldi, *Vita della beata Beatrice Estense II* (1631; reprint ed. 1723; reprint ed. Modena, 1843), is best on this poorly documented case.
4	88	1262	Collalto, Giuliana	*Acta Sanctorum*, September vol. 1 (Antwerp, 1746), pp. 309–17.
6	317	1269c	Gherardesca da Pisa	See Chapter 5, note 12.

Vol	Page	Death	Name	Source
4	595	1200l	Amata	See entry herein for Diana d'Andalò.
4	324	1200l	Cristiana di Assisi	Zeffirino Lazzeri, "Il processo di canonizzazione di S. Chiara d'Assisi," *Archivum Franciscarum Historicum* 13, fasc. iii–iv (July-October 1920): 463–64.
11	1345	1276	Sperandea (Sperandia)	See Chapter 5, note 12.
12	1483	1278	Zita, vergine, domestica a Lucca	Fatinelli de Fatinellis, *Vita beatae Zitae virginis Lucensis, ex vetustissimo codice manuscripto fideliter transumpta* (Ferrara, 1688).
1	894	1280c	Altrude da Roma	BSS.
4	124	1280	Colonna, Margherita	Livario Oliger, *Beata Margherita Colonna. Le due vite scritte dal fratello Giovanni Colonna senatore di Roma e da Stefania monaca di S. Silvestris in Capite* (Rome, 1935), provides a full treatment and the original texts.
1	412	1281	Agnese Peranda	Ludovico Iacobilli, *Vite de' santi e beati dell' Umbria* (Foligno, 1647), 1:291–93.
2	849	1289	Bartolomea (Mea) da Siena	BSS.
4	595	1290	Cecilia	See entry herein for Diana d'Andalò.
3	230	1292	Boiani, Benvenuta	See Chapter 5, note 21.
4	957	1297	Egidia da Cortona	The only notices are contained in the *legenda* of Margherita da Cortona.
8	759	1297	Margherita da Cortona	See Chapter 4, notes 4, 16, 21, 27, and 36.
10	1263	1298	Pupelli, Marsilia	BSS.
3	339	1300	Bonizella di Siena	BSS.
8	1170	1300c	Marina di Spoleto	*Acta Sanctorum*, June vol. 3 (Antwerp, 1701), pp. 665–67.
12	369	1305	Terebotti, Santuccia, di Gubbio	*Acta Sanctorum*, March vol. 3 (Antwerp, 1668), pp. 362–64.

Vol	Page	Death	Name	Source
6	556	1306	Giovanna (Vanna) di Orvieto	See Chapter 5, note 28.
6	559	1307	Giovanna di Signa	Saturnino Mencherini, "Vita e miracoli della beata Giovanna da Signa," *Archivum Franciscarum Historicum* 10 (1917): 367–86.
3	1217	1308	Chiara da Montefalco	Michele Faloci Pulignani, *Vita di Santa Chiara da Montefalco scritta da Berengario di Sant' Africano* (Foligno, 1885); also of interest are Giovanni Matteo Giberti, *Specchio lucidissimo di santità et miracoli nella vita, morte, e doppo morte della B. Chiara da Montefalco* (Fugligno, 1693); and P. T. De Töth, *Storia di S. Chiara da Montefalco secondo un antico documento dell' anno 1308 per la prima volta integralmente pubblicato tradotto e illustrato* (Siena, 1908).
12	94	1308	Tagliapietra, Contessa	*Acta Sanctorum*, September vol. 3 (Antwerp, 1750), pp. 309–11; and Giovanni Musolino et al., *Santi e beati veneziani: Quaranta profili* (Venice, 1963), pp. 156–59, for limited additional information.
1	751	1309	Aldobrandesca (Alda) da Siena	*Acta Sanctorum*, April vol. 3 (Antwerp, 1675), pp. 466–72.
1	1185	1309	Angela da Foligno	See Chapter 4, notes 4, 37, 41, and 49.
4	324	1310	Cristiana da Santa Croce (Oringa Menabuoi)	Vincenzo Checchi, *Una fondatrice toscana del secolo XIII e le sue costituzioni: S. Cristiana da S. Croce sull' Arno* (Florence, 1927), pp. 45–49, for her rules on fasting; and Giovanni Lami, *Vita della b. Oringa Cristiana* (Florence, 1769), for a *vita* that must be used cautiously.
12	818	1310	Umiltà	*Acta Sanctorum*, May vol. 5 (Antwerp, 1685), pp. 203–22; for writings attributed to her see Piero Zama, *Santa Umiltà: La vita e i "Sermones"* (Faenza, 1974); for a scholarly modern biography see Mauro Ercolani, *Vita di S. Umiltà: Fondatrice delle monache vallombrosane a Faenza e a Firenze* (Pescia, 1910).
3	182	1314	Bicchieri, Emilia	*Acta Sanctorum*, May vol. 7 (Antwerp, 1688), pp. 557–71; and G. G. Meersseman, "La bienheureuse Émile Bicchieri," *Archi-*

Vol	Page	Death	Name	Source
				vum Fratrum Praedicatorum 24 (1954): 199–239.
1	375	1317	Agnese da Monte-pulciano	See Chapter 5, note 29.
1	412	1319	Chiara de Ianua	Ludovico Iacobilli, *Vite de' santi e beati dell' Umbria* (Foligno, 1647), 1:291–93.
5	1256	1319	Francucci Bezzoli, Giustina	*Acta Sanctorum*, March vol. 2 (Antwerp, 1668), pp. 242–45.
8	756	1320	Margherita di Città di Castello	Marie-Hyacinthe Laurent, "La plus ancienne légende de la b. Marguerite de Città di Castello," *Archivum Fratrum Praedicatorum* 10 (1940): 109–31.
6	1241	1321	Giuntini, Diana	BSS.
3	1228	1300e	Chiarella	Ludovico Iacobilli, *Vite de' santi e beati dell' Umbria* (Foligno, 1647), 1:433–35.
7	513	1300e	Guidoni, Filippa	BSS.
3	1228	1300e	Illuminata di Montefalco	See entry herein for Chiarella.
12	782	1300e	Ugolina	BSS.
1	422	1326	Agolanti, Chiara, da Rimini	Giuseppe Garampi, *Vita della b. Chiara da Rimini* (Rome, 1788), and by the same author, *Memorie ecclesiastiche appartenenti all' istoria e al culto della b. Chiara di Rimini* (Rome, 1755), are lengthy but none too reliable.
8	773	1330	Margherita da Faenza	*Acta Sanctorum*, August vol. 5 (Antwerp, 1741), pp. 845–54; and see Mauro Ercolani, *Vita di S. Umiltà* (Pescia, 1910), pp. 129–41.
7	1076	1333	Lambertini, Imelda	Timoteo Centi, *La beata Imelda Lambertini, vergine domenicana con studio critico e documenti inediti* (Florence, 1955), collects the few existing documents.
6	1184	1341	Giuliana Falconieri	Davide M. Montagna, "La 'leggenda' quattrocentesca della beata Giuliana Falconieri," *Moniales Ordinis Servorum* 2, fasc. i (1964): 16–28, is to be preferred to the 1613 *vita* in the *Acta Sanctorum*.

VOL	PAGE	DEATH	NAME	SOURCE
3	993	1342	Caterina da Siena	BSS.
12	719	1343	Tuscana, vedova di Verona	*Acta Sanctorum*, July vol. 3 (Antwerp, 1723), pp. 860–66.
3	1225	1345	Chiara (Sancia di Maiorca), regina di Sicilia	BSS.
2	849	1348	Bartolomea da Siena	*Acta Sanctorum*, May vol. 4 (Antwerp, 1685), pp. 626–27.
3	589	1350	Bufalari, Lucia, di Amelia	Giovanni Lupidi, *Memorie storiche riguardanti la beata Lucia Bufalari Amerina* (Rome, 1928), provides what little is known.
9	466	1356	Michelina da Pesaro	*Acta Sanctorum*, June vol. 3 (Antwerp, 1701), pp. 925–37.
5	1008	1360	Francesca (Franceschina) da Gubbio	*Acta Sanctorum*, February vol. 1 (Antwerp, 1658), pp. 931–32.
3	369	1361	Botti, Villana	S. Orlandi, *La beata Villana terziaria domenicana fiorentina del sec. XIII* (Florence, 1976), is more thorough than the *Acta Sanctorum*, and see Anna Benvenuti Papi, "Il modello familiare nell' agiografia fiorentina tra '200 e '400. Sviluppo di una negazione," *Nuova DWF* 16 (Spring 1981): 80–105.
3	1234	1366a	Chigi, Angela	BSS.
3	196	1367	Biscossi, Sibillina, di Pavia	*Acta Sanctorum*, March vol. 3 (Antwerp, 1668), pp. 67–71.
11	115	1367d	Rena, Giulia	BSS.
11	1270	1367d	Soderini, Giovanna	*Acta Sanctorum*, October vol. 12 (Antwerp, 1867), pp. 398–406.
6	343	1300l	Giacomina (Iacopina, Pina) da Pisa	S. Barsotti, *Un nuovo fiore domenicano. La beata Jacopina da Pisa suora della penitenza* (Pisa, 1904), embellishes what little there is.
3	996	1380	Caterina Benincasa da Siena	See notes to Chapter 2.
10	76	1383	Panacea (Panasia)	*Acta Sanctorum*, May vol. 1 (Antwerp, 1680), pp. 164–65.

VOL	PAGE	DEATH	NAME	SOURCE
4	121	1387	Colombini, Caterina, da Siena	BSS.
3	940	1391	Castora da Gubbio	*Acta Sanctorum*, June vol. 2 (Antwerp, 1698), pp. 1006–1008.
8	792	1395	Margherita di San Severino Marche	*Acta Sanctorum*, August vol. 2 (Antwerp, 1735), pp. 117–21.
8	239	1400c	Lucia da Caltagirone	*Acta Sanctorum*, September vol. 7 (Antwerp, 1760), pp. 361–74.
9	1271	1410	Orsolina di Parma	*Acta Sanctorum*, April vol. 1 (Antwerp, 1675), pp. 723–39.
3	192	1411c	Bionda da Verucchio	BSS.
6	23	1420	Gambacorta, Chiara	Niccola Zucchelli, *La B. Chiara Gambacorta: La chiesa ed il Convento di S. Domenico in Pisa* (Pisa, 1914), includes (pp. 363–89) a *vita* by her contemporary and several of her letters (pp. 343–60); on her cult see *Super confirmatione cultus ab immemorabili tempore praestiti B. Clarae Gambacorti Viduae* (Rome, 1829).
8	626	1431	Mancini, Maria	Giuseppe Sainati, *Vite dei santi, beati, e servi di Dio nati nella diocesi pisana* (Pisa, 1884), pp. 202–17; Niccola Zucchelli, *La B. Chiara Gambacorta: La chiesa ed il Convento di S. Domenico in Pisa* (Pisa, 1914), pp. 121–28.
1	1231	1435	Angelina dei Conti di Marsciano	Felice da Porretta, *La beata Angelina di Marsciano: Storia e leggenda* (Florence, 1937).
5	1006	1438d	Francesca di Assisi	Ludovico Iacobilli, *Vite de' santi e beati dell' Umbria* (Foligno, 1647), 1:45–46.
6	105	1439	Gemma, vergine, reclusa a Goriano Sicoli	*Acta Sanctorum*, May vol. 3 (Antwerp, 1680), p. 182.
5	1011	1440	Francesca Romana	See Chapter 5, notes 32 and 33.
5	436	1441	Faciardi, Michelina, di Rimini	BSS.

Vol	Page	Death	Name	Source
9	258	1444	Meda, Felice	*Acta Sanctorum*, September vol. 8 (Antwerp, 1762), pp. 751–69; F. Meda, "Una insigne clarissa milanese: La B. Felice Meda (1378–1444)," *Archivum Franciscanum Historicum* 20 (1927): 241–59, considers the sources at length.
11	212	1447d	Rita da Cascia	Monastero di S. Rita, *Documentazione ritiana antica*, 4 vols. (Cascia, 1968–70).
1	1232	1450	Angelina da Spoleto	*Acta Sanctorum*, June vol. 5 (Antwerp, 1709), pp. 530–31.
3	365	1450	Bossi, Eugenia Felice, da Milano	A brief mention is found in the materials for Felice Meda.
3	707	1400m	Camilla di San Severino Marche	BSS.
6	1164	1400m	Giulia	BSS.
2	75	1455	Antonia da Siena	BSS.
1	764	1458	Alessandrina da Letto	Luke Wadding, ed., *Annales Minorum* (Quaracchi, 1932), 10:113–15; all Wadding entries provide only brief notices.
4	341	1458	Cristina da Spoleto	*Acta Sanctorum*, February vol. 2 (Antwerp, 1658), pp. 799–802.
12	886	1458	Valentini, Elena	*Acta Sanctorum*, April vol. 3 (Antwerp, 1675), pp. 247–58.
1	1233	1459	Angelina da Terni	BSS.
11	158	1459d	Riccardi, Costanza	BSS.
4	7	1460	Civati, Giacomina, da Milano	Luke Wadding, ed., *Annales Minorum* (Quaracchi, 1932), 12:17–18.
3	980	1463	Caterina da Bologna	Giacomo Grassetti, *Vita di Santa Caterina da Bologna* (1610; reprint ed., Bologna, 1724); Caterina da Bologna, *Le armi necessarie alla battaglia spirituale alla quale si aggiunge LO SPECCHIO d'illuminazione sulla vita della medesima santa* (Bologna, 1787), contains Illuminata Bembo's contemporary *vita*, and contrary to *Butler's Lives of*

Vol	Page	Death	Name	Source
				the Saints (1:539), may be found in this printed edition at the Biblioteca Universitaria at Bologna.
4	125	1464c	Colonna Calafato, Macalda	BSS plus the stories in materials on her daughter Eustochia.
8	793	1464	Margherita di Savoia	Serafino Razzi, *Vite dei santi, e beati del sacro Ordine de' Frati Praedicatori, cosi huomini come donne. Con aggiunta di molte vite, che nella prima impressione non erono* (Florence, 1588), 2:51–63. Hereinafter cited as Razzi, *Vite dei santi*.
1	826	1465	Alfani, Felice, da Perugia	Antonio Fantozzi, "La riforma osservante dei monasteri delle clarisse nell' Italia centrale," *Archivum Franciscanum Historicum* 23 (1930): 377–81, 489–92, mentions her briefly.
1	728	1465	Albrici, Maddalena	*Acta Sanctorum*, May vol. 3 (Antwerp, 1680), pp. 252–62.
10	550	1468	Picenardi, Elisabetta	Isodoro Bianchi, *Vita della beata Elisabetta Picenardi* (Monza, 1900); Davide M. Montagna, "Nuove ricerche sulla beata Elisabetta Picenardi," *Moniales Ordinis Servorum* 1 (Rome, 1963): 23–32, contains the earliest *vita*.
1	1311	1469	Annibaldi, Teodora degli	BSS.
5	305	1469	Eustochio, vergine di Padova	Giulio Cordara, *Vita, virtù e miracoli della B. Eustochio vergine padovana* (Rome, 1675).
3	140	1469a	Besozzi, Felicia, di Milano	BSS.
2	74	1472	Antonia da Firenze	Mario Morelli, *La Beata Antonia da Firenze ed il monastero aquilano dell' Eucarestia* (L'Aquila, 1971); Ciro Cannarozzi, "Due vite della B. Antonia da Firenze," *Studi Francescani* 57, fasc. 1–2 (January-June 1960): 319–42.
1	1190	1400l	Angela II di Ferrara	BSS.
2	768	1478	Barbara da Bergamo	Luke Wadding, ed., *Annales Minorum* (Quaracchi, 1933), 14:155–56.

Vol	Page	Death	Name	Source
3	991	1478	Caterina da Pallanza	*Acta Sanctorum*, April vol. 1 (Antwerp, 1675), pp. 643–54; Ferruccio Minola-Cattaneo, *Santa Maria del Monte sopra Varese* (Varese, 1931), pp. 143–83, for the *vita* by Benedetta Biumi, her contemporary.
11	1010	1478	Sforza, Serafina (Sveva)	Federico Madiai, "Nuovi documenti su Sveva di Montefeltro Sforza," *Le Marche* 9 (1909): 94–142.
3	978	1480	Caterina dell' Amatrice	Ludovico Iacobilli, *Vite de' santi e beati dell' Umbria* (Foligno, 1647), 1:7–8.
7	797	1481	Indusiata, Elguina	BSS.
3	662	1484	Calafato, Franceschina (Francesca), da Messina	BSS plus mentions in materials on her sister Eustochia.
3	660	1486	Calafato, Eustochia (Smeralda), di Messina	See Chapter 5, note 40.
6	1349	1487	Giustiniani, Eufemia	Luigi Carrer, *Anello di sette gemme o Venezia e la sua storia* (Venice, 1838), pp. 649–78.
1	1233	1490	Angelina da Spoleto	Ludovico Iacobilli, *Vite de' santi e beati dell' Umbria* (Foligno, 1656), 2:150.
11	749	1491	Scopelli, Giovanna	*Acta Sanctorum*, July vol. 2 (Antwerp, 1721), pp. 728–35.
10	1227	1492	Prudenzia	*Acta Sanctorum*, May vol. 2 (Antwerp, 1680), pp. 129–30.
6	1107	1495	Girlani, Arcangela	Ludovico Saggi, *La congregazione mantovana dei carmelitani sino alla morte del B. Battista Spagnoli* (1516) (Rome, 1954), pp. 221–24.
2	1088	1496	Bembo, Illuminata	See entry for Caterina da Bologna.
12	1050	1497	Veronica da Binasco	*Acta Sanctorum*, January vol. 1 (Antwerp, 1643), pp. 887–929.
1	1016	1498	Amodei, Elisabetta, da Palermo	*Acta Sanctorum*, February vol. 1 (Antwerp, 1658), p. 448 gives a brief notice.

Vol	Page	Death	Name	Source
3	238	1498	Bonaventura di Antrodoco	BSS.
3	1217	1500	Chiara da Foligno	Ludovico Iacobilli, *Vite de' santi e beati dell' Umbria* (Foligno, 1656), 2:4.
4	166	1500	Coppoli, Cecilia	Antonio Fantozzi, "Documenti intorno alla B. Cecilia Coppoli, clarissa (1426–1500)," *Archivum Franciscanum Historicum* 19, fasc. ii–iii (April-July 1926): 194–225, 334–84.
4	369	1500	Crivelli, Maria, da Milano	Luke Wadding, ed., *Annales Minorum* (Quaracchi, 1932), 12:18.
4	101	1501	Colomba da Rieti	See Chapter 6, notes 2 and 9.
6	1181	1501	Giuliana [Puricelli]	See entry for Caterina di Pallanza for Biumi's *vita.*
10	77	1503	Panatieri, Maddalena	*Acta Sanctorum*, October supplementum (Paris, 1875), pp. 168*-178*.
1	1170	1505	Andreasi, Osanna	See Chapter 6, note 14.
2	991	1505	Beatrice da Ferrara	Razzi, *Vite dei santi* (Florence, 1587), 1: 193–94.
8	780	1505	Margherita da Ravenna	Note that the entry for Molli, Margherita (9:538) in the *Bibliotheca Sanctorum* refers to this person. *Acta Sanctorum*, January vol. 2 (Antwerp, 1643), pp. 548–54.
2	74	1507	Antonia da Brescia	Razzi, *Vite dei santi*, 1:183–86.
9	358	1508	Mercadelli, Eustochia	Ibid., pp. 197–98.
3	984	1510	Caterina da Genova	See Chapter 6, note 19.
8	404	1510	Luzi, Marchesina	BSS.
3	1063	1511c	Cecilia	Razzi, *Vite dei santi*, 1:188–89.
10	880	1511	Pio di Savoia, Camilla	Luisa Lugli Raimondi, *Memorie storiche e documenti sulla città e sull' antico principato di Carpi* (Carpi, 1951), 12:76–81.
4	216	1512	Correggiari, Angela Serafina	Razzi, *Vite dei santi*, 1:191–93.

Vol	Page	Death	Name	Source
9	979	1512	Nicolosa	BSS.
3	590	1514	Bugni, Chiara	*Acta Sanctorum*, September vol. 5 (Antwerp, 1755), pp. 465–66 contains a mention; Giovanni Musolino et al., *Santi e beati veneziani: Quaranta profili* (Venice, 1963), pp. 255–60.
9	568	1514	Montaldi, Paola	*Acta Sanctorum*, October vol. 13 (Antwerp, 1883), pp. 207–25.
3	733	1515	Candida da Como	*Acta Sanctorum*, September vol. 6 (Antwerp, 1757), p. 105, gives a brief notice.
6	28	1515	Gambara Costa, Paola	See Chapter 6, note 20.
3	983	1516	Caterina da Gambolò	Franco Pianzola, *La b. Caterina da Gambolò* (Mortara-Vigevano, 1916).
2	975	1519	Battista di Piacenza	BSS.
4	853	1520	Duglioli, Elena	*Acta Sanctorum*, September vol. 6 (Antwerp, 1757), pp. 655–59.
11	603	1520	Salviati, Elisabetta	Giuseppe Maria Brocchi, *Vite de' santi e beati fiorentini* (Florence, 1761), 3:330–38.
12	950	1524	Varano, Camilla Battista, da	Giacomo Boccanera, ed., *Beata Camilla Battista da Varano. Le opere spirituali* (Iesi, 1958).
9	474	1525	Mignani, Laura	Antonio Cistelli, *Figure della Riforma pretridentina* (Brescia, 1948), pp. 56–103.
4	369	1527c	Crivelli, Isabella	Luke Wadding, ed., *Annales Minorum* (Quaracchi, 1932), 13:548.
1	873	1529	Aliprandi, Caterina	Giacinto Burroni, "Le 'memorie del monastero del Gesù' in Asti," *Rivista di Storia - Arte - Archeologia. Bollettino della sezione di Alessandria* 47 (1938): 106–9.
3	557	1529	Brugora, Caterina, di Milano	BSS.
6	167	1530	Gentile da Ravenna	*Acta Sanctorum*, January vol. 2 (Antwerp, 1643), pp. 910–15.
10	1318	1530	Quinzani, Stefana	Paolo Guerrini, "La prima legenda volgare de la b. Stefana Quinzani d'Orzinuovi secondo il codice Vaticano-Urbinate latino 1755," *Memorie storiche della diocesi di Brescia* (Brescia, 1930), 1:65–186.

Vol	Page	Death	Name	Source
1	717	1533	Albertoni, Lodovica degli	Aniceto Chiappini, ed., *Annales Minorum* (Quaracchi, 1933), 26:386–90.
1	1191	1540	Angela Merici	*Regola della Compagnia di* S. *Orsola dettata di* S. *Angela Merici* (Brescia, 1873), includes in Chapter 4 the saint's rules for fasting.
4	338	1543	Cristina da L'Aquila	Carlo Cremona, *La beata Cristina de L'Aquila agostiniana* (Rome, 1943), must be used with caution.
3	547	1544	Broccadelli, Lucia	Razzi, *Vite dei santi*, 1:179–83.
3	992	1547	Caterina da Racconigi	See Chapter 6, notes 15 and 17.
3	1056	1500m	Cavenago, Giovanna Maria	BSS.
3	1063	1500m	Cecilia da Piacenza	BSS.
3	1087	1500m	Cecilia da Siena	BSS.
4	678	1553	Domenica da Paradiso	See Chapter 6, notes 22, 25, and 28.
9	1274	1565	Osanna (Ozane) di Cattaro	Innocenzo Taurisano, *La beata Osanna da Cattaro domenicana* (Rome, 1929).
2	707	1577	Bagnesi, Maria Bartolomea	See Chapter 6, note 40.
12	1040	1587	Vernazza, Battista	Umile Bonzi da Genova, "La vénérabile Battistina Vernazza," *Revue d'Ascétique et de Mystique*, 16 (1935): 147–79.
1	382	1588	Agnese da Pescara	Ludovico Iacobilli, *Vite de' santi e beati dell' Umbria* (Foligno, 1661), 3:26.
3	1044	1590	Caterina de' Ricci di Firenze	Guglielmo M. Di Agresti, ed., *Santa Caterina de' Ricci: Testimonianze sull' età giovanile* (Florence, 1963), *Serafino Razzi. Vita di Santa Caterina de' Ricci* (Florence, 1965), *Santa Caterina de' Ricci. Epistolario*, 5 vols. (Florence, 1973–75).
12	948	1606	Vannini, Caterina	See Chapter 6, notes 29 and 33.

Vol	Page	Death	Name	Source
8	1107	1607	Maria Maddalena de' Pazzi	See Chapter 6, notes 34–36.
5	969	1617	Fornari Strata, Maria Vittoria	Umile Bonzi da Genova, "Mémoire autobiographique de la Bienheureuse Marie-Victoire de Fornari Strata, fondatrice des Annonciades Celestes," *Revue d'Ascétique et de Mystique* 17 (1937): 394–403; anonymous, *Vita della Beata Maria Vittoria Fornari Strata, fondatrice dell' Ordine della Santissima Annunziata detto le Turchine pubblicata nella occasione della solenne beatificazione di Essa* (Rome, 1828).
2	1241	1618	Benincasa, Orsola	Francesco Maria Maggio, *Vita della venerabil madre Orsola Benincasa napoletana originale da Siena dell' ordine del B. Gaetano fondatrice delle vergini della congregatione e dell' eremo della immacolata concettione* (Rome, 1655), remains on the Index because of its Jansenist tendencies and is definitely the one to use for this holy anorexic.
6	322	1640	Giacinta Marescotti	Leone Veuthey, "Un diario autografo inedito di S. Giacinta Marescotti, terziaria francescana," *Miscellanea Francescana* 40 (Rome, 1940): 187–96; and Aniceto Chiappini, "S. Hyacinthae Mariscotti vita," *Annales Minorum* 28 (1941): 604–46, provide the basic texts; also useful are Pacifico Deani, *S. Giacinta Marescotti* (Rome, n.d.), and Girolamo Ventimiglia, *Vita della beata Giacinta Mariscotti, monaca nel Monastero di S. Bernardino di Viterbo* (Rome, 1726).
10	69	1645	Paluzzi, Caterina di Gesù e Maria	Andreina De Clementi, "Una mistica contadina: Caterina Paluzzi di Morlupo," *Memoria: Rivista di storia delle donne* 5 (November 1982): 23–33.
3	346	1670	Bonomo (Bonhomo), Giovanna Maria	BSS.
12	1100	1670	Villani, Maria	Domenico Maria Marchese, *Vita della serva di Dio Suor Maria Villani dell' Ordine de'*

Vol	Page	Death	Name	Source
				Predicatori, *fondatrice del Monastero di Santa Maria del Divino Amore di Napoli* (Naples, 1674).
6	588	1673	Giovanna Maria della Croce	Teodorico Asson, "Vita della venerabile Giovanna Maria della Croce," *Studi Francescani* 25 (1928): 306–47, for a 1682 *vita* by Francesco Baroni.
3	1226	1675	Chiara Maria della Passione	Alfonso di S. Giuseppe, *La venerabile Madre Chiara Maria della Passione* (Rome, 1932).
1	875	1677	Allegri (De Allegris), Maria	Diomira del Verbo Incarnato (Margherita Allegri), *Scritti e detti* (Florence, 1979); Alessandro Ciolli, *Vita della venerabile serva di Dio Maria Margherita Diomira del Verbo Incarnato degli Allegri di Firenzuola* (Florence, 1872); the BSS entry confuses this saint with Maria Diomira del Verbo Incarnato (8:1058).
9	1244	1685	Orsini Borghese, Maria Vittoria	anonymous, *La vita della venerabile serva di Dio D. Cammilla Orsini Borghese principessa di Sulmona di poi Suor Maria Vittoria religiosa dell' Ordine dell' Annunziata* (Rome, 1717).
8	1053	1699	Maria Crocifissa della Concezione	Calogero Gallerano, *Isabella Tomasi (la venerabile Suor Maria* Crocifissa) (Sorrento, 1963).
8	966	1717	Maria degli Angeli	Elia di Santa Teresa, *La diletta del crocifisso: Vita della venerabile Suor Maria degli Angioli* (Venice, 1735), and Anselmo di S. Luigi Gonzaga, *Vita della B. Maria degli Angeli*, 2d ed. (Turin, 1866).
1	1322	1718	Ansalone, Rosalia	BSS; there appear to be good materials here, but I was not able to locate them.
2	1084	1719	Belloni, Antonia Maria	BSS.
12	1050	1727	Veronica Giuliani	See notes to Chapter 3.
12	1005	1728	Venerini, Rosa	Andrea Girolamo Andreucci, *Ragguaglio della vita della serva di Dio Rosa Venerini, viterbese, istitutrice delle Scuole e Maestre Pie* (Rome, 1732), is fundamental; also see Gilla Vincenzo Gremigni, *La Beata Rosa*

Vol	Page	Death	Name	Source
				Venerini (Rome, 1952), and Maria Eugenia Pietromarchi, *Vita della Beata Rosa Venerini, fondatrice delle Maestre Pie* (Rome, 1952).
8	1048	1731	Maria Colomba di S. Maria della Croce	Vincenzo Novaro, "Di una monaca domenicana viterbese," *Il Rosario - Memorie Domenicane* 26 (1909): 94–99, 157–60.
8	257	1732	Lucia Filippini	See the sources for her companion, Rosa Venerini, plus *Acta Canonizationum quibus Sanctissimus Dominus Noster Pius Papa XI die 22 iunii A.D. 1930 Beatis Catharinae Thomas et Luciae Filippini* (Insulae Liri, 1932).
8	1223	1737	Martinengo, Maria Maddalena	G. M. Pugnetti, *L'autobiografia della beata Suor Maria Maddalena Martinengo contessa di Barco, clarissa cappuccina* (Brescia, 1964), discusses the complex sources on this case, but I was refused permission to consult them.
5	969	1744	Fornari, Chiara Isabella	BSS; the worthwhile documents are at the Curia in Todi, but I never obtained permission to consult them.
11	663	1745	Satellico, Maria Crocifissa	Giovanni Battista Scaramelli, *Vita della ven. serva di Dio Maria Crocifissa Satellico* (Venice, 1748), for the earliest *vita*, which is on the Index because of its suspected Jansenism.
11	574	1748	Salandri, Maria Gertrude	anonymous, *Vita della ven. serva di Dio Suor Maria Geltrude Salandri, romana dell' Ordine di S. Domenico fondatrice del Monistero del Santissimo Rosario in Valentano* (Rome, 1774), details this conscious imitator of Catherine of Siena.
4	378	1755	Crostarosa, Maria Celeste	Jean Baptiste Favre, *A Great Mystic of the Eighteenth Century: The Ven. Sister Mary Celeste Crostarosa* (London, 1935).
11	1290	1758	Solimani, Giovanna Maria Battista	Giovanni Musso, *Una mistica del secolo XVIII: Vita della Madre Giovanna Battista Solimani fondatrice delle Romite di S.G. Battista* (Genoa, 1960).
3	1164	1767	Cevoli, Florida	Giuseppe Sainati, *Vita della venerabile Suor Florida* (Monza, 1873), and see her testi-

Vol	Page	Death	Name	Source
				mony in the canonization proceedings for Veronica Giuliani (notes to Chapter 3).
1	424	1768	Agostini, Maria Rosa	BSS.
8	1059	1768	Maria Diomira del Verbo Incarnato	anonymous, ed., *Vita della venerabile Suor Maria Diomira del Verbo Incarnato, cappuccina professa nel Monastero di Fanano, scritta da Lei medesima* (1788; reprint ed., Rome, 1916).
12	424	1770	Teresa Margherita del S. Cuore di Gesù	Ermanno del S.mo Sacramento et al., "S. Teresa Margherita del Cuore di Gesù (Redi), formazione, spirito, scritti," *Ephemerides Carmeliticae* 10, fasc. i–ii (1959): 3–480; for an insightful analysis of this saint's relationship with her father, based on their extensive correspondence, see the article therein (pp. 7–52) by Ferdinando di S. Maria.
8	1077	1773	Maria Lilia del S.mo Crocifisso	anonymous, *Compendio della vita della venerabile Suor Lilia M. del SS. Crocifisso vergine viterbese del Terz' Ordine di S. Francesco, fondatrice del Monasterio dell' Assunta in Viterbo e di altri quattro altrove* (Bologna, 1875).
8	1066	1791	Maria Francesca delle Cinque Piaghe	Maria Paola Adami, S. *Maria Francesca* (Bari, 1957), must be used with caution.
6	319	1800	Ghersi, Chiara Isabella	Giovanni Francesco da Marassi, *Vita della venerabile Chiara Isabella Ghersi* (Genoa, 1875).
3	750	1800e	Canori Mora, Elisabetta	BSS.
4	443	1826	D'Ambrosio, Maria Crocifissa delle Cinque Piaghe	*Acta Sanctae Sedis* 28 (1895–96): 686–89, describes her heavy mortifications, but in rather conventional fashion.
9	191	1831	Maurizi, Maria Luisa	Maria Luisa Maurizi, *Morali e divote riflessioni, a tutti utilissime e specialmente alle persone claustrali* (Rome, 1833), shows an unusual degree of concentration on Jesus.
2	849	1833	Bartolomea Capitanio di Lovere	Maria Clara Bianchi, ed., *Bartolomea Capitanio. Scritti spirituali: Lettere* (Rome, 1978), *Bartolomea Capitanio. Scritti: Il suo cammino spirituale* (Rome, 1979); Luigi Ig-